IT'S ALL IN THE LYRICS

How Music Helped Me Heal and Find My Voice

IT'S ALL IN THE LYRICS
Copyright © 2024 by Dualist Media LLC

Book Cover by Tony Kessel
Editing by Kit Duncan

ISBN: 9798227078254 (D2D eBook); 9798227607058 (D2D paperback); 9798339350026 (KDP paperback); 9798339350637 (KDP hardcover)

Second edition: September 2024

10 9 8 7 6 5 4 3 2

IT'S ALL IN THE LYRICS

How Music Helped Me Heal and Find My Voice

Tony Kessel

This project includes several stories that may be disturbing to people with mental health concerns. If you are having suicidal thoughts, do not suffer in silence. Reach out for help. For Service members, veterans, and their dependents needing assistance, contact the Veteran Crisis Line by dialing 988 and pressing option 1, by text at 838255, or by chat at www.veteranscrisisline.net. For those without military affiliation, dial 988 or visit 988lifeline.org. For non-emergent information on mental health issues, please visit www.nimh.nih.gov. It is never wrong to be broken. Please seek to understand your brokenness with the help of trained medical professionals.

RESOURCES

For a more interactive experience with this project, I've assembled these songs into a playlist. Scan your preferred music platform QR code below to find it where you consume music.

YouTube

Apple Music

Spotify

Amazon Music

Deezer

PREFACE

Have any of you genuinely traced your musical lineage? In 2017, I attended a Garth Brooks concert. It was a bizarre experience; one I didn't believe I'd ever have again after his retirement. That simple event caused years of memories to flood into my mind. How had so much time passed since those youthful days? How did I go from listening exclusively to GB, even feeling guilty for enjoying any other artist, to a metalhead?

I didn't have answers, but I committed to retracing my steps by building a song-a-day playlist from May 1, 2017 until April 30, 2018. After sifting through thousands of musical experiences, I decided to tell my story through music. I had to compress a lifetime to 366 songs. A tall order, indeed.

As I approached the end of the experiment, I realized my project held much more than daily blog entries. While I have yet to release a single song as a musician, I accidentally accomplished a separate life goal of writing a book. With refinement, this work not only explored my musical history, but also clarified my decision to write, record, mix, and produce my own music. Music deeply influenced by the songs I expound upon.

To start, I'd like to pose a challenge. Don't just explore my lineage; trace your own. Don't just listen to the songs; relive them. The extreme joys. The inevitable lows. The victories of life. The darkest valleys. Odds are, if you picked this book up, you value music as much as I do. Please retrace your steps. What path did you take to get to where you are?

If any of these songs resonate with you, let me know. Share your own entries. I'm curious how your musical journey panned out.

I'll admit, this project may appear self-involved. However, it was put together to heal myself and help others find restoration through art.

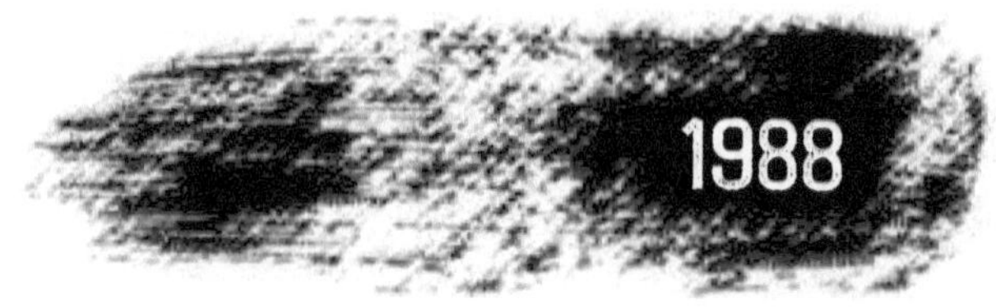

I Told You So / Randy Travis

My parents got divorced before my first birthday. I spent most of my childhood hoping my mom would somehow change her flaws and plead with Dad to bring the family back together. Through Randy Travis' *Always & Forever*, I expected reconciliation and a return to the life I deserved. I was too young to understand, but for the first time, I used music as a drug to digest the unpalatable.

That being said, it may be necessary to slap a warning sticker on this exercise. I wrote this book to highlight my desire to write and record music, spanning thirty-four years of my personal history. This project gets introspective, emotional, and dark at times. Since music's the consistent potion I reach for to process life, I often link experiences to song. Vacations, tragedies, love, professional development—it's all fair game. Rest assured, though. In the same way it coaxes me through darkness, it has provided so many lighter moments to illuminate my path along the way.

Forever & Ever, Amen / Randy Travis

Every entertainer has a story of how they first caught the bug. At four years old, I remember singing Randy Travis' "Forever and Ever, Amen" for my family. Maybe it was the lyrics. A quick hat tip to my frequently changing sandbox romances. It could've been a reference to my desire for lifelong love. I'm not entirely sure.

Maybe I enjoyed the thrill of performing for an engaged audience as I sang along with the music video. We 80s babies weren't treated with the same sense of importance as kids today are. For some reason, when I serenaded my family, they listened. What an incredible feeling! I finally found a way to gain an adult's attention.

Mind you, I'm not a career musician earning a living through ticket sales. However, I do love entertaining. Telling an engaging story. Charming rooms of people in speech. Being the life of the party. When I got that first adrenaline rush years ago, I had to pursue it.

Good Intentions / Randy Travis

When I was eight, my dad told me, "I tell you about my life's mistakes, so you don't make 'em." That's a powerful observation to share with a child. Though I remember this quote much later in life, he lived by that mentality. He had the best intentions. However, he was a flawed human being with an imperfect past. By sharing his flaws, he hoped to advance his children's lives.

Even at four years old, I teared up over Randy's character serving a Christmastime jail sentence. I doubt my awareness was this pointed, but now I live by my father's advice. If I'm lucky, I'll avoid making some of his mistakes. If I'm talented, I'll mirror his successes.

Runaway / Del Shannon

Del Shannon's "Runaway" might be my dad's favorite song. I could ask him, but he sang it with such conviction I choose to believe it is. Now, Dad isn't what most people would call a good singer. He could care less what people thought. Regardless of skill or ability, this track seemed like a therapeutic experience to him. He couldn't allow his pleading kids' cries to slow his healing process.

I still listen to "Runaway" today, but the newer, hipper Gary Allan cover. Like my father, I sing this song while carting my kids around town. I can only hope they don't judge my vocal talent. If so, they could at least possess the nerve to call me out.

Runaround Sue / Dion

Dad also loved "Runaround Sue." Again, and it bears repeating, Pops was not a good singer. I noticed when he sang with artists like Dion, Creedence Clearwater Revival, or George Thorogood, he sounded decent. Their rough, unpolished vocals made him a tad more tolerable to listen to.

Being a child of divorce was challenging. You longed for your parents' reunion, but the adult in me knows that's not possible. As a kid, I committed to two things: getting them back together or finding out why they failed.

Dad wouldn't tell me. Instead, he jammed out to these songs as tears welled in his eyes. He belted out life-changing guidance. He still hasn't told me what happened between him and my mom, but I believe I've figured it out. The moral of the story is sad but true. Son, you gotta keep away from Runaround Sue.

Nothing's Gonna Stop Us Now / Starship

I was born in the 80s. Yep, the 80s—the generation filled with hokey pop music, power ballads, and drum machines. Hilarious sounding drum machines. Starship's "Nothing's Gonna Stop Us Now" doesn't disappoint.

Riding shotgun, like kids did before laws existed, I have distinct memories of Dad driving my brothers and me to my mom's place. Distracting himself with the radio, he fought off tears as he sang his heart out. He didn't want to miss sections of our lives. We didn't want to leave him but wanted to spend time with our mom. Rather than feel our feelings, we did what we do best: made fun of him for being a bad singer.

Dad had the last laugh, though. If you were to check the contents of my aging iPod, this song's right there. Next to my other experiences. Depending on who's with me, I find myself frantically skipping it to avoid explanation. Dad, if you're reading this, I have it for you.

Happy Together / The Turtles

Divorce, through a child's eyes, is a beast. "It's my fault," and countless other clichés haunted me from a young age. Separating shortly after my birth, I was their final child. Constant guilt plagued me. Why didn't my parents stay together? For them? For us kids? Wasn't marriage supposed to be forever? If eternal commitment could end, couldn't divorce? I had a lot of questions, but only one answer. I'd do anything, and everything, to avoid putting my children through this despicable institution.

Eat It / Weird Al

I'm aware of the darkness of my story from the onset. However, I seriously pondered the status of romantic relationships in my earliest memories. Rest assured; I possessed unsolicited optimism. Life can't be all dark all the time.

When I was five, Dad remarried a woman with two sons. That's correct, five stinky boys in one house. We watched *WWE*, collected GI Joes, and loved, and I mean LOVED, Weird Al. He provided a ray of sunshine in an otherwise hopeless world. When I look back, I recall memorizing the lyrics to "Nature Trail to Hell," "Fat," and "Eat It." Amidst the abnormal transition, my brothers and I found comfort shooting marbles in the backyard, obnoxiously singing along with Weird Al songs we barely understood.

Blue Christmas / Elvis Presley

If you're listening to the playlist accompanying this book, I sincerely apologize. Odds are, this ill-timed holiday hit won't fall into the correct season. Again, I'm sorry, but it's a critical piece of the puzzle I'm assembling.

Imagine this scene: family celebrating together. Kids placing ornaments on a tree. A dark room highlighting the dull glow of Christmas lights. A Billboard mixtape providing the soundtrack for our festivities. Everything's perfect, except for one thing. A little boy, incapable of enjoying what he has, sobs from a secret place for the one thing he didn't.

I must admit to being that little boy. In a moment fit for a Hallmark holiday movie, the lyrics to Elvis' "Blue Christmas" played out. The season is all about family. Despite all I had, my mom wasn't there. I wanted her to be, but she was absent yet again. I didn't realize most Christmases would be like this one. All I knew, I needed my mom. She wasn't there, no matter how much I wished her to be.

Dizzy / Tommy Roe

Every aspiring musician remembers their first stereo. Mine was a record player with a broken tape deck. My first album, not sure where it came from, was Tommy Roe's *Greatest Hits*. I tried fixing the supply reel, unsuccessfully I might add, while listening to this record. In fact, I think I broke it worse.

Consuming a song entitled "Dizzy," spinning under the record needle, as I solved a complex problem is a little ironic. Several hours into the project, I was left with six extra screws and this record. My dreams of capturing Randy Travis songs from the radio would have to wait.

The Gambler / Kenny Rogers

We lived for recess in second grade. Boys chase girls. Tetherball. King of the Mountain. You know the games kids play to blow off steam acquired throughout our ever-so-stressful school days.

One afternoon, I engaged in a heated game of tag with a group of friends. A kindergartner kept tagging me. Every time. It seemed like he was becoming "it" on purpose just to come after me. Adding fuel to the fire, he knew we played without tag-backs. That little jerk trapped me in an unsolvable loop.

I left the game to beat him up, so he took off. As I closed in, my fifth-grade brother, Chad, stopped me. Putting the palm of his hand on my chest, he dispensed the same guidance Kenny Rogers gave while our parents drove around in our wood-paneled station wagon. "You gotta know when to walk away, know when to run. This time, you need to run away. Don't let him get you in trouble. Run away!"

I took his advice, but only out of confusion.

I reflect on this story often. Did my older brother really use "The Gambler" as a training aid? I wonder if he believes the tenets laid forth in the song. Does he know when to hold 'em? Know when to fold 'em? Does he ever count his money while he's sittin' at the table? It may not be fair to him, but when we're together, I still search his actions for compliance to the gambler's creed.

Eleanor Rigby / The Beatles

Chad loved the Beatles—and their independent releases: John Lennon, Paul McCartney and Wings, and George Harrison. He had records, eight-tracks, tapes, posters, pens, and board games. He studied them like a high school kid prepares for the SATs.

Interrupting my memory, I once got so mad at him that I chucked a box of his collection off a bridge. I thought I got even, but he beat me up. Today, I kick myself over discarding his small fortune. I definitely earned that beating. In the days to pass, his old eight-track tapes floated down the creek around town. Stupid, stupid, STUPID!!!

In tandem with my brother's obsession, my second-grade teacher read *Sadako and the Thousand Paper Cranes* to our class. For those who are unfamiliar, it's a novel about a girl who contracted leukemia after the Hiroshima bombings. According to Japanese folklore, folding a thousand paper cranes earned her one wish, which she planned to use to rid her body of cancer. Somehow, I knew death was inevitable. I listened to the story day after day, week after week hoping she'd catch her crane count. Unfortunately, Sadako never met her goal, as cancer destroyed her short life.

There was no hope for the little Japanese girl. No hope for Eleanor Rigby, or the preacher, from my brother's music. Maybe life was just filled with several unfair losses. While these people had pure motives—a thousand paper cranes, love, church attendance—none of them got their heart's desires. Instead, they received disappointment, even death. All at once, life's desperation became all too real.

Angel of the Morning / Juice Newton

My first day of the third grade held so much hope. I'm not sure how normal kids went home after school, but I got sidetracked playing, wandering around town, or catching critters. It wasn't uncommon for me to return late. Not to mention the surefire detentions I'd receive for talking or interrupting class.

However, first day detention would be in bad taste for a new year. I marched right home, excited to share the details with my family.

As I approached the dining room, my stepmom cried as she packed a box of my belongings. Enthusiasm faded as I begged for answers. "What's happening? Where am I going?"

"Please," she pleaded. "Your dad... can explain... when he gets home."

Arriving moments later, he also began sobbing uncontrollably. Hugging me with a sense of finality, the slight scent of failing deodorant lingered as I buried my face into his chest. "Tony, having eight kids is a great responsibility," he said. "You're going to foster care until I can sort things out."

As Dad and I held onto each other, the lyrics to Juice Newton's "Angel of the Morning" flooded my mind.

Where did life go so wrong? A few short years ago, our relationship was all we had. I remembered lying beside his bed waiting for his alarm clock to ring. I remembered sifting through lunch selections with him before he headed off to work. I remembered riding shotgun as we drove places, his little sidekick. I remembered rubbing my face against his stubble as he sang me to sleep. I remembered every painful memory we couldn't build upon anymore.

While trudging to my social worker's vehicle to leave for my new home, I couldn't look back. Even at that age, I knew seeing Dad's face would only make me more miserable. Cold callousness hardened my heart as I tried to believe what he promised me. Climbing into the car, I weighed in on what was supposed to be the temporary solution to our problems. Then, we slowly drove away.

That Summer / Garth Brooks

Garth Brooks entered my life at the exact moment I needed him most. In the confusion of going to a new home, I searched for answers. I wanted to trust these strange people, but I didn't know them. From the back seat of my foster parents' car, a gentle fall breeze teased my hair through the open window. "That Summer" played over the local radio station. Feeling the intensity, the desperation, of the song all at once, I found escape from my problems.

This Garth Brooks guy knew how to tell a story. My story. Had he directly observed aspects of my life? How else would he know how windy North Dakota was? The way wheat danced in the wind? How else would he understand the hopelessness of my situation? How on earth did he depict the wonder of blowing breeze and the desire to be carried away with it? He had to shadow me to be able to speak so clearly. All I know is GB and I had a four-minute conversation that day. For a brief moment, I believed that my life could improve.

I'd hate to put the cart way before the horse here, but after a lifetime of circumstantial change, after hearing a million songs since, "That Summer" is still my favorite song of all time. With every listen, I travel through time to that afternoon. The cool breeze blowing in my face. The desperation of rebuilding my life again. The search for answers to solve my pain. Every single time, I helplessly transport back into that seat and feel it all over again.

Standing Outside the Fire / Garth Brooks

Addictions never start with ill intentions. It begins with a sip or a puff. Name your vice, but they usually roll out slowly.

After hearing "That Summer," I had an insatiable desire to hear more from this Garth Brooks dude. I paid attention to the radio with greater interest. What else did he sing? Were his other songs good? Would he keep talking about my particular predicament? I wasn't sure, but Garth became the distraction, the elixir, I used to digest the intolerable pieces of my life.

Wild Horses / Garth Brooks

My foster parents bought Garth Brooks' *No Fences*, maybe due to the success of "Friends in Low Places" and "The Thunder Rolls." Maybe because I pestered them. I've chosen to believe it was because of me. Now, don't get me wrong. I liked both of his massive hits, but two different deep tracks caught my attention.

My hopeful desires seemed to conflict. I wasn't gonna get them all. Dad and my mom weren't getting back together. As much as I wanted to return home, I needed help to air out my experiences. What I wanted, and needed, were in extreme tension. Lacking awareness of the delicate balance between these dreams, I felt it when I heard "Wild Horses."

Wolves / Garth Brooks

It didn't take long, but I memorized every word to "Wolves." My sad story forced me to drink every drop—a cleft lip and palate, divorce, my mom, seven siblings, foster care, social alienation, the constant fear of judgment. In order to heal, I needed to hear it, but I also dreaded the process. Belting out the refrain with full force, I wasn't just singing. I legitimately prayed to God, that somehow, I could cease to be amongst the hunted.

The Night Will Only Know / Garth Brooks

Like any true junkie, a person will do anything to feed their addiction. By chance, my social worker owned Garth's *In Pieces*. I'd heard "Standing Outside the Fire." What other songs were housed in this potential masterpiece? I begged to find out every time she shuttled me to appointments, meetings, or counseling. She probably just agreed to give me hope amongst all the loss.

"The Night Will Only Know" was my go-to track from the cassette. Yep. That meant we either had to fast forward OR take in the whole tape to listen to one song. Once my research exposed the details of a section, another new mystery presented itself. I wrestled with the moral quandary of keeping a murder quiet to protect a secret relationship. I queried words, like innuendo, in the family dictionary. This was real entertainment, pure intrigue. For the next several months, I guilt-tripped my poor social worker into listening to this song until I pieced it together.

The Night I Called the Old Man Out / Garth Brooks

No matter how much I loved my dad, I didn't understand the concept of going to foster home. How could he let me slip through his fingers? I dreamt of the opportunity to call my old man out. Make him feel my hurt. Break him for breaking me. Drag him outside and deal with my aggression from moments he wronged me.

Then, there was this doubt. I'd once seen Dad take on a dude with a clear height/weight advantage. He didn't lose. Pops delivered the victory speech. He was the toughest guy I knew. Even if I grew some more, there was no way I could ever win a physical fight against him. I guess that's not what I wanted anyway. I needed validation that he cared amidst my pain.

All My Rowdy Friends (Have Settled Down) / Hank Williams, Jr.

Being in a new home meant I had to learn how to live, without context, among two new parents. When I was with my real family, I spent entire afternoons climbing to the highest part of any tree I could find. This hobby was forbidden at my new house. I never even considered how dangerous it was until I got in trouble the first time I got caught. My whole existence seemed flawed.

My new family loved traveling. Since there's no way of knowing when I heard these gems first, I've assembled what I call the summer driving medley. Sure, I incessantly interrogated them from the back seat, but I wanted to truly know them. I did it the only way I knew how: listening to their favorite songs to figure them out.

Let me start by describing my foster dad. After drawing a low draft number, he joined the Army and served a full military career, never discussing his experiences as a mail clerk in Vietnam. Post-retirement, he returned to North Dakota to be near his aging parents. He was a strong, quiet, good ol' boy who liked old country music. If I wanted to understand who he was, I'd have to watch. Mr. Man of Few Words certainly wouldn't tell me straight-up.

I'm Gonna Hire a Wino / David Frizzell

Song after song, trip after trip, I was reminded of my foster dad's mysterious past he never mentioned. Crazy nights drinking beer with Army buddies. A life he sacrificed for a social worker job with his family. He didn't resent it. In fact, I think he preferred the simplicity.

On the flip side, I had to imagine an abrupt end to his bachelor status. As he established life with a wife and three children, I believe there were some stern conversations from the doghouse about changing his ways. Mom seemed business savvy; he seemed to have party animal tendencies. What if they converted their house into a bar to save cash? Far-fetched, sure, but sometimes marriage requires this type of innovative compromise.

Luckenbach, Texas / Waylon Jennings

Vacations are about spending time with family. Hours in the car. Hours in cabins, tents, hotel rooms, and campers. We left the hustle of everyday life for a return to the basics. We kids didn't let that stop us. Striking at our foster parents' dropped guard, we tested the loosening of traditionally defined rules. The harder they worked to cement our make-shift family together, the more we attempted to unhinge the system working for our benefit.

Meet Me in Montana / Dan Seals (Ft. Marie Osmond)

I was raised in North Dakota. We took several family trips to Wyoming, South Dakota, and yep, Montana. The concept was funny, especially when my foster parents' adult kids traveled with us in a separate vehicle. I could only assume they were serenaded by the same old dusty Dan Seals tape on their youthful treks across the countryside. "Hey, you should 'meet us in Montana.' Get it?" I joked.

On these vacations, I witnessed my first example of true love. My foster dad reminded me of Dan Seals. Ma was a little like Marie Osmond. From the back seat, I watched as they shared quiet conversation, held hands, and snuck kisses. Their strange affection seemed foreign to me.

I can't help it, but when I drive through the mountains these days, I find myself longing for the simplicity of those family trips. To clarify the memories, I may even throw some old country music into rotation. What I wouldn't give to trade the rat race for some carefree shenanigans across Yellowstone National Park.

Livin' On Love / Alan Jackson

My foster dad is 6' 4" and weighed in at 220 pounds at the time. He's a gentle giant with a loud personality. For example, he speaks a few decibels above whisper volume (until he's mad) but sneezes hard enough to rock a building's foundation. His cold, expressionless face makes him impossible to read.

I couldn't fathom how this icy-cold killer enjoyed tender love songs by Alan Jackson. Through mysterious behavior, he taught me you can't wait for verbal expression from people. Sometimes, you need to acknowledge the subtle social cues. Their actions may say everything you need to hear.

He's a Rebel / The Crystals

My foster mom is entirely different than her husband. Where Dad had quiet, humble roots in rural North Dakota, Mom maintained a loud, fierce attitude from her upbringing in Detroit, Michigan. Dad's tough like men are supposed to be; Mom's tough because life made her that way. I still haven't fully learned this, but it isn't wise to cross her. She'll outlast you in vindictiveness just to spite you.

Then, you'd listen to music with her. With diverse, but sensitive, tastes, I can't daydream about a road trip when Motown wasn't playing in the background. Her music was symbolic to a generation and she developed in the heart of it all.

Most of her songs highlighted society's rejection of bad boys. I had to believe she dated tough guys by public perception with gentle spirits. She didn't detail her past either, but I learned her strength stemmed from some unmentionable challenges.

Un-Break My Heart / Toni Braxton

One of my brother Norm's funny kid's tapes said, "I can sing like a girl, I can sing like a frog." That's Toni Braxton. She's capable of hitting notes lower than I can. Not just a little either, but way lower. Through Toni's sultry vocals, I realized I didn't have to like my foster mom's musical taste, but she did recognize talent.

On a completely unrelated note, Toni Braxton highlights one of my key pet peeves: the male version of Tony is spelled with a "y." So, medical receptionists, call center employees, and anyone else with careers confirming the spelling of human names, listen to me. I've checked my birth certificate multiple times. It doesn't read "Anthoni." I have yet to meet another dude who spells it that way—end of rant. Please forgive me. I have to work these demons out somehow.

End of the Road / Boyz II Men

There was a time in the 90s when Motown influence morphed into the R&B scene. Take Boyz II Men, for example. As my foster mom's kids developed their own tastes, she appreciated them. That's the thing about her. She listened to most musical genres. It had to be interesting to hail from Detroit and hear her children's adaptation to the Motown movement. Even better, it was inspiring to witness her children inherit her love for music.

Only Time / Enya

My foster mom once made a nineteen-track mixtape alternating between only two songs. Welcome to the first. I DO NOT like Enya's "Only Time." Never have, never will. I'm not sure where the hatred stems from, but it reminds me of playful pixies engaged in a snowball fight. With that level of disdain at first listen, imagine hearing it nine out of nineteen times on one album.

You may be asking how I know this CD had nineteen songs. I had the distinct pleasure of watching the track count increase from the back seat while waiting for the torment to end. I hold a deep belief that disc could replace waterboarding as a viable form of human torture. Terrorists would divulge every piece of information you require. Personally, I don't even think it would take all nineteen lashes. When I mention it that way, it kinda makes my mom a hero. Only kinda, though.

My Heart Will Go On / Celine Dion

What would happen if this notorious nineteen-track CD was deployed in a torture scenario? It was, whether intentional or not, so I speak from experience. The enemy's spirit wouldn't break. At least, not at first. You see, Enya was akin to drilling a corkscrew through your earholes, but track two, Celine Dion's "My Heart Will Go On," provided the "terrorists" with ten opportunities to show our resilience.

My foster dad, younger foster brother Norm, and I changed the lyrics. We sang in obnoxious falsetto. Wailed along with pitchy flute imitations. However, none of our efforts discouraged the cruel and unusual use of this torture device. Every passenger got a turn to pick the music. Ma's selection was to be played until we broke. With this admission, I don't think we ever did. For several years, our punishment persisted every long-distance car ride.

Total Eclipse of the Heart / Bonnie Tyler

Most people my age were introduced to "Total Eclipse of the Heart" through Will Ferrell's *Old School*. I distinctly remember it on summer vacations, but the song was a staple around the Kessel household. While I may joke at my foster mom's expense, I related to this piece.

A part of me enjoyed the opportunities to go on trips around the country with my foster family. However, I wrestled with the fact I couldn't travel with my biological family. I honestly believed if I was happy with my foster family, I betrayed my roots. On the flip side, I thought if I experienced joy with my real family, I neglected my foster family's sacrifice. The heart's actual total eclipse was never being content with what I had, but seeking happiness through the unobtainable.

Take My Breath Away / Berlin

Have any of you listened to the *Top Gun* soundtrack? Once upon a time, I could sing along with the entire album. I even scatted over the theme song. Like any other computer with limited memory, I've managed to recapture most of the space it used to consume.

One particular romp through the tape, my foster brother spouted, "This'll take your breath away!" Imitating a machine gun, he sprayed imaginary bullets, and spit, in an oscillating fan motion from his booster seat. Norm was so young; he may've been the only one to get away with it.

Naturally, my foster dad and I burst out in nervous laughter. This angered my foster mom so much, she rewound the tape, cranked the volume, and replayed it from the beginning. "You guys are jerks! I never get to enjoy anything!"

Not daring to mutter a word, we let her have a moment with her precious song.

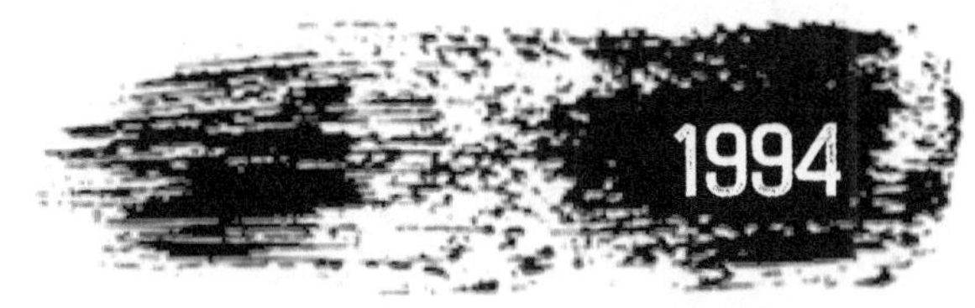

My Love / Little Texas

The first wedding I remember attending was for one of my foster dad's co-workers. He was a full-time social worker and a part-time Soldier in the National Guard. Sure, Dad was an Army vet, but this dude currently served. I became so intrigued by military personnel that I bought a G.I. Joe with my spending money during the trip. We're not talking about a regular-sized figurine, either, but one quadruple the standard size.

The wedding dance was plagued with slow songs. Instead of sliding on my knees while cocktail swordfighting the other kids, I was forced to watch years' worth of old love. Think about your parents' relationship for a minute. Gross, right? To avoid the discomfort, I wandered around collecting uneaten after-dinner mints. From the corner of my eye, I caught Dad's co-worker and his new bride dancing to "My Love." For some reason, when viewed from a different perspective, the magic of marriage amplifies.

Heart of Glass / Blondie

My foster mom owned a reel-to-reel player. Even with my level of exposure to music, I'd never seen one of these machines. That sucker was loud, too. When in use, you could hear it from a mile away. As I walked the two blocks toward my house after school, each lyric increased with clarity. Oh no! That noise only meant one thing: since Mom was working, I was working. Thanks, Blondie, for ruining my afternoon.

Life's a Dance / John Michael Montgomery

I got a suit for my tenth birthday. It was my birthday suit. Not that kind, you dirty pervert! Comprised of clothing straight from the Mr. Rogers collection: a maroon striped clip-on tie, a white dress shirt, khaki pants, and a forest green cardigan sweater. It was, hands down, the classiest outfit in my wardrobe.

I had to look sharp for my foster brother Danny's wedding. A lot transpired over a year. As a proud suit owner, I was dignified enough to dabble in the art of slow dancing. Sure, I danced with my aunt, but still, we danced. Was I any good? I don't know. John Michael Montgomery's "Life's a Dance" says it all, though. I'd figure it out along the way.

Mmm Mmm Mmm Mmm / Crash Test Dummies

After watching *Dumb and Dumber* once, my brothers and I fell in love. Studying the VHS seven times during the one-day rental, we memorized every word, every song, every quip, every facial expression. The movie's pure comedic genius, minus one part. Do you remember when Harry swaps driving responsibilities with Lloyd to find out he traveled several hundred miles in the wrong direction? Harry seethes on the road with his butt crack hanging out. "I'm only human, Harry!" Lloyd screams. To enhance the scene's emotion, The Crash Test Dummies' "Mmm Mmm Mmm" soars in the background.

A weird scene to hate, sure, but let me explain. You see, my brother Chad moved into the foster home I lived in. Since he also battles with severe music addiction, I'd heard the song long before the movie was released. Chad knew the dude's low voice and the lyrical content freaked me out. In our shared room, we listened to tapes through headphones after our parents made us go to bed.

What track could a demented older brother torture me with while fast asleep? Yep, "Mmm Mmm Mmm." Images of children convulsing on a church floor jolted me awake, screaming. Birthmarks all over someone's body? Gross. After years of therapy, I'm finally able to listen to it without freaking out.

Reno / Doug Supernaw

It was bound to happen. Fifth-grade brought about my first serious crush. A girl in my class, dressed like one of the Go-Gos, handed out Tiger Pops for Halloween. Despite my affinity for the multi-colored lollipop, I refused to eat it. She was so perfect and edgy. For over a week, I played out our relationship while spinning the sucker stick between my fingers.

I'm not superstitious, but that Tiger Pop was our symbol of unrequited love. The longer I kept it, the possibility of our future together was real. Chad tore into my love memento. He even went as far as swiping the artificial replacement I swapped in from my other Halloween candy.

If I couldn't maintain a sucker, how could I keep a girlfriend? It seemed as if my crush understood the sucker's power and conspired with my brother to avoid the whole mess. I understand how insane this sounds now, but it tormented me for days.

After losing my Garth Brooks tape collection as punishment, I was forced into radioland for two weeks. While sipping from a tall glass of self-pity, Doug Supernaw's "Reno" played during a late evening broadcast. I wasn't ready to abandon hope, but Doug convinced me girls had to be pretty evil. My fragile heart couldn't quite handle them yet.

Learning to Live Again / Garth Brooks

The Chase is, and will always be, my favorite GB album. Every track exposed different aspects of my insecurities. Through a simple lyrical misinterpretation, "Learning to Live Again" screamed loudest to me. Initially, I thought the burnt hand and cut face described finding love with a physical deformity. He had a scarred face, or so I thought.

See, I was born with a cleft lip and palate. After several corrective surgeries, I have scars in undeniable places. Unless wearing a ski mask in public becomes acceptable, I had to become more secure in my flaws.

As a child, I knew the dating scene, pursuing romantic interests, and getting married presented challenges for me. Garth seemed to depict this struggle so succinctly. He didn't, because that's not what the song's about; it's about re-entering the market after a traumatic break-up. That's not the point, though. Music became the conversation I didn't dare share with others.

Wheel of Fortune / Ace of Base

Most people alive in the 90s remember Ace of Base. I'm not sure why, but Chad always shared his musical treasures with me. The Beatles, Michael Jackson, Johnny Cash, and Ace of Base. Subtle lyrical nuances from the liner notes, observations from songs, and music videos. *The Sign's* kinda creepy once you slip into the deep tracks, but his enthusiasm was intriguing. Even more, I would've listened to anything he asked me to if it meant spending time with my big brother.

She's Every Woman / Garth Brooks

I've met some recovering addicts. They've all told me if they could rewind time and change things, they would. They can even pinpoint the exact moment they first clung to their vice. So can I. Not to make light of addiction, but my particular breed of obsession can be found in New Release Tuesday. For years, I've been seeking new music, new releases, new experiences.

I'd been a Garth Brooks fanatic for several years, but never during a record release. That's until *Fresh Horses.* Since Garth's key business strategy includes releasing albums near Black Friday, a junkie was required to wait for Christmas to get his fix.

Resorting to new lows to cure the itch, I had to willingly consume radio. It was my personal responsibility to ensure Garth performed well on the Top 40. I bought blank tapes, captured, and reviewed live broadcasts whenever possible to get the perfect version of "She's Every Woman." You know, that cut the DJ didn't talk over or end short.

This behavior can only be seen as addictive in nature. I hadn't been a part of the Garth phenomenon in this capacity. Where some of my fellow addicts express regret at the path life took them on, this one song began a journey of endless discovery.

The Car / Jeff Carson

In listening to the radio, other songs resonated with my experiences. My absolute loyalty was to Garth Brooks, but I dedicated one blank tape to capture these moments in time. For instance, my biological dad frequently diagnosed car problems by sound. He has a gift. After hearing a particular noise, he sold the part necessary to solve said problem.

Lying in the driveway as he fixed our old station wagon, I never acquired the fine art of automobile repair. By handing him tools as he worked, I was guaranteed to have the time I needed with him.

Someone Else's Star / Bryan White

Pondering my life in the sixth grade, it became evident I lacked in several ways. Yes, some kids started dating. Some thought they found love. It wasn't about that for me. When I looked at their lives, they seemed to be getting better. They had more friends, more things, and a romantic companion to share experiences with (I know; I was a kid, ok?). The wishes I had for myself were being given to those around me. When would it be my turn to be happy?

On the Verge / Collin Raye

After my first crush inadvertently crushed me, I steered clear of the female persuasion for the better part of a year. Then, I met my sixth-grade teacher. She was a recent college graduate hired a week into school to fill an unexpected vacancy. Although inappropriate, I acquired feelings for her.

She was my teacher. Her duty was to build the foundation for educational and workforce success, not serve as my romantic interest.

I kept weighing my situation out. Some days, I was ok with it. On other days, my feelings drove deep shame. I remember using elementary math to figure out our age difference. 23−11=12, twice my life experience. I definitely knew what I felt, but I continued to convince myself out of the predicament. If I wasn't in love, I had to be well on my way.

If I Could Make a Living / Clay Walker

Since I'm flirting with the concept of violating my absolute dedication to GB, allow me to tell you the story of how I finally did.

Chad hung out with his best friend most days we weren't in trouble. I always begged to go with them, but brothers find innovative ways to leave you behind. One afternoon, HE actually asked ME. When he went the day before, I asked him to go. He said no, I cried, he left. Was it possible my tears made him cave?

Of course, it couldn't be that simple. I was solicited for indentured servitude to his friend's chore list while they listened to Dire Straits and played *NBA Jam*. If I hurried, they agreed to let me play video games with them. The exact moment I finished the last item on the list, my brother announced, "All right, man. It's time to go home for supper."

No fair! I worked so hard but didn't get to have any fun. I used tears, once again, as a bartering chip.

Handing me a shoebox full of cassettes, my brother's friend said, "Here. Pick a tape for helping out."

Leafing through the box, he had nothing from the Garth catalog I didn't already own. Cautiously selecting Clay Walker's *If I Could Make a Living*, my betrayal was complete. In an ironic twist, I earned my first non-Garth album as currency for work. My conscience was clear, though. Someone else's money dropped on the countertop of a music store for this purchase. The folks over at Billboard would never know.

Nobody Wins / Radney Foster

From an early age, I was intimately aware of the winners and losers of love. Add several years, a little maturity, and massive radio consumption, I learned relationships only succeed in compromise. I knew love was messy. Sometimes, it wells shallow pride that generates arguments and destroys relational stability.

I knew the catastrophe well, witnessing it firsthand: doors slamming and yelling. Mean, unintentional words birthed into existence. Silence for days until the more guilty party issued an apology. Then, the healing could begin. As I explored how to behave in future relationships, I took note of less-than-perfect examples through lyrical exploration.

Not On Your Love / Jeff Carson

I often wonder if other children of divorce romanticize the concept of eternal love. We have the blueprint for love gone wrong. You'd think we have enough information to generate relationships toward perfect conclusion. At a bare minimum, we have the insight not to take them for granted.

Emulating a reverse slippery slope, the fantasies danced through my imagination. What if my parents resolved their problems on those challenging nights instead of walking away? If they dedicated to talking things out, no matter how long resolution took, we'd still be together. With our unified family intact, I would've never been shipped to a foster home. If only couples committed to this one thing, life could've been perfect.

She Can't Say I Didn't Cry / Rick Trevino

Where most kids say their dads were tough and withdrawn, my biological father wasn't afraid to express emotion. I CANNOT say I never saw him cry about any of his past regrets. Over my mom and their divorce. Over my departure from home. By society's definition of masculinity, he maintained subject matter expertise in fixing broken cars down at the auto part store.

I'm here to tell you: he cried. Every time he hurt. Every time he beamed with pride or expressed deep joy. Real men can, and do, cry.

Lipstick Promises / George Ducas

Have you heard the joke about what happens when country music is played backward? Your girl loads your dog in the bed of your truck before returning to you. The music video would feature grainy grayscale imagery of a solitary tear crawling up your cheek as your family reunites at the dining room table. Country music tends to pander to the sad people who listen to it.

As I consumed an increasing amount of the genre, I was left wondering how to avoid these heartbreakers I kept hearing about. At eleven years old, I contemplated what my future romances had in store. How could I escape putting my kids through any portion of my life? How was I supposed to trust any woman I met wouldn't turn out like my mom? Is love even worth it? Although I felt alone, it had to be better than being destroyed by another person out of blind faith. Not having answers, I dug through the radio to find them.

What Mattered Most / Ty Herndon

Imagine a kid's room littered with Kirby Puckett, Cris Carter, and Penny Hardaway cards, *Goosebumps* books, Garth Brooks tapes, magazine clippings, and a few composition notebooks. I wasn't allowed to keep it that way, but when I was in my room, I immersed myself in what I enjoyed.

Garth Brooks' name given at birth was Troyal. He was married to Sandy and had three kids: Taylor, August, and Allie. Kirby Puckett didn't have a middle name. In 1991, Dad and I watched him carry the Twins to a World Series victory. Cris Carter was drafted by the Eagles before being traded to Minnesota in 1990. My *Goosebumps* books were on the shelf in numerical order, without a book missing.

What if these meticulous practices were applied to a person I loved? Let's explore how Ty's character details his significant other. Did knowing this information help him cater to the emotional support she needed? In the end, he admits it didn't. As I explored my own interests, I missed the point. Obsessive knowledge lacking action doesn't equate to love.

Heart Half Empty / Ty Herndon (Ft. Stephanie Bentley)

Given the stories I've shared, it becomes easy to assume I drifted toward negativity. The truth remains, life can still be viewed through a cautiously optimistic lens. Why stop loving when everything feels lost? Why throw out positive memories due to a few negative ones? Somehow, with my tapes and radio, my glass would always be full.

The River of Dreams / Billy Joel

Despite my best efforts, I couldn't escape the crush I had on my sixth-grade teacher. Her youth made her super cool in ways most other teachers weren't. Case and point: she allowed us to bring music to listen to during art class. One particular Friday, I hand-carried Garth Brooks' *In Pieces* to school. Returning after recess, "Callin' Baton Rouge" blared over the classroom stereo. My girl was listening to my tape of my favorite artist!

Later that night, I abandoned my usual 99.1 Keys Country for a local pop station. A few hours after falling asleep, my bladder screamed at me to do its bidding. Billy Joel's "The River of Dreams" forced my teacher's imagery when I returned to bed. Out of all the tapes in her possession, she chose mine! We were pretty much set to get married or whatever people do when they fall in love.

Since there isn't a song for how she broke my heart, let me finish the story. When class resumed after Christmas vacation, my teacher announced her engagement. During a scheduled bathroom break, I overheard a female classmate ask how her fiancé proposed. Apparently, the jerk delivered gifts through a scavenger hunt culminating in a proposal. A knot formed in the pit of my stomach, triggering my gag reflex as I held back tears. It took months to get over her. But first, I had to painfully learn how to dismiss desire for something I could never have.

No Man's Land / John Michael Montgomery

One of the greatest moments in my life was the advent of CD. As people upgraded their collections, I got tapes for a cheap trade, even some at no cost. That's exactly how John Michael Montgomery's third album came into my life. My brother Chad gifted it to me.

My recollection isn't exclusive to receiving free stuff. That would be shallow. Around the time Chad gave me the tape, he moved out of our shared foster home. If he could be shuttled off without warning, couldn't I face the same fate? With his final gift in hand, I was forced into my own no man's land.

The Change / Garth Brooks

Do you remember attending school on days when tragedy struck? Teachers wheeled out TVs on carts to allow us to absorb historical significance in real time. Every class was momentarily suspended as we discussed implications and waded through the traumatic imagery: firefighters sifting through concrete shards, paramedics hanging their heads in defeat, innocent bystanders hosting candlelight vigils.

Before I saw the video for "The Change," it became evident Garth would respond to the carnage the Oklahoma City bombing left in his home state. My young mind couldn't grasp a gracious response to injured children being pulled from the rubble where their daycare once stood. What kind of psycho would do what Timothy McVeigh did? Didn't he understand how precious life is? How was I supposed to forget the wreckage his careless attack caused?

Yet, in the passing of time since, one of my most significant life philosophies has solidified. I have to get preachy for a moment, but we cannot allow other's hateful, malicious, fear-inducing actions dictate any other response aside from love. As I continued to process the tragedies of life through song, I learned this world's a dark place. Try as it may, I couldn't allow it to change me.

Little Rock / Collin Raye

In the 90s, fans leaned heavily upon music videos to round out the consumer experience. When done right, they intensify a song's impact. For example, take Collin Raye's "Little Rock." During the bridge, the video highlights Collin's character in a physical altercation with his spouse before chucking a whiskey glass into the fireplace. The disturbing imagery heightened the emotional investment behind the melody. If it wasn't evident throughout a normal listening session, the song painted a picture of alcohol abuse.

Now, add my personal experiences. Before any of his kids were born, my dad had problems with addiction. In one of those "if you learn from my mistakes, you won't have to make them yourself" kind of discussions, he pled with us to avoid the stuff.

It doesn't stop there. One of my earliest memories, at three years old, involved alcohol abuse. My mom, my two brothers, and I sat on the couch watching *Cheers*. As the theme song played, my memory of the night reflected a soft yellow hue. My recollection begins in a warm, safe place.

Without warning, the evening turned to a violent pounding on the door. Not the gentle tapping of a friendly neighbor, but a person seeking to hurt us. The surprise visitor was my mom's drunk boyfriend. Entering the room, he lunged toward my mom and brothers. My oldest brother, Kurt, protected me by tucking me behind the couch. Being a curious three-year-old, I witnessed this man hit, shove, and scream at my family.

In the age before cell phones and continuously connected society, somehow, Dad instinctively stopped by. He pulled my mom's boyfriend into the front yard. Dad is my frame, a skinny, nerdy dude. Her boyfriend was built like a truck. Dad beat him. I watched from the steps as he lectured my mom's boyfriend for hurting kids and a woman. I'm not sure how they left, but it seemed like Dad took him away.

All this to say, my dad was once an alcoholic. He had to deal with his own demons at one time. Besides, his kids, whom he hoped to keep away from those demons, would still be subjected to them. As I saw the music video for "Little Rock," it became easy to visualize in my life. As wrong as it may be, I wanted my mom's boyfriend to pay for what he did to us.

Smells Like Nirvana / Weird Al

Junior High—that awkward time in life capped by self-exploration and moments of frantic intensity. While my classmates were absorbed in finding themselves, I was at it with my core group of friends. We never hung out together but found commonality in Weird Al Yankovic. Over the next couple months, I acquired *Bad Hair Day*, *Alapalooza*, *Dare to Be Stupid*, and *Off the Deep End*.

Music is mainly serious business for me. During a time of intense self-discovery, I catered to the goofy streak within me. I had this weird desire to fit in. As hard as I tried to stick to my personal interests, I drifted away from expectations. The staple, Weird Al, was as close to normal as I could get.

Wipe Out / The Ventures

During seventh grade, I transitioned from music consumption to production by joining the band. Mind you, my friends had already been playing for a few years. I was behind AND the best instruments were taken. When I arrived on the first day of class without an instrument, I was escorted back to a boneyard. Of the two left, I chose the baritone. Basically, a mini tuba. All sixty-some pounds of me got to play the fourth-largest musical device available at school.

Further, I didn't know how to read music. A mere appreciator at this point, I plunged in enthusiastically. Learning how to play a D, I played the note every time my sheet music called for any noise. No progression, no rhythm, nothing. Just careless D notes strung together with abandon. Never mind technique, my music career was dawning.

Livin' in the Fridge / Weird Al

While my friends dated, joined sports teams, and established their identities, I memorized Weird Al food lyrics. They liked all kinds of new music I'd never heard before. I kept listening to Garth, which most of my friends had drifted from, and Weird Al. I liked song parodies without any idea of the original content. Aerosmith, Nirvana, Coolio? Who are they? As my peers pushed the boundaries, some might say they were living on the edge. Me? Yep, I was livin' in the fridge.

Living in a Moment / Ty Herndon

Around this point in life, several of my classmates entered the dating scene. They engaged in intense weeklong relationships that ended dramatically and without reason. It was the last thing I needed, but the first thing I wanted. While listening to music, I romanticized the idea of running into a girl at school. By surprise, I'd find a mate to share my life with.

Keep in mind, I attended an institution with a little more than three hundred students in total (kindergarten through twelfth grade). There wasn't a person I hadn't met. I could only rely on new girls or a fresh glimpse at one I hadn't considered before. In retrospect, I was too vulnerable to shower after Phy Ed back then. While I had no business being in a relationship, it was still everything I wanted.

Everything You Know Is Wrong / Weird Al

My Weird Al infatuation made way for a disastrous character flaw. As most subjects of his content trudge through life without a care in the world, they do so with flair, confidence, and a fashion sense south of normal. Not only was I oblivious, I acted as if everything was exactly how I planned it. I enlisted an attitude of unwarranted arrogance, mixed with a slightly off-center sense of humor. I'm sad to report; it took several years to learn how to use this to my advantage. At that time, in those moments, I was not a relatable individual to most people.

Cavity Search / Weird Al

Being born with a cleft lip and palate, I spent a lot of time in dental chairs. I didn't fear dentists like most people do. I was tired of them. And orthodontists. And ear, nose, and throat doctors. And oral maxillofacial surgeons. And speech therapists. I was tired of them all. I had caps, crowns, bone grafts, braces, spacers, fillings, root canals, and every type of dentistry imaginable, all by the time I was thirteen. Numb me. Drill me. Floss me. Bill me. Welcome to my life as a young person.

When Cowboys Didn't Dance / Lonestar

In the sawdust cloud kicked up by boot-scootin' boogies and achy-breaky heart line dancers, the flashiness of country music confused me. Living in town, I understand my story may contradict itself. Sure, my family helped move bales a few times, fed cows, and gathered eggs as a novelty. We took dips in farm stock tanks with my cousins on a few occasions. Played King of the Mountain on a stack of hay bales. Yet, I've never lived in the country. I am a hypocrite.

If listening to the radio taught me anything, country music was losing its roots. Yep, a Garth Brooks fan complained of decreasing genre authenticity. My biggest influence took country music into the mainstream in the most substantial manner. Again, I am a hypocrite. The conflict welled up as I contemplated the dwindling pioneer spirit depicted during the Wild West days. The more we wander away from tough times, the further we drift from understanding them.

Tequila Talkin' / Lonestar

My medicine became living in a past that no longer affected me and country music. Why didn't my parents fight to keep me or bring me home? Why was I born into a poor family? Did people think I was ugly due to my birth defect? Why didn't I have more friends? Why didn't girls like me? You get the picture—sob story after sob story.

These delusions drove weird mannerisms. With little social grace, I didn't know how to maintain normal relationships with people. Looking back, my social interactions bore a striking resemblance to end-of-evening bar conversations.

One-sided discussions filled with "she doesn't know what she's missing" followed by apologies later, justifying my comments in the first place. Sure, I'd stumble across the truth eventually. At my house. In my bedroom. With my stereo. Alone, but long after the abnormal interaction.

Daddy's Hands / Holly Dunn

Throughout my middle school years, Holly Dunn's "Daddy's Hands" was the anthem for most father/daughter dances I observed. The rest of the crowd watches a father dance with his little girl as a final send-off into married life. It's beautiful, but with parent issues, the onset of puberty, and constant identity crises, I had several minutes to contemplate my relationship with my fathers.

As a teenager, I never understood why neither of my fathers possessed enough intuition to help me through my internal struggles. Watching these intensely intimate moments made me squirm in contradiction. I had plenty of time to brew up admiration for their role in my life. Also, moments to consider why I didn't share a similar connection.

During this uncomfortable pause, I resorted to standing on the sidelines poking fun of the whole ordeal with my cousins. I loved the song, recorded it off the radio, but had to pretend to hate it in settings like this one.

No One Needs to Know / Shania Twain

Most people who listened to country radio in the 90s are aware of Shania Twain. It's rare for me to say this, but I hated "Any Man of Mine." My female classmates chanted this anthem everywhere: in the halls, jumping rope on the playground, and walking home from school. I gather her hitmaker, *The Woman in Me*, wore out its allure with my friend circle since it was gifted to me at the end of seventh grade.

I couldn't stand the premise someone would have the courage to challenge GB. However, in order to know your enemy, you have to study them. During a weeklong visit with my biological family, I took to the trenches to conduct a deep analysis of Shania's perceived masterpiece. Behind enemy lines, I was tricked into liking "No One Needs to Know."

Imagine every anticipated romantic interest I had to this point started and ended this exact way. I didn't dare to share my desires—expecting dates, weddings, and the future—to work itself out. Especially after Chad made me call my first crush. Never again. I could plan. I could dream. If I didn't act, I wouldn't get hurt. Surprisingly enough, a lack of action equates to a lack of results. It was far easier to process life in silent frustration.

Maybe We Should Just Sleep on It / Tim McGraw

At a young age, three years old to be exact, my mother taught me if you wanted material goods, you'd have to steal them. With time, the innocence faded. You don't bother asking when your parents couldn't make ends meet. Even in my new home, swiping items became more convenient than facing inevitable rejection. Baseball cards, Goosebump books, candy, and yes: tapes. While it's embarrassing to admit, Tim McGraw's *All I Want* was acquired via a five-finger discount from a local store.

When you steal albums your parents know you couldn't afford and they didn't buy them for you, it cannot be common knowledge. You have to live a double life. It was as if I owned two completely different music collections: the one they knew about and my secret stash.

Despite my severe social idiocy, I noticed people weren't invested in GB the same way I was. They were, however, talking about Tim McGraw. In my head, owning this album was a rite of passage to popularity. My friends had to put as much stock in music as I did. Night after night, I stayed up late studying the material necessary to pass the one test I couldn't crack.

Da Da Da / The Trio

On a crisp, cool fall night, I attended my first ever junior high lock-in. Our pick-up five-on-five basketball game faded to three-on-three into one-on-one when I was left alone shooting hoops until daybreak. Popular hits of the day, Sugar Ray's "I Just Wanna Fly" and The Trio's "Da Da Da," blasted from a boombox in the corner of the gym. Rules and responsibilities went out the window.

For one evening, it seemed like even adolescent politics disappeared. Growing up happens at the speed of life. Sometimes, you have to lock the doors to enjoy the process for a little while longer.

The Old Stuff / Garth Brooks

Some moments define who you are, the exact moment they occur. One afternoon, my brother Chad called me from his new foster home to tell me he had three tickets to attend a Garth Brooks concert in Bismarck, ND. Through careful coordination with my social worker, I was approved to go if an adult went with to supervise. For my first concert experience, I was fortunate enough to exist in the presence of my biggest influence.

I have no idea how normal people prepare to meet their heroes, but dedicated every free minute to studying every detail of Garth's on-stage persona. With his music looped, I reviewed every lyric to every song. I re-watched his televised performances, going as far as begging a friend to capture *Live from Central Park* on HBO for me. Not wanting to miss anything, I explored all aspects of his crazy live show. I used any remaining free time to record the radio to hear tracks from *Sevens*, his next Black Friday release. Between my studies, I lined out my outfit: a Garth Brooks t-shirt and *Ropin' the Wind* baseball cap.

On the big day, the wait for him to take the stage was unbearable. In a long-anticipated moment, Garth opened the concert with "The Old Stuff." Even better, he replaced "Detroit" with "Bismarck," as my research suggested he would. He screamed the name of a city one hundred miles from my hometown! Giving this show my everything, I stood the entire time and sang to every song.

My favorite memory of the concert was when my brother took me stage side. Our seats were in a great location, but he wanted to take me closer. With my social worker's permission, Chad, the metalhead, took me to the floor wearing his Marilyn Manson shirt. As we approached the stage, my heart pounded in my throat.

Thump-thump. Thump-thump. Thump-thump.

I was confident we violated some sort of venue policy, but there we were. Chad struck up a conversation with a stoic-looking security guard to take me to the edge of the stage. Behind his back, Chad motioned for me to come closer. As I crept forward, I heard him tell the guard I was the biggest Garth fan he knew.

"I don't care, kid. Get back to your assigned seat."

Amidst failed logic, my brother deployed mosh pit tactics to clear a path to the stage. Towering less than ten feet away, Garth strummed his guitar with the headstock pointed toward me. Making brief eye contact with my hero, paralysis overtook me. Daydreams of gifting him my hat ended abruptly as security bulldozed us away from the stage. My body trembled with adrenaline as I contemplated the wasted opportunity.

These songs capstoned most moments in my young life. Singing them with a unified crowd in North Dakota was an entirely different experience. I was already a Garth Brooks superfan, but that night, I got to witness the live show that earned him seven CMA Entertainer of the Year awards.

Belleau Wood / Garth Brooks

Per tradition, I got Garth Brooks' *Sevens* for Christmas. As I've explained, his genuine talent for storytelling forces investment into a song's content. Closing out the holiday, I sipped in the story of a time when music temporarily ended war. The historical impact of "Belleau Wood" had me contemplating the unifying potential music possesses. That evening, I went to sleep believing kindness could exist in the world if people simply took the time to invest in it.

It's Your Love / Tim McGraw (Ft. Faith Hill)

Since I have older siblings, I became an uncle at a young age. For some reason, the weight of pregnancy didn't resonate with my understanding of the biological process. It wasn't a problem I had to deal with when I couldn't tell girls I liked them.

At the helm of a simple music video, my sex education classes clicked. Unbridled passion somehow leads to this condition. When done correctly, the magic of raising kids looked beautiful. On the other hand, a fifteen-year-old girl I knew was navigating high school as an overwhelmed mother of two. Given my past, I was left to wonder if I even wanted children of my own.

Letting Go / Suzy Bogguss

Since leaving my mom's custody at four years old, I'd only seen her a few times. We exchanged a handful of letters throughout the years. On one desperate occasion, I went as far as to accept a collect call, costing me $70 from my first paper route check, just to speak with her. No matter how much I desired a meaningful relationship with this woman, it never seemed possible.

Since Chad lived halfway between us, he planned a trip to the Kirkwood Mall in Bismarck. After eating lunch at an alien-themed restaurant, we spent the afternoon bargain-hunting for Space Jam as a gift for my little brother. It was nice to see her and my two little sisters, but the visit left a void within my broken spirit. How had five years passed since I saw her last and this trip be such a bust?

I packed up my disappointment and carried it home with me for the hundred-mile journey. Returning to a note from my foster mom, I allowed Channel Twenty-seven, CMT, to babysit me until she returned. The cold black TV screen gained focus on the intro credits for Suzy Bogguss' "Letting Go." A simple tale of a high school girl departing her parents to start her own life.

In an act of vengeance, I wished the same torment plaguing me struck my biological mom. My irrational optimism was failing. For the first time in my life, I realized she probably didn't feel a thing. Somehow, sitting alone in the basement that afternoon clarified she would never love me the way I loved her.

Sweet Dreams / Marilyn Manson

Chad eventually moved closer to me with a different foster family. Sensing this relationship was important, my foster mom allowed me to visit Chad at his new house often. He lived in a beautiful home with shutters, a well-maintained front yard, and a white picket fence. If I remember right, they may've even had a toy poodle or some little dog. I'm not sure why this house impressed me so much. I had one exactly like it. Somehow, Chad hit the big time.

Going to Chad's room, a Kurt Cobain memorial poster highlighted his sad face, now deceased. I thumbed through his massive, unfamiliar music collection. Flipping on MTV to stomp out boredom, our hopes to catch *Beavis and Butthead* were interrupted by the music video for Marilyn Manson's "Sweet Dreams." Who was this freak? My saving grace was his new foster mom kept coming into the room, forcing Chad to change the channel. As soon as she left, he flipped back to keep watching. Sprawled out in a recliner, he only moved enough to ensure she didn't enter the room to bust him again.

Manson sang with passion and conviction, but he didn't sing of hopeful things. I remember the original Eurythmics version; this one was way different. I didn't know what to think. How was I supposed to relate to other kids if this is what they listened to?

One Sweet Day / Mariah Carey (Ft. Boyz II Men)

I may not need to explain this, but my initial journey into music production was a total failure. Near the end of my first year of band, I was encouraged to take private lessons or quit. Since Garth only played a brass instrument for "One Night a Day" during live shows, the baritone didn't appease to my true calling.

My band teacher was encouraging, though; he wasn't a jerk. Coaching me toward a smoother learning curve, he asked me to try choir out. Plus, he couldn't get dudes to join. I didn't tell him but I enrolled in chorus for a chance to hang out with girls.

Mr. Matthews was a sixty year old dude with diverse musical tastes. One day, I wandered into class as he listened to Tupac. Once again, I entered into another educational experience without natural talent, but as Mr. Matthews promised, the learning curve was less sharp. Plus, developing my singing voice was a worthwhile investment.

Tragedy struck Mr. Matthews as his wife unexpectedly fell ill and passed away. On my fourteenth birthday, our choir sang Mariah Carey's "One Sweet Day" at a fundraiser to ease his medical expenses. In a swift stroke of my own impending fate, my foster dad's mom was in Oklahoma undergoing treatment for cancer. We didn't believe she had long to live, either. For the first time, I wasn't just using music to process aspects of my own life. My classmates and I utilized art in an attempt to make Mr. Matthews' world a little more bearable.

The River / Garth Brooks

Most schools have spirit week shenanigans: Pajama Day, Hat Day, School Spirit Day. In 1998, we had a Hero Day. Who would I attempt to memorialize, you ask? Yep, I went to school sporting a dress shirt, jeans, boots, and a cowboy hat I borrowed from Dad. Minus the absolute fact Garth Brooks doesn't wear glasses due to severe nearsightedness and astigmatism, I proudly wore this near-Garth emulation.

I'm positive no one noticed my cosplay as much as I hoped. However, I did gain attention in one particular arena. Mr. Matthews' bereavement leave after the loss of his wife left our small-town school with few options for coverage. For my class, music education was delivered by our junior high algebra teacher, Mrs. Braunagel. We spent the next several weeks singing along with sample accompaniment CDs music teachers get sent to them.

On Hero Day, my algebra teacher called me out in front of the whole class. "If Garth's your hero, sing us a song. Be Garth!"

My female classmates stared at me, waiting for me to man up. The tension built up as I rifled through accompaniments in search of one of my staples: "That Summer," "Standing Outside the Fire," or "The Dance." All I could find was "The River."

In front of God and everyone, dressed like Garth himself, I delivered a passionate, off-key performance. Representing how he performs live, I put one arm out and the other over my heart to display sincerity. The cocktail of fear and adrenaline of singing for my family when I was younger came flooding back. I was no Entertainer of the Year, but for a moment, I pretended to be.

Because You Loved Me / Celine Dion

I'm no stranger to death. Three of my biological grandparents passed away before I ever met them. We lost my foster grandpa during my fourth-grade year. My step-grandparents, Dad's mom, and Granny Sue were still alive and well by this point in my story. Given most people only have four grandparents, I was doing fine.

Of all of them, I spent the most time with Granny Sue. Since she lived in town, I got to know her better than the rest of my grandparents. A few months after her lung cancer diagnosis, she traveled to Oklahoma to spend time with my aunt and receive treatment.

Cancer's an unrelenting adversary. Despite her best efforts to return home for end-of-life care, she didn't make it. In our last visit before she left North Dakota, our *Lion King* viewing party was interrupted by a surprise visitor. Sure, rewinding VHS tapes was a chore, but I had a moment in time captured. Since she passed away before returning home, I never got the chance to resolve our last act of business together.

At her Rosary, my aunt detailed heartfelt observations of her mother. She told the congregation Granny Sue was the type of person who always had music playing. Introducing my elementary school music teacher, my aunt dedicated "Because You Loved Me" to her memory. The performance included one trade-off: each instance of "baby" was replaced with "granny." They personalized the performance with her preferred nickname.

How hadn't I noticed we shared this passion? A majority of the time I was at her apartment, we watched hours of CMT together. She wouldn't need music if I played mine. Way too loud, turn it down. We never discussed any other aspect but the volume. Perhaps at my funeral, my family members will nominate me to the same humble halls of music aficionado superstardom they recognized Granny Sue with.

Chain Gang / Sam Cooke

I am a criminal. You read that correctly. I hold three criminal convictions through the Stark County Juvenile Court system. One for shoplifting candy from a grocery store. One for criminal mischief for unintentionally breaking a semi windshield during a rock-throwing contest. One for criminal mischief for leafing through a magazine in a customer's back seat while delivering the local newspaper. My last charge rounded out the experience with a reading of my Miranda Rights and a full pat-down. I am a criminal.

These occurrences happened during junior high. However, this story marks the beginning of my freshman year of high school. Even after my crime streak, my parents agreed the court-dictated charges was a sufficient punishment for me. At my last sentencing, I was promised incarceration at the juvenile detention center if I got in trouble again before my eighteenth birthday. Not even this weighty threat was enough to deviate me from criminal activity. My moral compass lacked the calibration necessary to find magnetic north.

During a blistering skirmish with my foster mom one afternoon, she took aim at my perpetually bad attitude by grounding me until further notice. What's that supposed to mean? Further notice has no parameters.

Sometimes, the words echoing in your head sound like the perfect silver bullet to kill the argument for good. "You'll get tired of me and quit! I will not change!"

With a smile, maybe even a scoff, she made it clear I'd just declared war. You see, we both knew I was perfectly content sitting in my room listening to music alone. Like a defiant dog, she tightened my leash to school, bed, writing sentences at the table, and doing chores. My punishment was defined by the length of time it took me to generate genuine life change.

With the backstory out of the way, we get to "Chain Gang." The argument was between my mom and me. What I didn't account for was her marriage to a veteran with a stint as a basic training platoon sergeant. Both parents knew morale-bending tricks to convert the most jaded people toward the path of righteousness. For anecdotal evidence, I once edged our yard with a pair of household scissors. It took hours. I was free to complete this task until further notice.

A few weeks in, my warden and her deputy struck up a heart-to-heart while I picked weeds. I grew militant to their psychological manipulation, refusing to show progress to their good cop shtick. My foster dad pointed me back to the soulless conversation I was having with the dandelions in our garden.

Before returning to his project, he called out, "Worked my fingers to the bone! What do you get?" I glared at him as he instructed me to answer with "Bony Fingers!" Through gritted teeth, I met his demands. "Come on now! You love this! Sing it like you mean it." The exercise persisted until I sang it happily, yet drenched with sarcasm.

Oh, the songs I learned: "Take This Job and Shove It," "Bony Fingers," and "Chain Gang." Countless pieces that could feature in a Time Life midnight infomercial entitled *The Best of Breaking Tony's Soul*. Picture this but with a modern twist, Carson Daly replacing Dick Clark to present anthems from my nostalgic teenage angst.

"Do you remember a simpler time when you tried punishing your parents for your unfair past? So does Time Life. We've put all the hits together in one convenient collection. Songs to celebrate your rebellion. Songs to make you shudder at the sight of landscaping rock. Songs triggered by the distinct smell of paint. For three easy installments of $19.99, you, too, can journey back to a time when your pride mattered more than your freedom."

Carried Away / George Strait

If you wanna break a person, take away what means the most to them. As Mom purged my baseball cards, Goosebump books, and tape collection, she narrowly missed my tape deck, headphones, and a blank cassette used to copy songs off the radio. If this was warfare, she slipped up.

In retrospect, I'm aware she left these items on purpose. She needed to line my prison with enough hope to see change was possible or leave me with one thing left to lose. No matter the intention, I kept my mouth shut for the first time in my life.

You see, I take everything I do to extremes. My addictive personality spawned this predicament in the first place. Three convictions later, I still hadn't learned healthy mechanisms to obtain the things I wanted. I couldn't admit it to my parents at the time, but quitting Garth Brooks cold turkey had me thinking as I scrounged radio broadcasts for his songs at night. Were my desires really worth this ill-defined punishment?

She Don't Know She's Beautiful / Sammy Kershaw

My parents answered my spiteful fight for resilience with a do-it-yourself home incarceration to avoid marking me with a permanent criminal record. Going to school provided a welcomed shift in scenery from a patch of grass, landscaping rock, a wall I was scrubbing, or my place at the dinner table.

Between my institutionalization and raging hormones, every girl became beautiful to me. One had a gorgeous smile; one was friendly; one was tall; one was short and cute. You get the point. Sheer beauty encapsulated in a cheap scent purchased from Bath & Body Works. One tiny problem: I wasn't available to hang out with any of them, at least until further notice.

I Am That Man / Brooks & Dunn

Since my social interactions dissipated due to punishment, I became more obscure than ever. My friends stopped inviting me to stuff. They stopped sharing what happened when they hung out. I witnessed frail, weeklong romantic relationships transform into stable, long-lasting ones. Other friendships were solidifying, while mine faded. Although I found respite in the change of scenery, I became a passenger—an inactive participant in life.

For another analogy, imagine observing life from the nosebleed section of a large stadium. Scuffles between friends. Long-term relationships crashing to a halt. Girls lamenting how all dudes are jerks. From my cheap seat, I witnessed all the action, but couldn't influence a thing.

It may sound like I was changing, like my punishment drove the compassion my parents hoped to achieve. Don't be fooled. While I strove to be a source of hope for others, the gloves slid back over taped knuckles the moment I crossed my house's threshold. I didn't want to be a constant disappointment, but already committed to this fight. I had to stick to my guns.

Everywhere / Tim McGraw

What was I missing by this little game I engaged in? In my soul-searching throughout the years, I've determined I have this little problem living in the present. Things were crystal clear; my past sucked. I had zero friends in foster homes. They didn't have to wonder if their parents loved them. Most of them were relatively attractive people free of birth defects, like a cleft lip and palate. Boohoo, allow me some time to collect myself over a Kleenex.

I also believed things nowhere near the realm of possibility. I cannot even begin to tell you how many times I practiced singing duets with Garth Brooks. It started realistically, like as a fan at a concert. Somehow, he'd invite me to sing on stage with him. After sensing our musical connection, we'd become writing buddies. Our tracks would soar the charts as I featured on his albums and toured the world with him. Outlandish, but somehow magically possible.

Both scenarios made me realize life was passing me by. If I kept a past-oriented, criminal mindset, I'd get caught in a cycle of frequent incarcerations. If I became famous, I'd be too busy pursuing my dreams to have enduring friendships. Constant travels would leave my interactions fleeting. Both scenarios freaked me out. What would I miss? Most importantly, who would I miss?

It's Your Song / Garth Brooks

Double Live was released during my makeshift house arrest. My low-quality live bootlegs, collected by holding a tape deck to TV speakers while watching

Live from Central Park, were no match for this professionally captured two-disc set. Not just Garth live, but double FREAKING live.

Featuring three unreleased tracks, I was drawn to the tribute from my hero to his hero. Since it was unlikely I'd become the mama's boy I wanted to be, my wild daydreams drifted to performing "It's Your Song" at his lifetime achievement award ceremony. "Garth, YOU gave me hope," I announced, fighting off tears before a flawless performance. "It's always been YOUR song."

Meanwhile, I was still grounded until further notice. Further notice was around three months and counting at the time.

Even after receiving the album for Christmas, my new treasure was escorted into hiding with the rest of my collection at the holiday's end. These crazy people I called parents weren't playing games. How was I supposed to defeat calloused enemies capable of robbing a child's joy on Christmas? Just to be sure, I couldn't drop my guard.

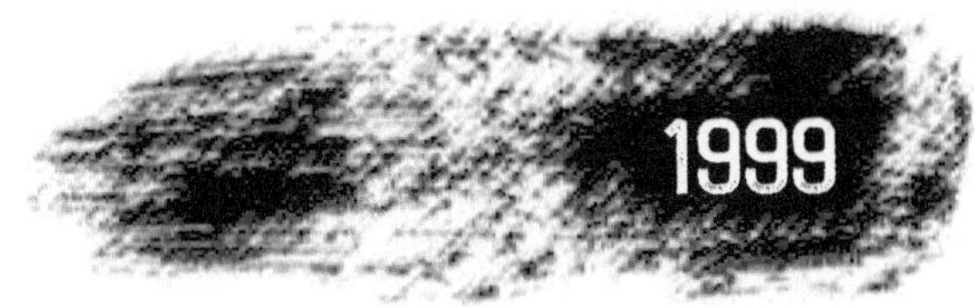

You're Still the One / Shania Twain

If I learned anything from my endless punishment, it was commitment and resolve to a cause. I declared war to obtain indisputable proof that someone, anyone, would commit to me. So many people wandered through the revolving door of my interpersonal relationships. It seemed like no one believed I could reform from the torrent of trouble I found myself in. My parents possessed absolute determination to this cause, despite probable criticism for their unfailing commitment to correct my course.

This concept directly translated to how I perceived romantic relationships. Every person would naysay my fantasy to find, and maintain, a marriage to my high school sweetheart. We would have to overcome a critical obstacle course to prove them all wrong. I'm not sure who "they" were, but my imaginary enemies could never separate me from the theoretical love of my life.

Please Remember Me / Tim McGraw

When older people learned of my predicament, I generally got the same warning. "You better get it together. During my rough phase, I lost fill in the blank (a grandparent, parent, significant other)." I wasn't having any of that. One, I wasn't them; two, they didn't know me; AND, three, that could never happen.

Welp, it did happen.

Grandma Marie was my only remaining biological grandparent. When her health began deteriorating, Dad begged my foster mom for one last visit. Less than a day later, she passed away. To better define the timeline, my punishment started in August 1998; Grandma's celebration of life was scheduled for September 1999. I still hadn't displayed the appropriate willingness to stray from destructive behaviors. Once again, Dad begged for me to attend the funeral, but my foster mom said no. At least at first. She relented under one condition: a single slip-up would send me to juvenile detention until my eighteenth birthday.

By this point, I engaged in two contrasting wars. I could either outlast my parents or dedicate to the reform most people didn't believe possible. While my foster mom drove me to meet Dad, she clarified the stakes one more time: one mistake and I was gone. She left me to drown in my thoughts as Tim McGraw's "Please Remember Me" played over the radio.

While I was off squandering existence, Grandma died. No more world-famous chocolate chip cookies. No more exploring her personal history during Minnesota Twins games. No more chances to say goodbye. I can't bring myself to believe Grandma Marie's hanging out in heaven watching over me, making my path straight. I mean, it's heaven. Peaceful paradise should trump continued service to her family. As selfish as it may be, I can only hope she knows I'm sorry.

Fade to Black / Metallica

Balancing the tightrope of respect and maturity, I managed to make the trip to Grandma's funeral uneventful. On the way home, my foster mom and I carried out one of our signature soul-searching discussions. This time, I avoided the deceptive trial-and-error phrases patched together in the correct order to cast the illusion of repentance. Raising the white flag, I informed her the fight wasn't worth it anymore. Too much of my life had been wasted. After several minutes of agonizing silence, she announced my punishment was over.

Exactly like being released from prison, I collected the items taken from me at incarceration. I was the proud owner of a Garth Brooks tape collection once again! Putting off my long-awaited reunion, I called my friend Derek to hang out. We spent the evening playing *Madden* and listening to Metallica. As this dark chapter of my life faded, everything was all but black. For the first time in a year, things began looking pretty bright.

Sad But True / Metallica

A lot of life passed me by in a year: friends moved away, kids were different, did different things, cared about different things. My classmates weren't listening to country music anymore, much less Garth Brooks. As I bounced between various friend groups to capture lost time, my soundtrack changed immensely. I wasn't afforded adequate time to fill the void in GB consumption. Imagine, if you will, the blurred musical hodge-podge during the day often centered around Metallica's *Black Album*. At night, I tucked away in solitude to reacquaint myself with the Garth Brooks catalog.

Stan / Eminem

Among the new music I was exposed to, rap was most popular with my friends. I had a hard time getting into the genre until Eminem entered the picture with his distinct blend of arrogance, self-deprecation, anger, and controversy.

I experimented slowly by listening to his music at friends' houses. My parents would never approve of this. Making unmarked copies, I attempted to sneak it into our house. My prediction was accurate. In one of two heated debates post-house arrest, Eminem was confiscated from me while Mom criticized its violent content.

Stan was a particularly rude awakening to my music addiction. Swap him with me and Eminem with Garth. Was I that crazy? Although I'd considered sending mail to the GB fan club, I never carried it out. The dramatic escalation of Stan's obsession over time was astonishing. Despite my mom's apparent hatred, another dude from Detroit taught me what she'd been trying to teach for years. Don't ever blur the line between normal fandom and unhealthy admiration.

The Number of the Beast / Iron Maiden

I have my musical preferences, but can listen to almost anything. If something makes me uncomfortable, I conduct an investigation. Are they saying things I disagree with? How come? Are they addressing topics I'd rather ignore? There are plenty of parts to music, but for me, it's all in the lyrics. What's this song trying to teach me?

There was one area I couldn't find comfortable. You see, one summer evening during junior high, my biological parents made my siblings and I watch a documentary called *Hell's Bells*. According to the film, rock music was the megaphone Satan uses to summon America's youth into performing his heinous deeds.

As I got older, I examined preconceived notions through three options: one, listen and be evil; two, listen and learn; or three, don't listen. *Hell's Bells* was obvious on how I should feel about AC/DC, route three for those jokers. It never mentioned my friend Derek's decision to listen to Iron Maiden and Iced Earth. As we played video games, I conducted lengthy good vs. evil discussions. Imagine being a teenager subjected to the following line of questioning:

"Did that dude say 666? Did he say the number of the beast?" I asked.

"Yup," Derek said. "It's not, like, devil worship."

"How?"

"Sometimes bands say stuff to get a rise out of people."

"Are you sure?"

"Yeah. People don't get metal. Like, the dude from Dio used to throw horns at concerts. People thought it was devil worship. It's not, though. The same sign people use for Satan was used in Italy to chase away evil spirits."

"Oh. So, people just misunderstand it? Also, who's Dio?"

My investigations were inconclusive. Derek was patient, but I simply didn't understand how all this confusion was happening. Isn't it better to stay away from dark ideologies? Did he ever play with Ouija boards? Who is Dio? Really, who are they?

Albuquerque / Weird Al

In the ninth grade, I agreed to take agriculture class just to be in shop. For a shot at building poorly fashioned footstools, I had to learn the entirety of the FFA creed. It was a small price, but power tools were involved.

What if I invested this same brainpower into memorizing what I thought was important?

One of my proudest life accomplishments is committing Weird Al's eleven-and-a-half-minute epic, "Albuquerque," to memory. Washing dishes, taking out the trash, walking to school, sitting alone in my room. Every waking moment of my day for several months was "A-a…A-Albuquerque!" I learned every word, a crowning achievement I still brag about to this day. As proud as I am, it's never mattered to anyone else.

Anonymous / Garth Brooks

If you've been paying attention closely, I was still the rightful owner of a tape collection in early 2000. Garth Brooks MADE me purchase my first CD. Since he didn't release his boxed set to cassette, I was forced to upgrade my collection for the six new tracks.

One small problem. I didn't have a steady income stream. Seeking out enough needy senior citizens, I mowed the exact number of lawns to pocket the $25 to purchase it from a girl I didn't like in my study hall.

Now, Garth has sold over 150 million records. I bought his entire pre-1997 catalog, thrice. All of them: *Garth Brooks, No Fences, Ropin' the Wind, The Chase, The Collection, In Pieces, The Hits, Fresh Horses, Double Live,* and *Sevens.* Sure, some were secondhand, but I also replaced a few because I wore them out. I've dropped some serious coin feeding this addiction.

Of the six new tracks, my favorite was "Anonymous." Since it was written by Tony Arata (who also wrote "The Dance"), I knew it would be good. Thumbing through the album liner in study hall, the lyrics seemed to speak to my consistent romantic predicament.

I cleared my schedule to test this theory later that evening. One by one, six CDs in a row, without skipping a song, I listened to every Garth CD to catch the new songs' context in the old order. All while holding the fifty+ page lyric book in my lap, following along. Even when imparted with this new technology, old habits were proving hard to break.

He Didn't Have to Be / Brad Paisley

When I was fifteen, I was assigned a new social worker. Being in foster homes for all but five years of my young life, this flawed system provided the only stability I knew. Although Dad promised the placement would be short-term, days turned into months into years.

My social worker and I touched base frequently to validate the resources I needed. During one of these meetings, she went over my parental phone visitation schedule. In the seven years I'd been in this home, I never had to obtain approval to call my parents. Out-of-town visits, sure, but phone time? After serving a year of deserved punishment, her lecture infuriated me. Despite any mistakes they made, and I made, we earned the right to a sense of normalcy moving forward.

My foster parents received a separate, but similar, scolding.

That evening, we held a family meeting to discuss options. They admitted this rule was made to keep children safe from dangerous parents. Since mine were decent people, they never followed it. If I agreed, they were willing to adopt me to remove these restrictions. Further, I had to request for both biological parents to terminate their parental rights.

To make my intentions known, I made the calls that night. Dad and my stepmom agreed without hesitation, citing a desire to give me the best possible life moving forward. My mom never answered, or returned, my call.

Six days after my sixteenth birthday, the process was complete; I was legally adopted.

Conducting such a heartbreaking exercise to wade closer to happiness drove deeper respect for my dad and stepmom. I only agreed to adoption to have unrestricted access to them. Imagine the psychology behind the question. The paranoia alone had enough potential to send them into a tailspin. In my adult mind, I'd want to explore motives and require more information than I presented them with. Yet, without hesitation, without question, they offered grace, love, humility, and faith.

As for my adoptive parents, how did they sacrifice so much? I was a nightmare, on purpose and unintentionally. Surgeries, dental appointments, counseling sessions, juvenile court hearings, probation officer meetings, parent/teacher conferences, insecurities, a million questions—the list goes on and on… I was a lot of things I shouldn't have been. I needed tough love, and they knew it. All the things I needed; they didn't have to be. I'm forever grateful they were.

I Will Still Love You / Britney Spears

For a moment, a brief moment, I fully embraced the concept of teen pop. 'N Sync, The Backstreet Boys, Christina Aguilera, Britney Spears, Mandy Moore, all those jokers. I thought my brother Aaron said I had to listen to them to get chicks. Since my methods were lacking, I did as instructed.

His recommendation didn't work, either, so I called him on his crap during my next coaching session. Offering further technical assistance, he asked me how often I listened to it. My listening schedule was a fifty/fifty split between Garth and pop. When did I listen to it? Often, but mainly at home alone. My mistake was evident when I said it out loud. It was almost too clear. He didn't intend for me to apply pop music serum, twice daily, to cure my insufferable woes with the female persuasion.

I won't take the easy road to stiff-arm potential harassment, but the high one. Britney Spears and Christina Aguilera still hold dedicated spaces in my CD binder. Judging by the massive amounts I've seen at used CD stores throughout the years, they aren't in high demand. My favorite tracks are still safely nestled in my aging iPod. I keep them because I like 'em. I need tracks, like Mandy Moore's "Cry," to smile upon my teenage ignorance.

When You Come Back to Me Again / Garth Brooks

A person never really knows how lost they are until they're out of the storm. My recent release from punishment and adoption made me consider the path I was headed on. Then, the one I diverted to. Doing what most teenagers would do in my position, I credited Garth Brooks for my return to righteousness. That lighthouse in the harbor guiding me home.

Sure, Garth was there for me in significant ways, but it wasn't like I could call him for life advice. Meanwhile, I gave little credit to the physical people around me. My troubled tendencies were over, but as can be seen, music was still my imaginary dwelling place.

Helplessly, Hopelessly / Jessica Andrews

I'm not a lucky person. Luck-based competitions tend to send my wild imagination on an emotional roller coaster ride. Life hadn't taught me that lesson yet. The radio and internet collided by allowing listeners to register for prizes on their website. Using my family's brand-new WebTV, I signed up hoping to win a Garth Brooks VIP concert experience, then skated off to bigger things.

While I was at school a month later, the station called my unsuspecting mother to confirm where to ship my winnings. I entered an online contest without permission? If our information got into the wrong hands, they could use it to track us, rob us, or worse, kill us. The irony doesn't escape me as I plaster my life story on all corners of the internet.

After dishing out enough head nods and apologies to appease her anger, I cautiously asked Mom what I happened to win. It was a promo CD from some artist she hadn't heard of. I paid attention to her piece, the least she could do was write the artist's name down. Nonetheless, the universe was shining its favor upon me!

After several weeks, a package reading "FRAGILE" finally arrived. I wasn't sure what that meant, but it sounded exotic. Out of curiosity, Ma made me open it in front of her.

Peeling the envelope flap, I was surprised to find a Jessica Andrews CD. Her crazy, piercing green eyes trapped me in a hypnotic trance when her music videos played on CMT. A mere two years my senior, I made plans to marry her if I ever became famous. Ma noticed she was pretty right away. After embarrassing me for a little while, I managed to duck out for my private pre-release listening party.

I'm minutely trying to be cute, but by the end of track five, I was helplessly, hopelessly in love. How in the world did her eyes get that shade of green? I can't recall why I stopped crushing on Jessica. Perhaps it was my infatuation with Jennifer Love Hewitt. I haven't thought about her in quite some time. I should pull out my dusty copy of *Who I Am* and see what she's up to these days.

Someone You Used to Know / Collin Raye

My high school only had two organized dances per year: homecoming and prom. As a breakthrough into the dating scene, I was dead set on attending both.

I began noticing a quiet girl in several of my classes. Maybe she thought I was obnoxious, or was interested, but whenever I tried to sneak a peek at her,

I'd catch her staring at me. We seemed to have promise. A quiet, good girl type would teach me how to behave. As an added bonus, her Soprano singing voice could feature nicely for duets on my future albums.

I waited for natural opportunities to speak with her, but we were never alone to talk. With the date of the dance fast approaching, I gathered the courage to write her a letter. Yep, a letter. I didn't dare admit my feelings, but asked if she wanted to go to homecoming with me. Presenting the best option to appease her shy nature, I gave her my locker number to deliver her written response. Tracking her for a few days, I strategically slipped the letter through the slit in her locker while collecting attendance.

After assessing her personality for several weeks, I anticipated her reaction. She was far too polite not to offer a response.

One day passed. Two. A week passed. Nothing.

I did stalk her, and if memory serves me correctly, I may have given her a deadline. She did go to homecoming. Alone. Who would choose solitude? I've avoided feeling this way for most of my life, but she chose it.

What I considered courage, she had to consider weird. With time, I understood her lack of response. Most of what I had done has gotten innocent women killed. Having clarity on past mistakes didn't resolve the embarrassment, though. I still had to see her everywhere. In the halls. In choir. In other classes. At school events. In every awkward interaction, we both had to ignore my failed attempts at striking up a romance.

Reflection / Christina Aguilera

For good measure, my pop phase had concluded. If country music was sad, pop ballads find better ways to stir the tender, broken pieces of the teenage psyche. Who better to describe my anguish than some other teen singing a sad song?

I still carried many stripes: ugly, criminal, liar, thief, punk, worthless. In my attempts to prove the doubters wrong, I found building a reputation's much harder than destroying one. There's no way of knowing how long construction would take. I had to be willing to wait it out.

This I Promise You / 'N Sync

I've heard and read the horror stories of blind dates past. They provide a distinct opportunity everyone should experience at least once during their lifetime.

After my failed attempt at getting a date, I was still available to take a friend's cousin to homecoming. Imagine a quiet, shy girl from a nearby town paired with a loud, awkward dude. Classmates slow dancing in a dimly lit gymnasium. Heads on shoulders as multi-colored lights traced their silhouettes. Rebellious couples rejecting restraint for the chance to make out where they receive education. And there I was, trying to add meaning to the lyrics blaring through the speakers. Even I sensed the tension of the situation.

Musical promises of eternal love resulted in an awkward email address exchange. I never heard from my blind date again. When our local paper printed a graduate recognition piece eighteen months later, I thumbed through the insert to find her senior picture. While it may seem fabricated, I know for a fact we went to a dance together. Yet, she vanished from my life as mysteriously as she entered into it.

I'd like a rewrite to the lyrics that frame my memory: "Until the time this dance is through, this I promise you." At least then, I wouldn't be made a lyrical liar.

The Dance / Garth Brooks

In the lyrics to "American Pie," Don McLean depicts the day music died. To him, the death of Buddy Holly, Richie Valens, and The Big Bopper signaled an ominous decline in American culture. While I can't confirm its final days, I recall one tragic October evening in 2000 when I almost lost my beloved art form.

To set the scene, I consider myself a night owl. The solitude and silence of a sleeping house provides a perfect backdrop for me to exhaust unresolved thoughts. Every so often, this pattern takes its toll on me and forces a rare early bedtime. Most nights during my teenage years, I lulled myself to sleep with music playing through my headphones. In my tossing-and-turning, I'd untangle the cable, shove them away, and drift back to dreamland.

October 26, 2000 was one of those evenings. Several days of perpetually exerted energy drove a reasonable bedtime most normal people are accustomed to. The warm embrace of my headphones enabled me to fade off to sleep quickly.

I'm not sure how I caught it, but the mere mention of Garth Brooks pulled me into immediate consciousness. As the night DJ announced Garth's retirement, he thanked him for his extensive catalog, exhilarating performances, and contributions to country music. Fans could expect one more CD release in November without a supporting tour. Garth gave us a large portion of himself, but now, he shifted focus to parenting his three daughters. Our journey together was over, at least until his girls went to college. The DJ closed his announcement with Garth's self-proclaimed masterpiece, "The Dance."

Every word reverberated on an endless loop, stabbing at my heart with each reflection. What was I supposed to do? Lying in my bed, sobbing, I eventually cried myself to sleep.

I liken the following day to the way a person would mourn the death of a close relative. Wearing all black, I wandered around school, breaking the news to everyone I knew. With one more opportunity for new music from my hero, what was I gonna do? Like I said before, music was given a terminal diagnosis for me. With two short months left to live, it was dangerously hanging on by a thread.

Maybe He'll Notice Her Now / Mindy McCready (Ft. Richie McDonald)

My friends can attest: ask me a simple question and I'll give you a complex answer. For instance, I played a game when asked about my favorite musician. Allow me to demonstrate: "Well, Garth Brooks is my favorite male singer, Mindy McCready's my favorite female singer, Lonestar's my favorite band. My all-time favorite would have to be Garth, though." That's a pretty obnoxious answer to a simple question. I don't think anyone cared. I probably told people without them asking.

I didn't just like Mindy McCready's music; I was insanely in love with HER. Right after Shania's "Any Man of Mine" business, I hated her. How dare chicks adopt an anthem to sing everywhere? Then, Mindy put out "Guys Do It All the Time." Catching the same media attention, I'm not even sure they're different songs. They blur together now. However, when Mindy did it, I fully supported it. Yep. Dudes do stuff like that. You showed us!

As I contemplated my next move, I didn't own a single Mindy or Lonestar album. Starting with Mindy, a co-worker offered me a used copy of *Ten Thousand Angels* for $5. Sold!

Listening to the album, I was reminded of Mindy's duet with Richie from Lonestar. The song was an ultimate victory of forgotten people. "He doesn't love you. Leave him, Mindy! Who would ever ignore you?!?" I didn't know the answer, but I did know one dude who vowed he never would.

Over and Over / Mindy McCready

Less than a week after I was adopted, I picked up my first job at the local Dairy Queen. I didn't make a lot of money, but every spare cent was spent growing my music collection. My parents refused to go out of their way to unload me at pawn shops to find affordable music. Friends would take me, but few had the patience to entertain my endless quest for hidden treasures. Often, I resorted to sifting truck stop CD racks at much higher price points than I would've liked.

That's exactly how Mindy McCready's *Superhits* came into my life. Purchased at a truck stop during my break, I returned to work to familiarize myself with Mindy while making people's cheeseburgers.

See, as the only guy on an all-female staff at DQ, they listened to classic rock and chick anthems. I wanted Mindy McCready. Do you have any idea how hard it is to pretend you're compromising with your co-workers by listening to a girl you're madly in love with? I was living a double life.

Cross Against the Moon / Mindy McCready

I grew to love Garth for how his storytelling challenged certain paradigms and inspired personal growth. My puppy love for Mindy McCready had no depth. I listened to her music because she had a pretty face. She was a strong, southern woman who wasn't gonna take crap from anyone. Message received. Nothing else to see here.

Then enters "Cross Against the Moon." The cocktail of childhood memories watching *The Wizard of Oz* combined with storytelling reminiscent of Garth's catalog mixed with a profound message presented by the most precious face on the planet. We're not talking about a chick anthem. We explored the actual difficulties one woman faced in chasing her dreams. Religion. Fame. Femininity. I didn't want to admit it yet, but maybe life without Garth was possible.

Come Cryin' to Me / Lonestar

Welcome to the Friend Zone! This unique place where girls confide in you and tell you their darkest secrets. You share intensely intimate moments with them. You attempt to comfort them. Hug them. Hand them a Kleenex. You suffer as much as they do.

It doesn't start there, though. It usually begins when the girl falls for a guy. They ask questions to gain your insight. You help orchestrate their relationship into existence. You ease the weirdness of early phase relationships.

Then, you watch them slide into momentary happiness. The couple falls in love as you become the uncomfortable third wheel. The dude's ok with you being there because you'll play video games with him. The girl's ok because you're safe. She won't ask you questions, but you're there if she needs an interpretation. The third wheel gets the discomfort.

You're there as the relationship starts to decline. Your friends don't see it, but you do. He stops being as affectionate. Overexerting playfulness, he pushes her into a snowbank. He blows her off to hang out with friends but invites you. You go because you want to socialize, but don't wanna go because you'll have to give a report. You see it ending, but they don't.

Then, the break-up. Heartbroken, she needs a sensitive person to listen to her. As she mourns her loss, you slam the gates on your tears. Dudes don't cry. So, you apologize for mistakes you didn't make, knitting cliché phrases together to make it through the night. Oh yeah, it might be a conversation at one a.m.

As you depart, she might thank you. She may even have the audacity to ask why there aren't any nice guys left. She might ask you that.

I'm not a hundred percent sure, but I think that's what happens in the friend zone. I believe that's what happens when you let girls cry to you. At least that's what my loser, third-wheel, friend-zoned friends have told me. I bet that same loser bought Lonestar's *Crazy Nights* at a Walmart in Miles City, Montana. What a loser!

Mr. Midnight / Garth Brooks

The Christmas season gave me ample time to ponder my next move after Garth's retirement. I binged his entire catalog with seasonal supplements provided by *Beyond the Season* and *The Magic of Christmas*. Per tradition, I waited for his last album, *Scarecrow*. Oddly enough, I wasn't in a rush to get it.

I compare this final experience to eating your favorite French fries. For me, it's Burger King. You shotgun the whole container, but that last one, you enjoy it. Searching the bottom of the bag, the bitter taste of salt lingers to remind you of the goodness you once had.

"Mr. Midnight" couldn't be a more accurate description of my life at the time. Listening to people call in requests, wishing the same for myself, then settling to move forward alone with my Garth collection. The story was as wild as my imagination. With my insane musical knowledge, I could find work as a DJ. In the meantime, I needed to develop my smooth radio voice.

With Arms Wide Open / Creed

Creed's *Human Clay* was the first rock album I ever purchased. I remember as it happened. Standing at the CD rack, I reflected upon how Scott Stapp's back story influenced his decision to share positive messages. The weight of eternity loomed in the backdrop.

At that very moment, I stood at the junction depicted in Robert Frost's "The Road Not Taken." With two choices laid out in front of me, this one action could force a completely different course than my familiar journey. An irreversible decision. Maybe rock music wasn't all bad. Perhaps a simple CD purchase wouldn't send Satan on a mad dash to steal my soul.

Inside Us All / Creed

Several things led me to Garth Brooks: his ability to inspire others, his desire to entertain, his willingness to be down-to-earth. I needed a hero to cling to, to inspire me. However, country music was simplistically dark. Most issues were relationship problems and I didn't have one of those.

My careful journey into rock tapped into my unfulfilled questions about darkness and true loneliness. Not the loneliness I passed off as wanting a girlfriend, but genuine isolation: feeling desolate in rooms full of people, navigating through past struggles like a lost stranger, wrestling to resolve my cocktail of emotions. There had to be a path to obtainable peace. Preparing for a journey of intense self-discovery, I took my first step toward the happiness I couldn't seem to find.

Maybe / Chris Gaines

When I tell people I'm a Garth fan, they ask, "What about his weird alter ego experiment?"

"You mean Chris Gaines?" I reply. "I especially like him."

For some backstory, Chris Gaines wasn't a failed attempt at an alter ego. He was a character Garth was cast to play for a movie entitled *The Lamb*. In an age-old trope, a sex-addicted rock star receives plastic surgery after a nearly fatal accident. Somewhere along the way, he rises back to glory.

At first, I wouldn't touch the rock-centric soundtrack with elements of R&B woven into the tapestry. Watching the *VH1 Storytellers* episode left me with several unanswered questions. Where's Jimmy? Why's Garth so angry? Did he really inject rap into the remake of a 1960s hippie song? Is Garth aware his Christmas album cover persona mirrors these same creepy vibes?

I didn't make a conscious decision to buy the CD. While on an economics field trip, I found a copy of the cassette at Sam Goody (RIP). After buying *Human Clay*, why not? Since I didn't own a portable tape player, I grazed the liner notes on the bus for over an hour with little context. Interrupting my studies, a girl from class challenged my purchase. "Is that Garth Brooks wearing spandex?"

Planting my feet, I began my first defense of Chris Gaines. "What's the difference between Wranglers and spandex? Either way, you see everything."

I have a one-question litmus test to determine a person's loyalty to GB: what do you think about Chris Gaines? If the person tells me they didn't hear, or like, the album, they're fake. I've only come across one other Chris Gaines fan and he doesn't even like Garth Brooks.

Suit up, people. If you want to be a REAL Garth fan, you must be willing to walk a mile in his tights.

Lonely Grill / Lonestar

I worked at Dairy Queen for three years in high school. After learning how to be a fry cook, my manager moved me to the front of the store to take orders and make ice cream concoctions. I took a lot of pride in that job. Where my friends had Michael Jordan posters and chicks in bikinis on their bedroom walls, I had old Blizzard and chicken strip basket promotional material plastered between my Garth Brooks memorabilia.

The trick about fast food is you need customers to have employees on the clock. Since I wasn't a bill-paying adult, I usually got sent home first when business went bust. During these slow periods, I had to assert relevance by inventing things to do. Let's just say, I could teach a masterclass on stainless steel cleaning practices. Down at the lonely grill, armed with a razor blade, degreaser, and a steel wool scouring pad, trying to stay productive enough to protect the purse strings that sustained my music habit.

Don't Let's Talk About Lisa / Lonestar

An artist has to perfect their craft. I decided to cut my storytelling teeth through a creative writing class. When my cousin Nate drafted a haiku highlighting the accidental vehicular homicide of an innocent squirrel, the class exploded with laughter. Classmates winked and pointed in the hallway before quoting the iconic last line: "Scamper, scamper, screech."

After hearing a poem so legendary its fame left the classroom, I devoted my energy to goofy drawings and funny poetry. My projects never warranted a reception as warm as Nate's.

Before long, I began practicing at home. If any of my pieces were good enough, I took it to class to read out loud. One of these attempts resulted in the accidental creation of my first song entitled "Let's Not Talk About

Rachel." The verses were gibberish, nonsensical phrases. The chorus praised Rachel for clarifying my confusing life. I was so sure this piece would lead to my inevitable fame I rehearsed interviews in my room. "How do you do it?" my interviewer asked.

"You know, it just comes to me. I think it, then I write it." I'd reply nonchalantly, wearing sunglasses for some stupid reason.

One day while listening to Lonestar, the déjà vu was overwhelming. I've been here before. Frantically running to my writing notebook, I read the lyrics of my song over "Don't Let's Talk About Lisa." Yep, pound-for-pound plagiarism. The rhythm. The tempo. The phrasings. How do I do it? I write the songs I've already heard.

The world didn't need another Lonestar. They needed whatever brand of what I was set to become. I just needed to discover what that might be.

Smile / Lonestar

After overcoming the shame of blatant plagiarism of "Don't Let's Talk About Lisa," I geared up for my second writing attempt. What if I didn't have to be goofy? What if I exposed my vulnerabilities like I learned from Creed?

My efforts resulted in a scathing review about my mother's absence entitled "Where Were You." For a second time, this song was lifted from Garth Brooks' "Which One of Them" with elements of Lonestar's "Smile." I only chose not to throw this other plagiarized piece out because it was my first attempt to tug at the strings of what bothered me.

I wrote lyrics for over thirty songs in my composition notebook that year. Tracked rough demos on my tape deck before my family woke in the morning. I don't have 'em anymore. At some point, I discarded the art unfit for public consumption in its rightful place. I just wish my insecurities didn't force such a rash decision. Those archives are likely to hold many other pieces I inadvertently ripped off.

Wonderful / Everclear

My past mistakes still haunted me. It felt as if people had seemingly low expectations of me. With big dreams and a dark past, the weight of my predicament became clear. My whole life was formed by the legendary divorce, poverty, foster home, and juvenile court. As a part of a vicious cycle, I was condemned to a lifetime of failure. Nothing more. Nothing less.

Garth hadn't taught me any of this. He led me to believe, through hope, I could change my circumstances.

Everclear was a little more honest with me. My music habits changed to match this realization. Time on CMT and country radio started to split with VH1 and the local pop station. After learning about the triumphs of the human spirit, it was time to enter the darkness.

Blue Moon / Steve Holy

I have a reclusive cousin who liked to evade social events. To make amends with his girlfriend, who wanted to go to our junior prom, he set us up to avoid the whole ordeal. Take it from me, it's ethically impossible to break into the dating scene when you go to a dance with someone else's partner.

The inside pocket of a tuxedo jacket is too small to carry a Walkman. In a rare scenario, I didn't have it with me. Walking home by myself that evening, the light of a full moon illuminated the darkest recesses of my true situation. I was alone. Rather than feel my feelings, I serenaded the glowing orb to a Steve Holy song.

Hemorrhage / Fuel

I can tell you the exact moment I traded country for rock. During a commercial for *Now That's What I Call Music, Volume 6*, quick shots scanned a band fronted by a dude with fake blonde hair singing his heart out. A five-second snippet was all it took to initiate the mission searching for this phenomenon that made me feel so alive.

I wasn't about to buy *Now 6,* though. A girl in my class let me scan through her store-bought copy as we drove around town in her red Pontiac Grand Am. My quest led me to a little song called "Hemorrhage" by Fuel.

I searched VH1's schedule to find the twenty-minute window they planned to play the music video next. "Hemorrhage" is featured on Fuel's album *Something Like Human*. The blonde mop-topped front man displayed the passion and conviction I was accustomed to seeing with Garth. Gripping the microphone with urgency, he delivered a message of rectifying wrongs before it's too late. I wasn't sure who this Brett Scallions dude was yet, but I was a big fan. I needed more.

Innocent / Fuel

Late-night programming was a staple to my high school years. After getting a TV for Christmas, I recorded Leno, Conan O'Brien, and Saturday Night

Live to re-enact skits for my friends. Leno taught me wordplay through his monologue and funny headlines. Conan opened my eyes to inserting cultural absurdity into everyday situations during his "Men Without Hats Conversation Channel" skit. Chris Farley coached me in the fine art of motivational speaking and breakdancing. I recorded, studied, and mimicked hours of comedy content for mere emulation.

When I saw Fuel had a spot on Leno, I gripped the edge of my seat for a live performance of "Hemorrhage." Instead, they performed "Innocent." It turns out, a friend gave me this song on a mix CD. Following some intro chords on a clean electric guitar, Brett sings the first lyric, "Satan." Nope, next. I blindly cast judgment after one word I didn't like.

Now that I knew who Fuel was, I paid attention to the lyrics. The listener wasn't being coaxed into Satan worship; we examined how coming of age detracts from our innocence. If I wanted to better understand the human experience, I needed Fuel's new album.

Bent / Matchbox Twenty

It may be hard to believe, but there once was a time when people couldn't rapidly consume music when they wanted. If we wanted to hear a song, we relied upon chance interactions through a radio broadcast. To better dictate what we listened to, we purchased the CD to listen to at a time of our choosing.

Specific rock albums sometimes proved to be a difficult purchase in Southwest North Dakota. When scrounging truck stop music racks didn't warrant success, I'd have to sweet talk my parents into stopping at Sam Goody (RIP) to buy Fuel's new CD.

During my wait, I sought enlightenment from peers to find more content from the world of rock. This turned out to be a disaster. As I found out, most people don't share my taste in music. Please accept this recent, real interaction I had with a friend as proof. "What are you listening to these days?" I asked, making polite conversation.

"It doesn't matter. You probably wouldn't like it anyway," my friend responded, shutting down the inquiry. Ouch! I never meant my quest for quality music to be pretentious.

Busted / Matchbox Twenty

I fall hard for obscure songs that should have been hits, but mainstream didn't quite recognize. It wasn't long before the radio-friendly musings of Matchbox Twenty lured me into quitting radio for good.

Once I dipped my toes into rock, I quickly realized living in rural North Dakota would be challenging for music consumption. The menu offered to me included trusted favorites from the world of country and classic rock. I chose to cover these genres by collecting recommendations from friends.

With all of this newfound free time, my music exploration evolved into finding hidden gems in popular rock albums acquired at local pawn shops. If there was a single defining moment in my music consumer experience, it was wanting to be familiar with any song/artist mentioned in discussion. With my spies in the trenches, I began my quest to become everyone's musical genius.

We Shall Be Free / Garth Brooks

At the end of my junior year, my adoptive father forced me to attend Boys State, a weeklong camp sponsored by The American Legion. I didn't want to go. I wanna make that perfectly clear. This meant burning money for a week without making any, slowing my music purchases. He didn't care. I went anyway.

The American Legion is a veteran's service organization aiming to breed a sense of Americanism while giving former military heroes an outlet for continued community support. I'm not against that. I was against losing income for a week. Plus, a bunch of ancient dudes told me it would be fun. I wasn't buying it. When these same old guys traded details of receiving enemy fire, getting doused in CS gas, and war with excitement, I was a little reluctant to agree upon shared understanding of recreational activities.

After Dad registered me for the event, I learned of an annual talent show associated with the camp. I was committed from that moment on. Consulting with my dad, I dug through the Garth Brooks catalog for a song to perform during the talent show. I landed on "We Shall Be Free." If the American Legion symbolized patriotism, this piece would land with my target audience.

I sang "We Shall Be Free" in front of two hundred people in my first solo performance. I had nothing to lose. If these people didn't like it, I'd leave at the end of the week. If they did, I'd become a star. Or so I thought. The possibility was open the moment I stopped dreaming and started performing.

What About Now? / Lonestar

When you live in a small town, nothing fascinating ever happens. As a kid, you love home, but you dream of leaving as soon as possible.

Working at Dairy Queen on a slow, overcast day, I overheard our regular customers discussing a commotion at the truck stop across the street. Popping my head out of the drive-through window, I saw a tour bus sporting a custom vinyl wrap from Lonestar's *I'm Already There*. Could it be a band from Texas was passing through my sleepy town? Grabbing a Sharpie and mix CD with "Amazed," I took off hoping to meet my boys from Lonestar.

Running toward the truck stop in a full sprint, I saw Keech Rainwater, the band's drummer, standing by the bus. I called out to gain his attention before they packed up to head off to their next tour destination. "Keech! Can I get an autograph?"

Since no one ever knows the drummer, he quickly rounded up Dean and Michael. As I handed over a CDR, the disappointment on their faces was immediate. "I know this kinda looks stupid, but I love you guys. I just took *Crazy Nights* and *Lonely Grill* out of my CD case last night," I offered up as damage control. "This wouldn't be complete without Richie's signature. Could you, maybe, get him to sign it?"

"He's asleep," Michael admitted. "Let me see what I can do." He disappeared into the bus to appease my request. After several minutes of waiting, he returned with my signed CD. I thanked him and scurried off.

Knowing their names seemed to be the only saving grace in this wildly awkward scenario. See, we 80s kids didn't have ready access to Google from a smartphone. I had to walk into that interaction with knowledge of who Richie McDonald, Michael Britt, Dean Sams, and Keech Rainwater were. I was a true fan. As I walked back to DQ, I fantasized about the day I didn't just know their names. They would know mine.

Open Your Eyes / Staind

That summer, my boss' little brother, John, began working at Dairy Queen. As the only other dude on an all-female staff, we became fast friends. With a common interest in music, we bonded by swapping musical recommendations in the greasy kitchen CD player.

We started with 90s country, which morphed into Weird Al, which morphed into spoken word comedy CDs from The Bob and Tom Show and Adam Sandler. Once he found out I was dabbling in commercial rock, the floodgates opened to lesser-known punk, hard rock, and metal gems. There's no telling what auditory delicacies we'd be cooking up when innocent bystanders passed through our kitchen.

Until I met John, I avoided listening to Staind. Casting further blind judgment on yet another rock band, I assumed their connection to Fred Durst would mimic the rap stylings of Limp Bizkit. Then, John made me listen to *Break the Cycle*. Once again, I was surprised when Aaron's lyrics spoke of teenage angst, family dysfunction, and struggling to find positivity in this negative world. The more I listened to the album, the more I realized music told the stories people wouldn't pay attention to any other way. By gravitating to Staind, I further rejected my biological family's belief that rock was evil. I was destined to use it for good.

Loser / 3 Doors Down

When listening to sappy music, I interpreted the content as fact. Everything was magical, if only I believed. By listening to rock, I started looking at myself realistically. Maybe what I considered entertainment wasn't amusing to my social circle. For example, I ran into a cute girl from school while wearing a navy-blue shirt with a skull, snake, and a stripe of orange/yellow tie-dye across the shoulders. She said hi, then complimented my shirt.

In an attempt to make her smile, I responded, "Thanks! Doesn't it look like I threw up on my shoulders?" After giving me a strange look, she left me to wallow in a pool of wasted opportunity.

Several months later while wearing the same shirt, I ran into the same girl. Don't be surprised, but she said hi, then complimented my shirt again. Forgetting the painful lesson from my recent history, I said, "Thanks! Doesn't it look like... Never mind."

She looked concerned, followed by relief, like, "Yeah! You're getting it!"

Sure, I was a loser. Pondering interactions like this one, I'm grateful this girl was willing to give me a second chance. Through her kindness, she taught me I didn't have to stay that way.

Excess Baggage / Staind

As summer progressed, I found myself hanging out with John more frequently. We entertained his parents for hours with impromptu observational humor coupled with goofy-sounding piano ditties on his 1970s-era Casio keyboard. As our musical trek got more serious, I asked him to teach me songs on his old classical guitar with a missing bottom string. Since most guitar players learn "Smoke on the Water" first, he started there.

I guess I figured I was an idiot savant whose knowledge of music would translate into musical talent. After agreeing to let me take his guitar home to practice, I got to work. I'd start with "Smoke on the Water," then nonsensically noodle along with songs I wanted to learn. When it didn't keep my attention, I moved to writing my own music. Although I had a lick written and recorded to tape, my second attempt at learning an instrument was failing.

While listening to Blink 182's *Dude Ranch* one evening, John and I explored the concept of starting a band. Checking on my progress with "Smoke on the Water," I finally owned up to wanting to learn a different song.

"Why didn't you say something sooner?" he asked.

After running to my house to fetch his guitar, I memorized the four-chords needed to play "Excess Baggage" that night. A few days later, I plucked along with the whole song. Now, if I could learn how to sing and play simultaneously, rock stardom would be mine.

Glycerine / Bush

When John found out I learned "Excess Baggage," he offered to teach me another song. For rock songs, we'd enter into the whimsical world of power chords. They were perfect for John's classical guitar because you don't need the bottom string to play them. After about an hour, I memorized the repeating progression to Bush's "Glycerine."

Alternating between the two songs I knew for hours, I sought to stroll the guitar player's rite of passage recommended by Bryan Adams. However, playing until my fingers bled proved difficult with nylon strings back in the summer of 2001.

It's All About the Pentiums / Weird Al

I was nominated for homecoming court. Now, I'm no conspiracy theorist, but I believe my nomination was a cruel joke. What unseen web of underground activities placed me in this lineup of popular athletes and cheerleaders? Allow me to present the facts I've collected through shoddy investigation.

It all started when a Boy's State camp counselor, affectionately referred to as C-SPAN due to his expansive knowledge of current events, heard me dropping Weird Al rhymes in the foyer. He suggested I close out my talent show set with "It's All About the Pentiums." No backing track, just odd pockets of silence injected between insults about weak computer performance.

Later in the week, some of my peers asked how I got so good at freestyling. Clearing the air, I wasn't a parody writing genius, just a massive Weird Al fan.

Fast forward to the night king and queen were announced. While collecting the breadcrumbs of my absurd fortune, the announcement was made: "Your 2001 Homecoming King is…Tony Kessel!"

Imagine how ridiculous I looked at the time. A nerdy kid with glasses and a Minnesota Vikings cap, leaning on crutches due to a flag football-related incident, gripping a clipboard used for taking stats. I was not royalty material, much less a guy who wins homecoming king. This honor was usually bestowed upon the most popular dude in school, which I was not.

Fast forward again, I arrived at the dance wearing my crown and a borrowed tie Dad wore at his own homecoming king coronation in the late 60s. Parading around the gymnasium, my collected clues confirmed the condition of my predicament.

It turns out, a friend from Boy's State promised our underclassmen, behind my back, I would rap at homecoming. When a group of sophomores came to collect on false campaign promises, I denied them.

"We only voted for you because we heard you'd rap if you won," they said, proceeding to take me on a guilt trip.

My initial plan was to approach the DJ, get shot down, then tell my peers it wasn't allowed. Yet, upon speaking with him, he only agreed to appease my false royal title. In front of God and everyone, I assumed the throne through a ceremonial acapella performance of Weird Al's "It's All About the Pentiums."

Here's the kicker: I know my set was captured on tape. Floating somewhere in this universe, a video exists of the whitest, nerdiest dude sporting a crown and A-shirt, chopping at the air with knife hands, dropping rhymes about beta-testing operating systems.

Now I wait in quiet caution. With one tragic misstep, the lizard people have enough videographic evidence to send me into viral super-stardom for all the wrong reasons.

Coma White / Marilyn Manson

Hot off the heels of my homecoming performance, I was approached by my friends John and Jordan to front their new band, Cixelsyd (dyslexic backward, get it?). I mean, why not? I'd been singing alone in my room for years in preparation for this moment. Pausing to make it seem like I had other options, I said, "Sure. I'll sing for you."

Since three out of five of the members were massive Metallica fans, I figured we'd be covering all Metallica, all the time. For a shot at stardom, I'd be willing to imitate James Hetfield.

At our first practice, we reviewed the setlist: Linkin Park's "One Step Closer," Marilyn Manson's "Coma White," and a working metal version of Garth Brooks' "The Thunder Rolls." No Metallica, but as we've already established, Manson is a satanist. "My mom doesn't let me listen to Manson," I argued.

"Dude, we picked Garth for you. Plus, it's not like that, man. It's an anti-drug song. Like, 'all the drugs in this world can't save her from herself.' It's cool, really."

Solid logic. What if we burst onto the scene with our cover of "The Thunder Rolls" (present me would interject: a decade before All That Remains did it)? "OK. Let's get to work." Who was I to allow this little squabble to distract from my dream of becoming a rock star?

I Don't Have to Wonder / Garth Brooks

Despite my newfound interest in rock, I still listened to Garth. A person should never forget the journey that brought them to where they are. Here's how I justified the switch: Garth Brooks had loads of rock influences from KISS to Billy Joel. His live performances (i.e. climbing rope ladders, spraying people with water, jumping on drum cages) are what left me wanting in other country artists. After following him for so long, it's difficult to watch other country musicians stand in one place, without a drum cage, wearing a fancy shirt, strumming on a guitar.

The darker content in GB's catalog presented new mysteries. "That Summer" becomes much clearer when examined through a smoky lens. The song explores the need to be connected in some way, the loneliness ensuing after the loss of a spouse coupled with the sexual curiosity of a teenage farmhand. It might've been wrong, but it captures the desperation of the human spirit.

As a country fan, I thought "I Don't Have to Wonder" journeyed through a dude watching a girl he loved marry another man from a distance. He didn't have to wonder if they should be together because she married someone else. I was too naïve to catch that the lead character kills himself. As he discards the ring meant for his love interest, he jumps right behind it, ending the torment of moving forward without her.

What could possibly drive a person to want to end it all? I'd been through quite a bit by this point, but death was never an option. Had I ever chosen to quit before, I never would've been where I was. It seemed like a permanent solution to a momentary problem. What if the lead character stumbled across a prettier, smarter, better partner to endure life with? He pissed the chance away. If life taught me anything, I found out if you wait it out and tough it up, all bad things crawl to an untimely demise.

With You / Linkin Park

In the fall of my senior year, my whole biological family met at my brother Chad's house for a week. In total, we got thirteen people together from four different cities throughout the Dakotas. It was a feat that hadn't happened since 1999 and hasn't been repeated since.

Different paths lead people to change. However, I discovered during that trip, family limits your growth to who you were when you last saw them. I tried so hard to fit in with my older brothers, but it wasn't happening how I envisioned it. It was as if I, front man for a band covering Marilyn Manson, was seated at the kid's Thanksgiving table.

No matter how hard they tried excluding me, I inserted myself into every activity I wasn't welcome in. "Going to the gas station? Me too! Let's go!"

Chad had his work tools stacked in the back seat.

"No problem! I'll move 'em over! See! I can fit. Let's go!"

He wasn't happy with me tagging along, but I wasn't gonna let him shake me off. I was going with the cool kids. We went to the gas station together, but it felt like we went separately. With aisles wide enough for three people, they checked out without me and waited in the parking lot.

As soon as I got into the car, Chad pulled out of the parking space. One little problem: my leg was still hanging out of the vehicle. I yelled for him to stop, which he did, right on top of my left foot.

After getting in with the door closed, I confronted them on their distance.

Refusing to make eye contact in the rearview mirror, he replied, "No offense, but you're a loser." Believe it or not, injecting a strategic "no offense" before a hurtful statement does very little to soften the blow of said observation. It's merely a head's up. Here you go, this is gonna sting!

Chad calling me a loser hurt more than him running over my foot. I'd spent most of my life trying to gain his approval. It didn't matter what anyone else thought; if he liked me, I believed I was cool. For the remainder of the car ride, he continued lecturing me about my Garth Brooks and *Goosebumps* infatuations. I refused to grace his ignorance with a response, but he remembered the thirteen-year-old version of who I was when we were still close. I'd updated, upgraded, and changed. He hadn't bothered to notice.

When we got to his house, my family decided to watch *Final Destination*. Nope, not gonna do that. I did want to express my dissatisfaction by throwing some stuff around before grabbing my Walkman and storming off. Maybe the flagrant pageantry would ping Chad's sympathy enough to beg me to come back inside.

He did no such thing.

As I sulked on the curb by myself, Dad came out to find out what happened. He encouraged me to share my feelings with Chad. Being the man of the house, I expected him to force us together to work things out like he always did. See, I fell victim to not seeing the changes others made in life, too.

I was still pissed off, so Dad recommended I take a walk to clear my head. Wandering aimlessly for several hours, I listened to Linkin Park's *Hybrid Theory* until my batteries died. I pondered the past. People's perception of me. About being a loser. About my obsessions. All the while, I allowed the lyrics to lament my current life situation.

I was still pissed off as I crept in for fresh batteries. I didn't want Chad, or any of my family, to lure me out of my anger cage. As I approached his apartment, a police car pulled into a parking space near the complex. I passed by a house party in the neighborhood several times during my walk. Did they bust it and think I fled? After midnight in a city, I was, at a minimum, breaking curfew.

All at once, my probation officer's voice echoed in my head, "One more mistake and I'll send you to juvenile detention until you're eighteen." My hard work swirling down the drain over a curfew violation.

Powerwalking past them without acknowledgment, I frantically entered the apartment. "The cops are here! I didn't do anything wrong. I was just listening to music. I promise."

The knock finally happened after what seemed like forever. Asking for my stepmom by name, the police escorted my parents outside to talk. A few moments later, they returned to the apartment in tears. These young officers were given the unfortunate task of notifying them that our thirteen-year-old cousin, Jamie, was killed in a car accident.

This was no longer a time to hold a grudge. Our family needed to be together. We shared old memories, dug at decades of hurt and loss. We talked about distance, about how we'd grown apart, about how to move forward from this moment.

See, life was changing for all of us. We were being pulled in different directions. It wasn't fair to assume we wouldn't adapt to these changes. As I said earlier, our entire family hasn't been together since that trip. We've made unfulfilled plans, even going as far as Facetiming Phat Matty into our last gathering in 2014.

I still reflect upon that night every time I hear *Hybrid Theory*. It symbolizes the anger, confusion, pain, and torment of my misunderstood youth.

If You Could Only See / Tonic

As my taste in music grew harder, I rarely dabbled in country, pop, and the childish musical antics of my past. The allure of my new music was the increasing distance I felt from the world. In search of so many different things, I kept coming up empty-handed. Take the dating scene for example. Most romantic relationships around me cast the appearance of intensely one-sided, convenient exchanges. It became easy to diagnose others' shortcomings from the outside.

With life blaring in the backdrop, I purchased one of my guiltiest pleasures of all time. Being in pawn shops on random treasure hunts, I gave Tonic's *Lemon Parade* a go. These guys weren't hard rock or metal by any stretch, but there were a lot of solid slower, love-type tracks I gravitated to. Sure, I passed the album off as decent, but in secret, I had the disc in heavy rotation.

I believe that's why I started seeing love songs as total garbage. They're all gross exaggerations of what life's like. The movies of the time, the music of the time, most commercial products being put out sold this lie that everything was flawless. All you need is love. Where my outward-facing persona rejected the idea, my internal monologue refused to let that concept go.

Nothing to Gein / Mudvayne

Along came my second season on the basketball team. Serving as a bench warmer for both seasons, I only played when I couldn't hurt them worse than they were already performing. I'm not bitter about that now. At the time, I didn't understand my teammates had played basketball in a competitive setting for seven years. I showed up and gave my all, but I came onto the scene way too late. Why would Coach reward my lack of basic skill with playing time?

In an attempt to make up for my inadequacies, I'd put some music in and return to work after my teammates left. Practicing lay-ups. Punishing myself with sprints for missed shots. My lofty aspiration was to consistently exceed Shaquille O'Neal's free throw percentage. I practiced for hours on end, listening to music until they made me leave.

My favorite part of basketball was the pre-game. Getting in a uniform. Studying court placement in the event I got to play. Fantasizing I'd do something spectacular if I got called in. The anticipation didn't start in the locker room; it began while queuing up one of two essential CDs. Since Mudvayne's *L.D. 50* worked so well for me, I'd move it into the team's CD player to pump them up.

A few games into the season, I was asked to settle on the team's copy of *Jock Jams*. It turns out, a song written from serial killer Ed Gein's perspective freaked my teammates out. I sacrificed by getting into the locker room earlier to prepare alone. When the rest of the team showed up, I'd move the CD to my Walkman, tuck it into the back of my shorts, and practice dribbling. Playing the game well was important, but preparing the stage for the audience was the rush I pursued.

Left Behind / Slipknot

The other CD in my warm-up arsenal was Slipknot's *Iowa*. Although I loved the performance aspect of basketball, my senior year was disappointing. In my last season with the team, I played less than the year prior. I know because I kept track, down to the second, both years.

Entering into the playoffs, we were slotted to play against the region's best team. This was probably gonna be my last basketball game. I took extra time in the locker room that day to my chosen soundtrack of Slipknot. Did we wanna win or get "Left Behind?" A win meant more time in the season. A blow-out, which was expected, meant more playing time for me. We'd have to wait, but this could be the last time I touched a basketball in a competitive setting.

The game went as horribly as anticipated. We went down early and never came back. The worst part was going into the fourth quarter, more than twenty points down, watching the other team's second-stringers file in. Coach kept me parked on the bench.

At the four-minute mark? Nope.

How about three? Not a chance.

Two? Nope.

I got sent in with one minute and nineteen seconds left to play. Coach gave the team one direction: pass the ball to Tony.

Up to this point in the season, I fired off seven shots without making a single basket. In that last minute, I shot the ball three times. Shot one was an easy, unguarded attempt from inside the paint. I missed it, cracking under pressure. Shot two was from a little further out with half-hearted coverage. Another miss, but this time, it was a complete airball. My third shot was further than the last one. I didn't want to risk it, but with less than ten seconds remaining, I had to settle, square up, and shoot. This was my final chance to prove the whole season wasn't a waste.

Without time to dribble, the guy guarding me stepped off to let me take the shot. Like in the womb, all sounds dulled to a murmur, minus the sound of my rapidly beating heart. Still sailing through the air, it looked like it had what it took to make it.

Three….Two….One….

The buzzer rang out. I could feel myself age by seventeen years as the ball dropped right through the net.

I'm not sure if I've driven this point home, but I was not a talented basketball player. For me, it was never about the thrill of competition. Drawing from that is difficult because where there are winners, there are losers. I'm too sympathetic to the other side's peril in defeat. It was about performance, dancing in the spotlight for the crowd's entertainment. It's like Rudy from the movie *Rudy*. Despite the loss, the "little guy" provides hope by doing the impossible. The victory sitting squarely in the middle of defeat wasn't Rudy bringing home the W; it was ol' Rudy closing his career out in a big way.

My Own Prison / Creed

After basketball season, I was left with nothing but time on my hands. Our band couldn't be viable if we practiced once every four months. Before I could get to work, I overheard classmates chatting about the recent Cixelsyd practice. I ran into our drummer listening to Chevelle at the gas station where he worked. "I dunno, man. We're all pretty busy."

In talking with John, he was down to play but hadn't spoken to anyone about it since our October jam session. Cool, I would have to serve as momentum. Someone fell victim to a rumor, but it was about to be correct.

A few days later, I asked the rhythm guitarist about jamming while washing our hands in the men's bathroom. He didn't seem to know either.

"How is it none of you are aware of a practice everyone's talking about?" I asked him.

"We are practicing. We just don't need you in the band anymore. We decided you're out." I got canned by the rhythm guitarist in the bathroom.

"What if we practiced more?" Nope.

"I can learn the songs!" Nope.

"Fine, I hope you fail. You guys suck anyway!" In my betrayal, I resorted to six-year-old tactics: condemnation blended with name-calling before a heated storm off. Take that, establishment!

For the next few days, I contemplated life by sulking and listening to music alone. Why did everything I touch turn to crap? I conducted intense soul-searching to Creed's first album. Committed to rebounding, I needed some time to dwell in my misery. So, Scott and I hung out, comparing our respective prisons. In a *Dawson's Creek* kind of way, I still believe mine was worse.

Soldier's Daughter / Tonic

I'm not sure what songs I expected them to play at prom, but I attempted mastery of three breakdance moves before the big day: the worm, the headspin, and the turtle. If I had time, I'd learn to switch the turtle into a jackhammer.

For some strange reason, I selected Tonic's *Lemon Parade* and Matchbox Twenty's *Mad Season* as background ambiance to these escapades. Neither of them is appropriate for breakdancing, but I practiced to them anyway. Take it from me: it's tough to skip to the faster songs in the middle of a ten-minute headstand. Also, you'll have ample time to ponder song lyrics, not necessarily the brain function, but the time.

As mentioned before, my dad's a veteran. He was too jaded by memories of the Vietnam War to understand my hobby. Catching me practice late one afternoon, he called me out. "What're you doing? Go do something more productive."

Nope. I was a rebel, a breakdancer. Ironically, I weighed in on being a Soldier's son while standing on my head, listening to music, and attempting to dance. He was really killing my buzz. Let me dance, Dad. Just let me dance.

Wherever You Will Go / The Calling

After a short grieving period, I committed to starting another band. It turns out the prima donnas in Cixelsyd were purging members left and right. They replaced John. They auditioned another rhythm guitarist and rejected him. Out of spite, I collected talent in their wake to form a rival band. When we got signed to a record deal, they'd regret getting rid of me.

John agreed to join right away. His first request was to cover "Wherever You Will Go." Once we lured people in with the hit of the day, we'd release our own stuff to broaden our fan base. We planned to entice the rejected rhythm guitarist by promoting him, effective immediately, to lead guitarist.

Keep in mind, neither of us had heard him play a single note. Shooting hoops one afternoon, we nagged him to join our band. He wasn't having it. Lacking any real type of commitment, he agreed to jam with us just to shut us up.

The only drummer we knew was in Cixelsyd. He was also the sole percussionist in our school's pep band. Without other options, we had the daunting task of convincing him to join a side project. Oh yeah, then the inevitable avoidance of his Metallica cover recommendations once he joined. Somewhere along our rise to fame, he'd leave Cixelsyd for us. He'd have to. We had The Calling.

Believe it or not, our unnamed band failed to launch. My coercion of the lead guitarist did very little to motivate him toward solid commitment. Out of respect for Cixelsyd, we never approached the drummer. Instead, our band practices consisted of John and me hypothetically playing the best songs in the best band that never was.

Naked / Avril Lavigne

As the school year drew to an end, my focus shifted to prom. Since my desire to plan often conflicts with the audacity to dream when deadlines are involved, I have to account for lost time while this internal war is waged.

After narrowing down potential choices to a primary date and a backup, I wrote my speech. I carefully selected the exact words to practice with perfect inflection. You can't accomplish that through mental rehearsals or whispering. You also can't go to prom if your parents send you to a psychiatric hospital for having conversations with secret people. To set the tone for my delivery, I rehearsed my speech over a hundred times by masking the murmurs to Avril Lavigne's "Naked."

When the time was right, I gathered the courage to ask my first choice. Despite all my rehearsals, she said no. I wanted to know why, to improve upon performance, but she refused to give me a reason.

See, this is why backup plans are necessary. I had enough time to shift focus to my second choice without having to panic. When the topic came up naturally one afternoon, I launched into my speech. We WOULD HAVE had a great time. She seemed disappointed, but already had a date.

With no backup plan to my backup plan, I appeared to be dateless. The day was drawing too close to rent a tux in time. Plus, I didn't think I could handle another rejection.

Sitting at lunch a few days later, a buddy asked if one of us single dudes would take his little sister to prom. She was a freshman but a sweet girl. Although this wasn't the situation I dreamt out at all, I offered to take her. With my string of luck, she probably managed to find a date in the ten minutes since asking her brother for help.

My canned speech was reduced to a nonchalant effort: "Hey, your brother said you wanted to go to prom. Let me take you. We can go as friends." She agreed. I didn't dare admit it, but the more a person exposes their insecurities, the less embarrassing it becomes.

Sunburn / Fuel

When I was a junior, I tried out for a local music festival my school choir participated in. What I considered a triumph ended in the astonishing news that my entire performance was pitchy. I was offered summer voice lessons and returned to choir to try my luck again during my senior year.

Through scales and sightreading, I improved enough to perform an acapella version of "Amazing Grace" at the next festival. I practiced the piece, written for a tenor, for several months at an octave lower. On performance day, I was so nervous I sang it in the original key. I didn't place, but my personal victory rested in the opportunity to sing for real people.

As with most school trips, we stopped at the local mall after the festival. Rather than exerting energy digging for a new treasure, I snuck to the bus to memorize Fuel lyrics in peace. A sophomore girl, sitting in front of me, ruined my plans by making conversation. "Whatcha listening to?"

Intending to start my private party, I kept my answer short. "'Jesus or a Gun' by Fuel."

"What's that supposed to mean?" she asked from behind a disgusted sneer.

"It's not how it sounds. Check it out." Mere seconds into the song, her concern was readily apparent. "Here, try this one." Skipping to "Sunburn," relief crossed her face as she settled into the more hopeful lyrics.

Handing my headphones back, she said, "The second one was better. I'm not sure about that Jesus song, though."

For the rest of the trip, I kept listening to the album. In the event she could hear my headphone bleed, I skipped "Jesus or a Gun" and went directly to "Sunburn." How didn't she understand the last-ditch effort? The desperation of needing a savior? Nonetheless, I never thought my music would offend anyone.

To this day, I find myself analyzing the lyrics to "Jesus or a Gun." If the doubt surrounding the song's meaning becomes overwhelming, I skip it and wait for "Sunburn."

Mary Pretends / Fuel

My biological mom's name is Mary. Enough said.

Mourning / Tantric

Around the time I graduated, the local Catholic church opened a teen center to keep us out of trouble. We stopped by the club on rare occasions to fulfill the societal obligation behind our parents' nagging. "If you don't go, they'll close it down. Then, what'll kids do next year?"

When our first visit to the club got boring, I promised to walk my two female friends home. Stopping by my cousin's ex-girlfriend's house first, we chatted about hearing Tantric's "Mourning" at the teen center. Maybe one day, we'd put the poetry we exchanged to music.

Speaking of our personal aspirations forced us to focus on our rapidly approaching graduation. Where would we go? What would we do? With so many questions and so little time left in high school, every minute possessed unparalleled intensity.

Walking the other girl to her house, she asked me to make her a mix CD. Somehow, I knew "Mourning" would make the list she promised to give me. After I left her house, I took the longest route home possible in a tiny town, reflecting on the lyrics to "Mourning." It seemed to capture a snapshot of these weird emotions. Joy. Pride. Sadness. Fear of the unknown. Hope. Camaraderie.

I'd taken the ACTs and was accepted into the local college, but for the first time, the reality of life after high school set in. Maybe I was just tired. Problems this huge are never solved in a day. Maybe things would make sense again in the morning.

Spiders / System of a Down

My stale music collection needed new life. I pestered my classmate daily until she provided the "Mourning" mix CD track list. Pop, the Goo Goo Dolls, Ja Rule, blah, blah, blah. I totally judged a book by its cover, but only one song had potential: "Spiders" by System of a Down.

Aiming for the jugular, I downloaded "Spiders" within the first hour at my house. Who were these guys? Why hadn't I heard of them? The other half of my dial-up internet facilitated slow research into these Armenian geniuses. If I expected to track my amazing finds, I'd have to put them to paper. Thus began my album purchase wish list.

Don't Stop Dancing / Creed

Creed's *Weathered* came to me at a time when I really needed it. Contemplative tracks challenged my past, reflected my present situation, and encouraged a bright future. It's not fair to compare my life to the Native American plight found in "Who's Got My Back," but I could, at a minimum, relate. Who was watching out for me? With zero college graduates in my family circle, how was I supposed to last longer in that environment than them?

Using Brad Delson from Linkin Park as a spirit guide, what steps should I take to become a lawyer (my back-up plan to potential stardom)? Through Creed's encouragement, the only thing I knew to do was keep dancing. I felt like no one was watching, but at the same time, everyone was. Could I measure up to the mounting pressure?

Seein' Red / Unwritten Law

I. Am. A. Music. Snob.

Keep in mind, I don't actively troll YouTube by launching insults at songs I don't like from underneath the bridge. Making the civil decision, I allow most music the opportunity to captivate me. If the artist/band doesn't, I respectfully decline and move on. As this list should show, some acts I pass on at one point in life may captivate me later. It's not a death sentence, but, at that particular moment, I pursue what I'm looking for to feed current sentiment.

In one last act of fellowship before graduation, our class decided to go to Evan's Plunge in Rapid City, SD. I was sent on a separate mission by my boss' nephew, Brad: find Unwritten Law's *Elva*.

Brad had spiky blonde hair like Chester Bennington and a set of contact lenses that changed the color of his iris to light blue. He was my hometown's scene kid, miles ahead of everyone else. Like it or not, he never gave a bad recommendation for a new band. I'd known my classmates for the past twelve years, so nothing magical was gonna happen on this trip. That CD, though: I needed it; WHEREVER IT WOULD FIND ME.

Despite my evident hatred for alcohol in earlier life, I attended most major parties during my senior year. The night before the trip, a few of my classmates had a small get-together. My two best friends and I weren't ready to quit drinking for the night. We moved the party, jamming out to The Bloodhound Gang.

As the main party instigator, I accidentally forced our younger friend into inebriation. In my own state of intoxicated guilt, I nursed him to sleep and established watch to keep him from choking on his own vomit. I slept until thirty minutes past our departure time. For some crazy reason, my class convinced the bus driver to wait for me before heading out of town.

I spent most of the two-day trip hungover. Take it from me, water slides and lazy rivers are less enjoyable with a pounding headache. Plus, this water park thing was a necessary evil. My ticket to Rapid City mall attendance. I was merely marking time.

The next day, we went to the mall. After searching several stores, I wandered into Target. Not only did I scratch the CD off my album wish list, but it sold for the sweet rate of $9.99.

Staring at the album art, a chalk portrait of a person in pain, a bright red promo sticker guided my listening experience to "Seein' Red." Flipping back to the beginning of the album, I listened to the CD on repeat for hours. It wasn't until a road sign announced our arrival home that I finally took it out to listen to the *Scorpion King* soundtrack. I needed a break to digest my musical meal. Somehow, *Elva* managed to capture every emotion I felt in those moments.

Now, if I'm allowed to justify my snobbiness, it all comes down to one principle. If an artist wants to win my attention, they need to speak to me where I'm at, at that exact moment. It took me several years to figure out the formula. Hang tight. There are still plenty of opportunities for me to prove this point.

Chop Suey! / System of a Down

As graduation money rolled in, I made grand plans to binge on new music. Mom didn't let me. With $100 to enjoy for myself, the rest went into college savings. Since it's difficult to purchase metal in North Dakota, I bought what I could find, where I could find it. Sure, truck stop prices limited my purchasing power, but I needed new tunes. In order to test out System of a Down's *Toxicity*, $20 was the price of admission.

The album was fantastic, but I soon discovered people weren't receptive to my diversifying musical tastes. My parents hated it. My co-workers asked me to turn it down in the kitchen at Dairy Queen. Even then, the older customers still complained. Why listen to yelling at whisper volume? If I wanted that, I wouldn't be listening to metal. One simply does not whisper in the state of anger and confusion. How was I supposed to work that out quietly?

My Life / 12 Stones

My friend Derek picked up the *Scorpion King* soundtrack for Godsmack's "I Stand Alone." I listened to it for the deep tracks. All my friends were talking about Creed and Nickelback. What about Lifer, Sevendust, Coal Chamber, and Flaw?

Through personal circumstances, my attention was drawn to 12 Stones' "My Life." "Are you going out again tonight? Why do you stay up so late? Did you submit your college application? Are you saving money? Bring me your bank statement."

"It's MY LIFE, MOM!!!!"

When I ran into Brad again, I thanked him for Unwritten Law. What's next? He pitched 12 Stones' self-titled album.

"Yeah, yeah. I've been jamming out to 'My Life' a lot lately."

He continued the sale. "Dude, it's not even the best track on the album."

Accepting my next assignment, I paused all active searches until I found it. Several weeks on the hunt warranted no results. Finally, I cracked, asking Brad to burn it for me until I could buy my own copy. Having music without liner notes and album artwork isn't the same experience.

As I approached graduation, the anthem to my life was 12 Stones. The songs flirted with teenage anger and confusion. My regrets called out to me. My hopes to establish a better future were ambiguous. In fact, nothing possessed clarity. I didn't know how to deal with it all but engage in intense music therapy provided by their first album.

18 and Life / Skid Row

Life in a small town as a teenager sucks. In the incessant quest for adventure, we chased nostalgic happenstance by ritualistic romps through symbolically dead-end streets. Driving around in Derek's van, we discussed his travels to Montana. In Nate's '57 Chevy, we recalled his frequent absences from school due to medical issues. My worn-out tennis shoes led us through many heated games of hacky sack. Our anticipated departures left Will navigating life in his 80s clunker, void his entire friend circle. They were trying times indeed, but we couldn't be bothered by that. If we stayed busy enough, we stalled the inevitable.

Now, we were not a musically diverse group. Nate and Derek preferred 80s metal. You know the likes: AC/DC, Metallica, Def Leppard, Motley Crue, Skid Row, and Ozzy. Will and I were into nu-metal: System of a Down, Limp Bizkit, The Bloodhound Gang, and Coal Chamber. Since Derek or Nate took up driving responsibilities, we got more 80s than modern rock. You drive, you pick the music. Rules is rules.

The four of us drove the same route most nights. Conoco: check. Superpumper: check. The weird loading dock in the vacant lot near the movie theatre: check. Any new spots? Nope. Let's see what everyone else is doing. Nothing? Right on.

With enough inspiration, we'd go into Dickinson on weekends to drag main. If Will's friends failed us, we went bowling or wandered around Walmart. At a bare minimum, I could chip away at my album checklist.

Such is life when you're eighteen in a small town. You always had nothing going on, but still pursued adventure. Our endless sentence was eighteen and life. The only problem was finding it.

Eden / The Mayfield Four

Graduation is terrifying enough as a regular kid. Try being legally adopted with abandonment issues. The whole concept was a forced departure from everything I'd finally learned to accept. From people I worked so hard to gain approval from. Life, as you know it, ends and you walk away, willingly. After being forced to say goodbye to people I never should have, I don't deal well with goodbyes.

The process of graduation seemed inherently superficial to me. People I disagreed with for all twelve years of school were presented as turnkey companions. For a moment, we became best friends based upon the torrent of a confusing situation. What was I supposed to do? Forget the criticisms, perceived hatred, and playful jabs of thirteen-year-olds lingering in my memories?

At the same time, I knew departures. When a person throws deuces, you'd hate to reflect on these monstrosities. Instead, you hope to illuminate the impending doom with unicorn tears and dancing rainbows. So, you hang out with them to present one more opportunity to leave a lasting impression. These perceived wrongs don't have to mark you forever. Allow me to arrogantly allow you to add to the chapter before the page turns.

Even more, my version of that chapter could benefit from some gentle housekeeping. You have to give grace because you need grace.

I didn't want to walk away. I had plenty of that, but graduation makes you. Life forced me to leave, at the exact time I conquered the bittersweet beast that is high school. I longed for the opportunity to move on, but first, I had to break through the pain of turning another page.

Mama, I'm Coming Home / Ozzy Osbourne

The departures began immediately. Derek left North Dakota, where his mom lived, for Montana, where his dad was, to work for the summer. He'd figure the rest out later. After graduation, we partied in a barn outside city limits, crashing in the living room until dawn.

As Derek and I drove on dirt roads the following morning, his Ozzy CDs came to mind. Right there. Although he wasn't going home to his mama, I didn't have the mental capacity to draw a better comparison. Less than twenty-four hours into post-high school life, I lost one of my best friends. Derek, the facilitator and vehicle for most of our shenanigans, was gone.

Running Out of Pain / 12 Stones

If there's any song in my arsenal that could EVER nudge Garth Brooks' "That Summer" from the illustrious top spot of my all-time favorite song list, it's 12 Stones' "Running Out of Pain."

The panicked sense of uncertainty drew parallels between going to foster home and going to college. The cool breeze from a decade earlier forced me to choose a new anthem as my friends and I drug the same streets. Observing life from the back seats of similar hand-me-down commuter cars, it became easy to apply 12 Stones, like extra-strength ointment, to the reaggravated injuries of departing home, yet again.

I had my whole life in front of me, but I also had my entire past behind me. From my vantage point, my run of good luck appeared to be just that, good luck. What if I depended on my parents' supervision to make the right choices? How was I supposed to be better at life than them? What if the unknowns of adulthood were more difficult than they depicted? Was I truly running out of pain?

With uncertain futures and endless confusion swirling in the atmosphere, there were many painful conversations reflecting upon unpursued/wasted opportunities. I listened, but who was I to dole out advice from the same boat? My role became a human Kleenex dispenser to people making questionable decisions to vacate discomfort. Maybe they'd go to college, too. Get some roommates and run away from it all. Having been in uncertainty before, all I could do was lead the charge into unchartered territory.

Identity / Greenwheel

As confusion continued calling, I answered with intensive retail therapy. Through deliberate discovery of desired discs, maybe I'd stay busy enough to forget all that. Most CDs on my checklist carried parental advisories. One problem: my family's love for Walmart limited my options to kid-friendly radio edits. The adult in me didn't need a filter. However, the unlicensed driver in me required pleading with my parents for rides to regular CD stores.

One such trip left me quarantined, on my parent's timeline, to the Walmart music section. Sampling song snippets through dirty headphones, my heart raced at the thought of making a colossal mistake purchase. A crap CD taunting the primal instinct behind impulse as I flipped through the pages of my collection.

With time ticking toward an embarrassing intercom announcement to meet Mom at the customer service desk, I picked up a commercial rock album. Two white strips framed a bright scenic picture of an unrecognizable band standing in a field. Give Greenwheel and their mediocre song titles a shot, then go.

Slamming into the brick wall known as "Identity," I struck up a conversation with myself. "Hold up! Back arrow that sucker. Hmmm." *Soma Holiday* was solid, but this track was gold. If I expected to find myself amidst the changes of graduation, this CD needed to be in my life.

When we got home, I'd have to help put the groceries away. After that, I planned to take in *Soma Holiday* and shoot hoops under the dull streetlights.

To this day, it's planted firmly in my top ten favorite albums of all time. Every time I listen to this crazy, unheard-of band purchased on a whim, I can recall, with clarity, kicking away landscaping rocks some kids threw on the court. Nothing to see here, just a dude playing basketball as I'd done for years. I remember the collision of pink and orange in the sky as the sun set. I remember anticipating the panic of getting lost on a huge college campus. Most importantly, I remember wishing every first-time album listening session was similar to the experience I had with *Soma Holiday* that evening.

Payback / Flaw

Like the impeccable timing of the ocean's tide, I managed to pull in a copy of Flaw's *Through the Eyes* at Sam Goody (RIP). You see, a few short days later, I found myself in our turquoise Ford F-150 blazing trails toward Wyoming for a family vacation to Old Faithful.

For old time's sake, I tried getting into the music of the vehicle. Dad set the stage with some Alan Jackson. When Dad and I dared to parody "Ave Maria" after the fifteenth time hearing it in a row, we received the all-too-familiar lecture. "You all wanna be goofy? Fine, it's Norm's turn."

Ray Stevens' "Harry, the Hairy Ape" is funny, but scripted humor cannot trump on-the-spot observations delivered in operatic falsetto. My selection, Linkin Park's *Hybrid Theory*, was out of the CD player by the end of "Papercut." "You shouldn't be listening to music about paranoia. Don't you have enough to worry about?"

Snatching my CD, I put Flaw into my Walkman to sulk alone. Guess what? You suck! Every time my family annoyed me on that trip, I retreated to the chorus of Flaw's "Payback" to avoid making an angry, irreversible comment.

In retrospect, I went to spend time with my family before leaving for college. Then, I skirted any meaningful attempt at connection by converting fear, sadness, and vulnerability into the sheer anger represented in "Payback." The path to manhood was already littered with the bitter tears of my youth. Preparing to take flight, it was time to man up and grow up.

My Letter / Flaw

What I deliberately failed to mention in the entry for "Payback" was I always allowed *Through the Eyes* to guide me into "My Letter." "Payback" gave me permission to be angry. "My Letter" forced me to ponder why.

As Chris Volz lamented his personal torment, I penned an imaginary letter of my own. With two years since our last interaction, I hadn't heard from my biological mom at all. Was she proud of my recent high school graduation? Was she aware of the daily damage she caused by choosing to remain vacant? What did I have to do to capture her attention? To finally earn her love? The one dangling carrot I could never reach, I wanted more than anything.

There was a lot to ponder. My trip to Old Faithful with my family was annoying me to no end. I needed time to sift through the shards of my psychological damage. I needed the opportunity to be angry, the chance to be scared. Like our temporary stay at KOA, I couldn't allow myself to camp there long. The future was calling, but moving forward required reduction of some unnecessary baggage.

11 a.m. / Incubus

If I haven't established this point yet, I'm an emotional hoarder. Not a physical hoarder of things, but a hoarder of emotion. I can't honestly tell what to hold onto and what to let go of. That may sound odd, so allow me to explain.

How was I to assess which experiences, good or bad, were good for me? I had to retain the positive stuff. Why get rid of that? These memories are essential to the foundation I was building. People kept reminding me of a bright future chocked full of potential. You can't set forward on the path of life without some cheap bricks of arrog…, I mean, confidence. People needed to believe in me as much as I pretended to. I needed the good stuff.

Keep it.

Now, the question of the bad stuff. Most of my past didn't need replication. It had to go. Then again, how can a person progress with the possibility of disappointment and failure lurking in the distance? Keep these threats in cache for immediate recollection used in defense or avoidance mechanisms. Also, failing to learn from all aspects of history condemns its repetition. To me, nothing's worse than discarding a previously owned experience. But what to keep?

Not sure, keep it all.

Sorting my emotional baggage for a fresh start didn't resolve much of anything. In fact, I wasn't even sure how this junk fit in the suitcase to begin with. Clean-up would have to wait for a different trash day. In the meantime, I had the daunting task of coaching each Tetris piece back into its designated space.

Ghetto / POD

After graduation, most summer evenings were spent either booze cruisin' or walking around town. Seeking divine protection, we seeded the blatant Christian message of POD's *Satellite* into dangerous, illegal activities. As an added precaution, we mainly drug country roads to evade law enforcement and town gossips. With any luck, we'd stumble across a discarded cardboard box large enough to get stuck under the vehicle. Using the box as a makeshift plow, we wagered how long it would hold up before exploding to pieces in the rearview mirror. The excitement would have to last until next time.

When gallivanting around in secrecy got boring, we'd meet up at The Dam Park (Look it up. The Dam Park is a legitimate fishing destination/ playground located in sunny Belfield, ND). With car doors opened, we applied the thin veil of POD, yet again, to our intense games of drunken hacky sack. Intoxication eventually impedes a person's hand-eye coordination and balance into ineffectiveness.

Then, and only then, we'd sprawl out on the hood of the car, stare at the starry night sky, and discuss the deeper stuff. The meaning of life. The future.

Relationships. By that point, our commitment to inebriation left us unable to return home to face our parents in a drunken stupor. For one last time, we allowed POD to coax us into a restless night of uncomfortable sleep in the bucket seats of beater cars.

Hold Me Down / Tommy Lee

My album quest lingers in most of my memories, and finances, of that summer. Lacking a money management system, Mom forced me to deposit half of my earnings into savings. The rest was used for music, Little Debbie snack cakes, and odd-flavored Mello Yellos. Poor financial planning mandated lopsided periods of feasts to fat-cat album purchases followed by the famine of using my college computer to research my next binge in music chat rooms.

With enough cash for one CD from my twenty-album wish list, I stumbled across Tommy Lee's *Never a Dull Moment* and Adema's self-titled album at the local Kmart (RIP). In a fight to the death between each album's lead singles, it was "Hold Me Down" vs. "Giving In." The first shots of this metaphorical battle rang out, BUT which act held the deep track stamina necessary to win?

The fury of war waged over the in-store sample player for thirty minutes. Only the victor could journey the space from the shelf and cash register before landing in the audio promised land of my Walkman. Not to mention, the glorious travels thereafter. Every other selection was marked, like a headstone, to my album wish list graveyard.

Giving In / Adema

Seriously, though: Tommy Lee, legendary rock drummer for Motley Crue vs. Mark Chavez, half-brother to KoRn singer Jonathan Davis. Tommy Lee's album was much weaker than Adema's. Could I trust the context of the available song snippets?

To level the playing field, I conducted a scientific comparison of these selections against my unbiased opinion of Jerry Cantrell's *Degradation Trip*. The outstretched arm with pins and strings featured on the album cover looked sweet. The songs sounded old, reminiscent of Derek's dusty Alice In Chain's CDs. Since Tommy Lee was closer in age, and style, to Jerry Cantrell, my decision was made. Adema reigned supreme. Scientific analysis would have to hold me over until next payday.

I meant to leave the subtlety of how much weight I put on a simple CD purchase and let the reader figure the irony out. I have to be more blatant. It strikes me as curious how little thought I put into any of my actual life decisions. Without a second thought, I sat through the four-hour ACT, submitted applications, and registered for classes recommended by my advisor. I had no idea what I didn't know. Void of hesitation or fear, I moved forward in the lines I was told to stand in. Yet, mere moments before this challenging purchase, I'd just left college orientation.

I can't fully understand how, or why, I went to college, but I can tell you, with precision, why I own Adema's self-titled album. Going to college may not be a science. However, selecting the perfect CD depicting current sentiment definitely is.

Blind / KoRn

Years ago, I was launched into Garth Brooks super fandom after hearing the hook to "That Summer." One magical moment established a plight of endless pursuit. To avoid going all out and losing everything again, I remained cautious about putting another musical act in that coveted seat. I'd fallen in love with so many bands, but none of them captured my full attention. I was looking for a band with tenure. You know, a band that would never leave me. Nonetheless, I was still taking applications for a band to put my faith in.

You can't listen to the types of music I do without stumbling upon KoRn. After picking up, and liking, *Follow the Leader*, their other four albums began calling my name.

My quest was clear, with one evident problem: who starts eating a hot dog from the middle? You have to start the journey with the self-titled album where the torn relationships, hurt feelings, and unsorted emotions were in their rawest form. Where the darkness of my personal history collided with the lyrical content of "Blind," "Chutes and Ladders," and "Daddy." With such strong opening remarks to the KoRn discography, the jury had a strong set of facts to review. Evade haste, Tony. There are still three more exhibits for consideration.

Falling Away from Me / KoRn

No story's complete without the introduction of dramatic tension. Something has to come along to make the audience question fate. For me, the plot killer to the KoRn discography is *Life Is Peachy*. Two good songs? If I was a fan in real-time, without knowledge of *Follow the Leader*, I might not've stayed.

To gather confidence in my journey, I skimmed through *Follow the Leader* for several days. An enthusiastic friend provided encouragement to complete my collection by offering up *Untouchables*. His contribution was welcomed, but out of order. With one album left, I acquired *Issues* at a local pawn shop. Your Honor, all evidence has been presented, closing arguments concluded. The jury is prepared for deliberation.

Dead / KoRn

During my last family vacation to South Dakota before going to college, I used every spare moment to deliberate my decision to dub KoRn as my new favorite band. Armed with the entire discography, the genius behind *Issues* was enough to seal their fate.

KoRn was my replacement for Garth Brooks. Garth was welcome to provide hope from the sidelines. Maybe if he returned from retirement, our paths would merge again. For now, my teenage angst required a different megaphone.

Let's face it. With college starting in less than a week, I was no longer a free man. By choosing to live at home, I could continue working at DQ on weekends and keep in touch with old friends. I had my rides to campus, my class schedule, and my wardrobe (now complete with several brand-new KoRn t-shirts) all figured out. Like Hannah Montana, I had the best of both worlds. This scary life transition was my first shot toward future happiness. And that was all I wanted.

Somewhere Out There / Our Lady Peace

For most of my senior year, I quit on the concept of romantic relationships. Going to college reignited my potential to enter the dating scene. However, I knew if I wanted to be in a relationship, I needed to make a ton of personal improvements.

First, girls like getting shuttled around. It's hard to have a girlfriend if you don't have a driver's license or a car. You see, I was told foster kids weren't allowed to get their license for liability reasons. I had to fix that soon. Then, as much as saving money for non-music purchases killed me, I needed a car.

Second, I needed a guitar. In my head, that Boy's State songwriter had a girlfriend because her love's depth couldn't exceed his musicianship. While scouring local pawn shops for CDs, I scanned the acoustic guitars dangling from hangers on the wall. By playing and writing music, I could deliver subtle, scripted messages, with confidence, to the female persuasion without the need for awkward conversational exchanges.

If I were to take a girl out, I had to be prepared to pay. I needed money to buy the stuff I wanted, leaving a little extra to take care of a chick in time-honored tradition—meals, presents, jewelry, the things girls want. I needed to keep working, maybe even get a second job in my college town. While money doesn't buy happiness, it does pay for the things that made me happy. I couldn't hurry the process. If I kept moving firmly in the direction of my dreams, I'd find the right girl somewhere along the way.

Driven Under / Seether

To pass time while downloading lesser-known KoRn content on WinMX, I logged into music discovery chatrooms with my trusty screenname: kornflake197. Perverts on the prowl for pretend online romances called out, "ASL? ASL?"

No thanks, dawg. "18, Male, North Dakota." Enter. "Anyone got hard rock/heavy metal recommendations?" Enter.

On rare occasions, I'd sit at the feet of fortunate rock fans taking in tales from the mosh pit. Amidst the frequent crickets, a compassionate stranger pierced the desperate darkness of date seekers with a good band recommendation. Both Seether and Breaking Benjamin entered my life in this exact way.

In my last week of freedom before college, I pondered my next steps to Seether's *Disclaimer* during late-night walks around my hometown. Void of tangible life, the dark streets sprawled out like a post-apocalyptic movie set. The aging signs of vacant storefronts indicative of a town past its potential taunted my deep-seeded beliefs of grandeur. Then, the familiar summer breeze seemed to signal my attention to the east. Others may stay in this wretched place, refusing to leave known comforts, but I couldn't. It was time to run.

Campus was nice, but I wasn't about to enter it alone. If I could cite one source for calming my nerves to this new experience, the blur of Seether's *Disclaimer* spinning in my Walkman's tiny window takes strong precedence. Let's face it, every class began with calloused instructors ritualistically reading an eighty-person roster to a roomful of thirty-two students. Where were the missing kids? In response, I paced the journey between one-word performances of roll call to *Disclaimer's* driving rhythms.

Further, I burned free time and negative energy through travels, on foot, comparing acoustic guitar prices at local pawn shops while waiting for Dad to give me a ride home after work. Testing campus library printouts of *Disclaimer* tabs, I imagined which guitar would be most effective to swap loneliness with Student Center visitors after completing my assignments.

As the unknowns of college became clear, my transition was cemented by my first instance of companionship: Seether's *Disclaimer*.

Downfall / Trust Company

Every Thursday evening, after Dad left for home, I had a three-hour English comp class. As I waited for the family friend my parents arranged me to stay the night with, I skimmed tracks from Trust Company's *Lonely Position of Neutral*. I'd ushered this best-of-both-worlds scenario into existence by holding onto home after beginning college.

Yet, my understanding of the formal, suit-and-tie bureaucracy of daytime campus life collided with the hopeful spark of what it contained at night. While perched on the steps of Kleinfelter Hall waiting for my mom's friend, a delivery guy frantically searched a grassy field to drop off a pizza ordered in the middle of a heated two-hand touch football tournament.

For quick backdrop, I was aware my mom's friend was a single mom with two kindergarten-age autistic twins. What I wasn't aware of was what managing life with autistic children truly looked like: their sensitivity to lights/ noise, the tantrums ensuing after unmet expectations, the apparent bribery to accomplish tasks necessary for survival, and the extreme patience/love her children required. I felt like a resource-sucking leech about this arrangement before my brief exposure to life with autism. In my head, her job as a social worker was already chaotic. Now, add me to the mix for eighteen weeks.

After a late-night, made-to-order supper, comprised of her twins' compromised food preferences, I snuck to the guest room to focus on my reading assignments. Disappointment in my collegiate experience wove a two-strand rope in my head with sorrow for being a siphon to a person who had to suffer to help, rendering my reading comprehension impossible. Somewhere between the second and third listen through *Lonely Position of Neutral*, I drifted to sleep.

As we headed toward campus the next morning, I shared my concerns about our arrangement in the brief pockets of silence between necessary affirmations to her twins. With a kindness capable of unintentionally driving guilt, like a railroad spike, further within me, she said, "Tony, you are NOT a burden. We all need help starting out."

"I understand, thanks. What'd you do when you went to college?"

She continued, "I promise you're not a burden. It costs more money, but my favorite part of college was living on campus. Some of my best friends, to this day, lived in the dorms with me."

Before exiting her car for my first Friday morning class, I thanked her one more time.

You Know You're Right / Nirvana

That morning, I inquired about a dorm room at the residential life office. They agreed to reserve their last male bed if I got my tuition adjusted with financial aid. As I presented the cost charts to my parents that evening, they fully supported my decision to live on campus.

After an hour of collegiate bureaucratic rituals on Monday morning, I crossed the threshold of an open door containing my first adult living experience. The room, and the whole building, reeked of BOD body spray. With Dad holding a box of my stuff behind me, I announced my arrival over the loud trash-talking of two young guys playing Bond. A nerdy-looking guy wearing glasses greeted me with a handshake. "Willie Nelson."

Yep, his name was Willie Nelson. Glancing back at my dad's smile of approval, my imagination ran wild. Were his parents old school country music fans, too? I only hoped he wasn't a pothead.

Returning from my first two-hour block of classes, nine dudes, being dudes, exchanged insults and N64 controllers while spitting Copenhagen juice into old Mountain Dew bottles. This was the dream. I was free to join in on the shenanigans at any point, but first, my parents would've wanted me to settle in.

Murphy's Law dictated nothing fun would happen when I was ready to play. In our first moment alone, Willie was putting laundry away with Nirvana's "You Know You're Right" playing on MTV in the background. For our first real conversation, we shared lifestyle expectations, gave music recommendations, compared our experiences of homecoming king selections at our respective schools, and agreed upon continuation of Will's enthusiastic open-door policy.

With this college thing figured out, I needed a job in town, my license, a car, a guitar, and I'd be set. I was still nervous, but this time, at being in control of my own destiny.

Your Love / The Outfield

Let me rewind for a minute. What was my exact expectation for college life? I have the perfect story.

A few weeks after moving onto campus, I returned from class to the sound of The Outfield's "Your Love" playing down the hall. I wasn't aware of this band, or song, at the time. Willie told me he listened to a lot of different types of music. This hilarious sounding, yet serious, ditty was one of those nuggets.

Entering through an already open door, I prepared to roast Willie's poor music taste. My scripted burn was ruined by one of his friends lying on his bed, serenading his girlfriend, karaoke-style, over the phone. He saw me walk into the room, said hi, then went on singing to his chick like I wasn't there.

The spontaneity of the situation is what I thought college would be. I didn't dream of debauchery and constant partying. I dreamt of the freedom affording late-night video game sessions intermingled with music downloads and ramen noodles. You know, the things my parents scrutinized when I lived at home.

I took the whole experience seriously, refusing to skip or miss class. I wanted a degree. I also wanted the social part: campus events, dances, concerts, and cafeteria food. I wanted to create new memories. "It was weird. He laid on my roommate's bed obnoxiously singing this gem from the 80s to his girlfriend. Man, we were so crazy! Living the college life, you know?"

I still tell this story in social settings. For flair, I conduct a dramatic reenactment with the most annoying falsetto voice possible. Maybe you just had to be there.

The Quiet Things That No One Ever Knows / Brand New

One of my favorite aspects of campus life was made-to-order omelets in the cafeteria every morning. It turns out, your average college kid doesn't prioritize breakfast over sleep. I, on the other hand, practically opened the cafeteria. Monday through Friday, I grabbed my omelet, a bowl of Lucky Charms, a glass of half chocolate/regular milk, and some orange juice. If I missed one of my ten meals a week, I lost money. I did not miss.

Breakfast was the only meal I didn't socialize at. Grabbing my usual table right in front of the TV playing music videos, Brand New's "The Quiet Things That No One Ever Knows" became a critical part of my routine. I wouldn't leave the cafeteria without my daily dose. Don't worry, though; I never waited on it.

The video has two highlights: the silly guitar slide between the intro and the verse "Beeew, Beeeeeer" and that clip where Jesse Lacey belts a note, bringing the lead actress into momentary consciousness during an apparent soul exchange. OK, sweet. I got my breakfast, got my table, and got my music video. Time to get to class.

I Feel So / Boxcar Racer

I exploited the transition to college for the opportunity to reinvent myself. Concealing my country music roots, I cast the appearance of a 2000s era rock front man: clean-cut, gelled hair with frosted tips, dark-colored band t-shirts, edgy designs etched on back pockets of JNCO jeans, and a fresh pair of laceless, white Adidas. In my head, lead singers epitomized unprecedented quirkiness. My quirk was, while I mastered the art of shoe-tying, I was far too busy to be bothered by that nonsense.

"Did you know Blink 182's Tom DeLonge has a side project called Boxcar Racer? Did you know Chester Bennington jumpstarted Linkin Park fame through his first band, Grey Daze? Are you aware the lead singer of Dashboard Confessional splits singing responsibilities with Further Seems Forever? Have you heard of 12 Stones? No? Ok, so Paul McCoy, the screaming dude in the breakdown of Evanescence's 'Bring Me to Life,' sings for 12 Stones. They're way better than Evanescence."

That guy sounds annoying, but unfortunately, it's the staple holding my mess-of-an-identity together. At least once per week for the past seventeen years, I declare disdain for the gimmicks of radio. Somewhere in the universe, a notification bell chimes when I say, "Oh, I don't listen to the radio…" Ding! Got it. Please remind me again next week.

Lastly, the final plague of the rock genius know-it-all is a constant surge of unbridled anger. The artistry is in keeping others guessing the source of your torment. Radiate anger to keep people mystified. Did he have a rough childhood? Maybe. Was college not going the right way? Probably. Did he follow a stock tip and have one of his investments go south? Sure. They needn't know my anger's source, just THAT I was pissed off. With my desired persona nailed down, point me toward the mic.

Guilt (Hold Down) / Fingertight

Along with anger came flagrant disregard for certain types of music: techno, pop, punk-pop, emo, and rap. Wait, my feelings for rap wavered depending upon the level of irony involved. Baller, Shot Caller! You see, they're broke, but spare no expense for some sweet twenty-inch blades. Is that really necessary? What a mockery! You see the quirk in that, eh? Lead singers are loud and opinionated.

If my life was a play, Fingertight would've entered stage right.

My breakfast routine had me hearing "Guilt" once a day. This band was categorized as emo, and if they weren't, their song title says it all. Guilt? Yep, unless guilt triggers intense acts of aggression, it isn't in the authorized category of allowed emotion. It did not. Dude wronged someone, now they're in a wheelchair, and he can't fix it. He feels straight-up guilt.

In this mock play, my previously expressed loud opinions forced me to take a strong negative stance.

How's this for irony? A purchased copy of *In the Name of Progress* stayed safely tucked away to the confines of my collection. If it played at supper, I'd take a moment to listen, to make it seem like honest assessment, then rip it to shreds. In essence, listen by night and criticize by day. I guess, if pushed for an explanation, Fingertight was my version of installing twenty-inch blades on an Impala.

Again & Again / Taproot

Without a car, I had to hoof four miles for replacement ramen noodles and toiletries. One afternoon, I stumbled across a used Ford on sale for $650. Without a license, my dad agreed to test drive it for me. "It's a great little car!" he reported. "For the money, it's worth it. Runs well enough to get around town. Start with this, but save up. It probably won't last longer than a year."

Great car, good price. Got it.

It turns out, Dad had already called the bank to set up a loan appointment. Like movies depict, I put on a shirt and tie for the meeting. With a co-signer, $100 down, and bi-weekly payments, this beauty was mine. Deal! My parents could store the car at home until I got my license. Leaving the small-town community bank, a proud car owner, I strutted with the confidence that foot travel would soon be an option, not a requirement.

A couple weeks later, I scheduled my driver's test. Despite bombing the parallel park, like every other kid in history, I was a card-carrying, licensed driver. Since my dainty old lady sedan quivered in fear as semis stormed past me, I opted to keep my radio off during our maiden voyage. Maybe on my next trip, I'd parade around town to music blaring with the windows down. I mean, that was the dream.

After dropping every spare cent on registering and insuring my car, I couldn't afford a $20 tape conversion kit. To listen to music while driving, I plugged computer speakers into my Walkman's headphone jack, resting a speaker on both sides of the dash. Let's be honest, Taproot's "Again & Again" was barely audible over the sorry cries of my 1984 Ghetto Blaster. I'd come so far so fast to allow my dreams to be dampened by reality.

Poem / Taproot

That Ford, birthed into existence the same year as me, became my pride and joy. Also like me, it needed some work. With one side mirror, which was apparently street legal in 1984, I drove to every auto parts store in town to complete the pair. The once-maroon carpet faded to the color of stewed carrots after twenty years of exposure. The nagging sag of ceiling fabric brushed the top of my head, a constant distraction while driving. The tape deck begged for an upgrade to the modern era: CD player, speakers, amp, and a ten-inch sub. For aesthetics, I made plans to spray-paint KoRn album art graffiti pieces to her plain white body.

Waiting to earn the money needed to convert my car into a metal machine, I kept my daily driving ritual. To combat the crisp fall breeze, I turned the heater up, cranked the windows down, and added clothing layers to keep warm. The ambient sound of my Taproot mix CD was barely audible over my makeshift stereo.

Come to think of it, the innocent dog walkers I drove by had to imagine my loud singing was necessary to mask the tragedy of a broken radio. As for me, I couldn't be bothered with appearances. This was MY dream.

Always / Saliva

Believe it or not, my car was not reliable. Sometimes, old girl felt her years of faithful service. Sometimes, my youthful zeal caused the engine to flood. Sometimes, North Dakota, nearing winter conditions, intervened on our relationship. Regardless of causation, I walked to my new job at Hardee's at least once a week.

Here's the good news: my makeshift car stereo transformed to accommodate my travel needs. Either way, Saliva's *Back into Your System* was queued up in preparation for the pending, unplanned walk. My weapon of choice, the Swiss-army knife, fitting for my makeshift system. Love 'em, or hate 'em, Saliva was versatile enough to fuel the carousel of cyclical teenage emotion: anger, pity, and introspective self-reflection. All within the timespan it took to stroll to work.

Pretty Girl (The Way) / Sugarcult

After getting to work amidst car issues, the blur of new co-workers spotlighted one heartbroken girl sorting through the pieces of her first break-up. Every employee fixated on her trashy ex-boyfriend dumping her for another chick. Sure, she was cute, but we only maintained communication on work-related things.

She took orders; I cooked 'em.

She barked order substitutions; I yelled, "Order up!" when said food was ready.

That was the extent of our relationship. She came to work, did her job, and went home. I sustained the viable income stream conducive to car upgrades, band t-shirts, and layaway payments toward my turquoise acoustic guitar at the pawn shop.

After closing the store one night, she lamented her situation with the assistant manager over the restaurant intercom system. Scrubbing the grill, I overheard her droning on about her ex-boyfriend. She missed him, but needed to focus on work and school. She never should've left gymnastics to appease their relationship.

She was single. So? That meant nothing positive for me. To avoid my previous woes in the friend-zone, I pretended to be so busy with work I couldn't hear her. That her situation didn't affect me. That I didn't observe, on a daily basis, charming, good-looking college jerks rope girls in, sleep with them, then dump them. Also, that I didn't observe, on a daily basis, chicks mistaking these lies for true love.

Despite my interest, I refused to reduce myself to circling the skies above the scent of vulnerability. When the right girl decided to exit the charade of cat-and-mouse relationships, they'd know where to find me.

The Taste of Ink / The Used

For several weeks, this girl continued talking about her break-up, but never with me. By that point in time, I'd shared hundreds of these moments with heart-broken girls. I knew the exact concoction of murmured words to console her pain. However, none of them seemed to change the situation. Almost every time, they'd either crawl back to the dude who dumped them or date a different guy with similar qualities. I wasn't about to invest in the fruitless endeavor of wasting shoulder space for this girl's tears.

One particular night, the store was slammed by two different buses of hungry football players. After the chaos was over, I scrambled to catch up on my closing routine. While the front people cleaned the lobby, they put our co-workers in goofy, hypothetical relationships over the headset. Pairing this girl with the creepiest guy we worked with, she shot back, "Tony's the only guy at Hardee's I'd ever date."

Shocking news to me, but I ignored it.

The assistant manager, not letting the comment slip, bum-rushed me at the sink to play cupid: "She's into you, man! Make a move!"

He nudged us further together by sending her to the kitchen to help me clean. Our anti-climactic conversation, seeded with my first attempts at intentional flirting, was the most significant leap I'd ever made toward a relationship.

The next day, the assistant manager, her, and I had lunch shifts together. Our pissed-off general manager handed us task lists from the night prior. For me, that was stocking freezers, cutting vegetables, and traying hamburger patties.

Admittedly, the promise of a potential relationship kept me up all night. This was it; I'd been waiting for this moment forever. Hope tangoed in my head with the incoherent ramblings of exhaustion as I opened the next box of patties. The rusty utility knife snagged the tape before plunging into the webbing between my left thumb and pointer finger. Removing the blade, immediate adrenaline caused blood to pulsate from within the gaping wound. A cut so deep, I was carted to the hospital for stitches and a tetanus shot.

To recover, the ER doctor made me take a week off. As fast as this girl and I were becoming an item, was it possible she'd move on while I healed? Didn't have her number; couldn't visit her at Hardee's. All I could do was wait it out and hope for the best.

The day I returned to work, she was scanning a newspaper before her shift when I went on break. She greeted me with a hug, "Can I see it?"

After carefully wrapping my wound, she put her hand on top of mine. "I'm sorry you cut yourself." She smiled, leaving me in a daze as she clocked in. Was this real life?

In the weeks to pass, our conversations became more frequent, more natural. Gathering the courage to ask her out, I received a yes. I was so nervous to screw the relationship up, the only meal I could stomach was cheap apple cinnamon oatmeal with dissolving dinosaur eggs meant to enhance the breakfast experience for children.

Everything was working out how I planned it. Job: check, car: check, guitar: check, college: check. The last empty box next to girlfriend, check.

Buried Myself Alive / The Used

After being love-drunk for the Christmas season, the cold of January set in, forcing honest sobriety.

As much as I didn't want to be a vulture, it never occurred to me I could be amongst the used. Most of our conversations centered around investigative findings of her ex-boyfriend's new relationship. It became clear; I was a space filler, her rebound. If given the chance to reignite her old romance, I believe she would've left me in a hot second.

To avoid conflict, I allowed my feelings to fester. I could empathize with the pain surrounding her first heartbreak. For what, though? To sacrifice myself at the cost of her past entrapment?

When this jerk was the centerpiece at our next private dinner, yet again, the blister burst. "Listen, I like you a lot. I really do. I'm trying to be present, but you're not here with me. Your last relationship failed. It's over. I'm sorry, but unless you want us to end too, you have to give me a chance."

I couldn't be timid in this thing. If love is, indeed, a battlefield, the contents of my heart required guarding. With her foot on my neck, I finally had her. Right where I wanted.

A Box Full of Sharp Objects / The Used

After calling things like they were, our relationship turned around.

I realized the potential from the onset; I was bound to a destructive path. You see, love resembles a box of sharp objects. Every fear, vulnerability, insecurity, hope, or dream possesses individual danger. Pure exhilaration comes from the potential the box wields. Well-constructed, carefully packed containers control the danger of each particular item. Yet a shoddy box, void of proper packing material, weaponize these same objects into an unstable grenade, unsuitable for any type of meaningful movement.

I can't pinpoint the exact source, but my sole goal in life was to enter one single, enduring romantic relationship. It wasn't from religious conviction;

I was a self-proclaimed agnostic. Maybe it came from my parent's divorce. From the frequent departures in my life. From a desire to protect my partner, and future kids, from past pains.

I can't put a finger on it, but the moment we both committed to each other, we committed to the long haul. This box of sharp objects was my first true test to correct my life's history.

I Hate Everything About You / Three Days Grace

After my plea for recognition, our relationship changed for the better. We became momentarily happy as the seeds of our relationship took root. We allowed ourselves to fall in love.

Once she invested, I noticed a definite difference as I transitioned from her distraction to the center of her attention. From the awkward new fry cook in the back to the matched investment of matrimony in the front of her mind within a three-month period. Maybe Dwight Shrute was right, although it's exactly what I asked for, I couldn't handle her undivided attention. Investing in this way, at that young an age, left very little room for growth as individual people.

Mere months after my heart-to-heart with her, I had to have one with myself. She made the decision to invest in this relationship, like I asked her. Like so many others, she could've beat feet to leave me to my own devices, but she didn't. That's how she was different—she stayed, even after getting to know me.

With frantic indebtedness, the favor of her kindness required repayment. I had to teach her, and learn myself, how to pursue our goals as a team.

Home / Three Days Grace

Once my parents and I agreed moving to campus was my best option, they joked, "Now, don't be calling home every day, crying about how much you miss us!"

Packing my stuff that weekend, I finished my last two weeks at Dairy Queen and came back for my car. I returned home for Thanksgiving dinner and Christmas Day. My dusty phone knew not their number. While their comment bordered upon bad dad joke and tension-breaker to a sorrowful situation, I carried it out to the opposite extreme. There's a kernel of truth to every joke, right?

You see, I did reasonably well in college. Unlike my small-town high school, the instructors didn't have to juggle three different topics. They were more versed, and passionate, in their subjects. I maintained perfect attendance my first semester out of genuine pursuit of knowledge.

The basic freedom offered by the collegiate environment called me to question the contained ecosystem of my upbringing. To establish myself as an independent free-thinker, I needed full-fledged separation from my parent's familiar systems.

Anything Right / POD (Ft. Christian Lindskog)

As pressure began to mount, already limited time converted to valuable currency. My girlfriend, the chief recipient, saw invested time as a primary sign of love and affection. My parents shifted playful passive-aggression into direct demands for help around the house. Seeking a supervisor promotion, Hardee's expected shift availability at a dime's drop. My freshman election to student government, and committee assignments, required several hours of weekly meeting attendance. My friends cracked jokes about a guy, named Tony, they used to hang out with; did he fail out? All the while, an acoustic guitar sat in the corner of my dorm, collecting the microscopic pieces of my rock star aspirations. I, one simple human, couldn't cram myself into the mold I made.

Even worse, the fear of failure was pressing. If time is currency, when would I over-extend to a dramatic breaking point? For those who didn't choose the college path, every illustrious brick laid to its foundation represents a student who tried, and failed, in advanced academia. If everyone succeeds, the value of a degree diminishes.

To further establish this rite of passage, many syllabus reviews to my basic level courses concluded with this speech: "My class is difficult. Most of you will not receive passing grades. Look to your left. Now, look to your right. One of those two people won't possess the fortitude necessary to pass this class."

Wow. Ok. That's pretty pessimistic, even for my continued, fake rock star persona.

Although I despised this canned speech, it was reasonably accurate. With the precision of an avian plague, I watched most of my peer group drop, like diseased birds, as first semester ended. My roommate came catastrophically close.

To attempt plague evasion, I started second semester with a room change. The feeling of failure as a destination was too overwhelming. With no other choice, I plowed forward. The empty seats to my left and right already declared this round's victory.

Enigma / Trapt

Darkness creeps in slowly at first. Somehow, the pursuit of happiness in unchartered territory, and this fake rock star persona, began consuming me. Where people had high expectations, to the point of audible encouragement, I chose to believe they wanted me to fail. I needed to fuel my lack of fulfillment, that next empty checkbox on my to-do list, as a means to success. Haters, and fans alike, would contribute from the sidelines, "Stay out of his way! He won't stop until he gains his rightful place."

It was essential to my quirky persona. Rock stars exemplify distance; it's the space from crowd to stage that casts mystery and admiration.

"What an enigma?! How does he do it?"

Like every other person throughout history: time management, prioritization, and a tish of piss/vinegar.

"How does he know what he wants?"

He doesn't. He's a college kid, drifting frivolously through life.

I hoped to convey a dark, mysterious figure capable of effortlessly accomplishing the impossible. In the end, I wasn't very much of a mystery. I was a little bit of an idiot.

Mechanical Animals / Marilyn Manson

If my only snag to true happiness was a band opportunity, I'd have to trade passive rock front man cosplay for the raw aggression of pursuit. My first chance came from a flyer for Fist (with an x over the i). Too easy, I overheard the rhythm guitarist, a personable guy with long, curly hair, jamming while returning to my room after class. When I asked about the band, he redirected my audition inquiry to the lead guitarist.

After calling the number on the flyer, I met another dude with long greasy hair and a braided goatee. Upon a visual inspection, he weighed in, "Nah, we got enough guitar players."

"That's perfect! I'm a singer!"

For a second time, his eyes scanned me from head-to-toe before casting final judgment. "Nah, we're good."

Without hearing a single note, my fate with the band was determined by short, frost-tipped hair, a beardless face, and Adidas shoes.

A few weeks later, I met with a local high schooler from a family of performing musicians. Rumor had it, he practiced guitar for six hours every day. The three guitars he noodled on during our first jam session each touted a more expensive price tag than my car. That's correct; I said guitar(s).

This Spencer Chamberlain-looking dude, sporting a long, black duster, was forming a Machine Head cover band. Handing me an eight-song setlist to learn by next practice, we never hung out again. On the plus side, I walked away a Machine Head fan.

Cranking KoRn while closing at Hardees, a new employee asked if the CD was mine. This guy, Stickel, was a massive Marilyn Manson fan. After a brief conversation about guitar playing technique, he offered to host a jam session.

"No, thanks. Manson's a satanist," I said. "Something else maybe?"

With a hysterical laugh, almost like I'd told a great joke, he responded, "No, he's not. Come play with Daddy sometime."

At our first practice, we rehearsed songs from *Mechanical Animals*, seeded with the occasional Godsmack ditty, for over four hours. While Stickel played his seafoam-green Jackson through an amp, I couldn't hear a sound from my sorry acoustic guitar. I just memorized his finger placements to perfect the pieces at home. After an acoustic performance of "Coma White," the band was born.

With that, we needed a name. Stickel recommended a series of Manson-related fragments. Even though we started as a cover band, I wanted to transition to writing our own masterpieces. Why restrict ourselves to a gimmick? After almost settling on the too obvious Sex Cells, we cast our final vote.

Between practices, I designed our logo in Microsoft Paint: an old-school black bomb with "Lost Cell" in yellow lettering inscribed on the body. For Stickel's review, I threw together a Netscape website, threatening rock world domination. In our bio, we promised to change the way rock music was produced, listened to, and perceived, all without a second practice.

Disassociative / Marilyn Manson

Both Stickel and I considered Lost Cell a serious effort. Our non-conventional practices often included trading his electric guitar with my acoustic between songs to critique playing technique. Once Stickel bought us a bass, he became the band's full-time guitarist and I took up vocalist/bassist responsibilities. Since we couldn't be bothered to recruit a drummer, we played over original recordings to keep time.

When that got boring, we rewrote Manson lyrics to match our situation; some serious, some straight-up crazy. To be honest, Lost Cell hinged upon his talent until I established more confidence as an artist.

Like most bands, our first song was a cover, a ruthless rendition of Manson's "Disassociative," entitled "Bipolar Disorder." It was popular in the underground scene, namely Stickel's basement, with our fan, Stickel's mom. Containing the exact instrumentation as "Disassociative," Stickel rewrote a lyrical depiction of bipolar disorder's unmatched ecstasy crashing to extended depressive depths. In essence, swapping one psychological disorder for another to raise awareness. How's that for forging new paths into the world of rock?

Close Friends / Adema

My pleas for KoRn covers were often silenced. Caving, Stickel offered to play "Blind" once to establish a need for seven-string guitars, tuned to Drop B, and a guitar tech. Proving his point, the song fell apart after the intro.

Reaching for KoRn's baby brother, I convinced him to play Adema's "Close Friends." It was the most cost-conscious course of action to get KoRn adjacent. Joking, we discussed how we, close friends, memorialized our friendship to this track. A quick lyric review says otherwise, but negotiation sometimes requires unethical tactics.

Since the Lost Cell experience transcended music, we incorporated a healthy ratio of one actual practice per four jam sessions. To play well in a band, you have to mesh well under the ruse of unscripted shenanigans. Our practices often consisted of enticing the creative process through mobile album reviews in Stickel's Chevy Lumina. It was speeding through the mall parking lot, after hours, to strike carts in a twisted game of bumper cars. It was tailing unknown, unsuspecting drivers for several blocks around town. Most importantly, it was searching for night walkers, slowing the vehicle to a stall, blaring one of ninety-one tracks from our mix CD of varied fart sounds, then shouting obscenities from the open windows as we peeled off.

You see, Lost Cell was an experience. We existed for the sole purpose of shaping the music consumption landscape. Somehow, someway, we accomplished that goal.

With or Without You / Dope

Band "practices," and other obligations, carried me through freshman year. Lazy summer days, free of the constant distractions I submersed myself in, forced me to assess my situation.

My band was more of an MTV prank show than a musical outfit. Oh, we talked. Skimmed songs for ideas. Searched online for equipment: better instruments, cabs, heads, effects pedals. We even "auditioned" a DJ to enhance our industrial sound: a fifteen-minute roast of his immense synthesizer knowledge before tucking him in Stickel's backseat for some shopping cart bumper cars. We had a blast, but fun doesn't earn a record deal or touring schedule.

For the first time in six months, I sat alone in my summer apartment. To flee the feeling, I decided to take a drive. Dope's *Life* thrust my actual condition to center stage. Although I was never physically alone, the desolation of a life without destination settled in. I hadn't made time to notice.

What was I doing? Was this the life I wanted? Without answers, the questions began accumulating.

In an act of classic avoidance, my biological mother seized my thoughts. Every single accomplishment was an effort torpedoed at capturing her attention. If I performed enough, she'd have to stop ignoring me. If I fixed her broken baby. If I educated myself. If I became famous. If only I was precisely opposite of why she left, she'd have to come back to me.

In less time than it takes to press replay on "With or Without You," the realization hit me. My mom was emotionally unavailable to serve as a captive audience. If I couldn't accept the truth, my whole life would masquerade in an endless pursuit of the unobtainable. With the finality of a funeral, I gave myself permission to cry one last time. Then, I said goodbye to her forever.

Nothing (Why) / Dope

After my tears dried, I continued driving around town with Dope's *Life* riding shotgun. Some tension alleviated, yet a separate, invasive burden remained an unwelcomed passenger that afternoon. Since Stickel, my girlfriend, and roommate were at work for a few more hours, I forged forward on my journey of self-discovery.

With the pressure of a vacant mother out of the equation, my actual condition slapped me square in the temple. Simply put, I didn't love my girlfriend anymore. By appealing to compassionate rationale, I convinced her to invest in us. Then, I proved incapable of offering her the same level of investment. Our relationship, from my perspective, was over.

Great, but what to do with this information? My actual problem was evident, but I couldn't bring myself to break her heart. In search of a solution, I drove around for hours, even scripting a break-up speech. Here's the answer: where I was dissatisfied, she was content. We didn't need a messy breakup. Staying with her forever would solve that. Sure, I'd also be miserable, but it beat being alone.

Whole / Flaw

As I delved deeper into darkness, my costume crept from the cute commodity of playful mock jock into the gothic visualization of visceral torment. Challenging work grooming regulations, I grew my hair out in the front and dyed it jet black. My middle fingernails, jet black. When I wasn't at work, I wore a KoRn ball chain choker. My favorite KoRn shirt was an animated band portrait tucked behind an oversized hand flipping the middle finger. With leg openings larger than the waist, my baggy, black Hot Topic pants were cinched with a black leather belt. A silver skull belt buckle pierced through the dark abyss. To garnish this gothic sundae, I purchased a drama-faced, full-finger ring with a two-inch metal claw on eBay.

I draped myself in discontent to gain attention. Gathering from the stares, finger points, and whispers, a very effective practice. Once enticed by my goth rock costume, their disgust triggered my primary purpose for the claw ring purchase. I required additional pageantry to add a live action middle finger to the backdrop of my graphic tee. Even on a college campus, my edge depended upon being willing to step outside the cultural norms of rural, southwest North Dakota.

Imagine my former fourth-grade teacher's surprise during a chance encounter with me in full costume at the local Walmart. She was the first, and only, person in my life to approach me on it. "Tony, this is a family store. I don't think it's fair for you to wear that around children. Please don't wear that shirt in public. You're a smart, good-looking young man. Please think of how others might perceive you."

I said little in response, but I certainly pondered perception while dressing this way. I believe this outfit said everything. "The path I'm heading down is perilous. Please help me."

Now or Never / Three Days Grace

I chose to buy the lie that the world was after me. The exact week I penned the check for my final car payment, the transmission blew, giving me the year Dad promised. All the freed-up money for music gear was diverted to yet another car payment. With a setback so simple, and a hateful heart, it became easy to believe the world was conspiring against me.

Yet, at the exact time of my first payment's due date, a job opportunity, with an exactly equal monthly salary, was handed to me. Despite my full-time income, becoming a resident assistant eased the initial tension of the situation. Here's the thing: I was offered the job based upon an observation of my tender handling of a child's ice cream order after a direct recommendation to consider me. More importantly, this job's main function was to help my fellow students acclimate to college life.

As angry as I was, I still sought opportunities to help others. I hoped to topple the pretentious tower that proclaimed "50% of you will not pass my class/succeed in college." This job put me in place to make the most of the bed I forced myself to lay in.

Leaving Only Scars / Systematic

What was wrong with me? On most accounts, I'd obtained my heart's desires. In my endless quest for blessing, I was left with the continued gaping void of a tangible music production outlet, writing jams to give the scene what it gave to me. Lost Cell once possessed great potential. Over time, we transformed more from a band to a bad experience. Was my pursuit of happiness pursuing me?

For the millionth time spanning two years, I took inventory, yet again. Who am I? What do I really want? What path would take me there? What was my contingency plan when everything fell apart again? Each of these inventories were soundtracked by music that screamed out what I didn't dare admit myself.

In my efforts to pick up the pieces, was I causing more damage than good? Was digging at old wounds a direct refusal of the healing process? Maybe one day, if I ever finally healed, my visible scars would declare the mysterious victory.

Down / Motograter

During this fragile time, I didn't actively pursue music, not even as a consumer. My symbol for life continuation, like a fuel gauge, was dwindling from hopeful fulfillment to empty agony. To be frank, most days I ran on fumes.

Aside from the subtle hint cast by my costume, I pretended like everything was perfect while forcing fake smiles. The truth was I laid in my bed at night, praying to a God I didn't believe in that, somehow, I would die in my sleep. I still saw suicide as selfish, BUT, an accidental death, for whatever reason, could still be viewed as honorable. If I were to slip away silently, I could depart the increased lingering of performance anxiety. Sure, some people would hurt in the process, but in this way, I could exit without having to witness myself hurt others.

Alone I Break / KoRn

Without a musical outlet, I took creative writing during fall semester to hone my poetic prowess. My final portfolio required a screenplay, one-act, or video treatment submission. Since music videos fit best into my plans, I wrote a treatment for KoRn's "Alone I Break."

At the time, I planned to enter their promotional contest for a fan-directed video. As an added bonus, the lyrical content frequented my nightly destructive fantasies.

In my treatment, the band enters into a hypnotherapist's office lined with leather-bound books in floor-to-ceiling bookcases. The therapist, a Sigmund Freud knock-off with thinning hair, a goatee, and black blazer with elbow patches, welcomes the band to their group therapy session. A hypnotic state coerces Jon's darkest, repressed thoughts through lip-synced lyrics. Self-realization overtakes Jon, jolting him awake to avoid further transparency. In one last act of brotherly unity, the band destroys the office, leaving the therapist to clean up the psychological aftermath represented by overturned shelves, splintered wood, and floating pages of manuscript.

When this piece was presented for critique, another class requirement, my peers complained of my depiction of mental instability. Some Christian chick even had the audacity to recommend, "Maybe if you try lighter material… Most of your submissions are, umm, unnecessarily dreary."

Even my target audience, the other band shirt-wearing classmate, betrayed our sacred bond with criticism. "You're telling me that a rock band destroys a room, jams out, then leaves? That sounds like every video of the genre."

Yep. Spot on. I wasn't aiming at originality. I was crying out for help.

Xmas Day / Sevendust

Thanksgiving morning, 2003 was destroyed by my girlfriend's confession. Over the next few months, this pattern continued to countless breaks for self-exploration. I didn't need a pause for that; I conducted mine in minute-by-minute stride.

As we grew further apart, I couldn't bring myself to dump her, and she couldn't declare, for certain, if she wanted to be with me. I continued committed to this lifelong metaphorical bed that sucked the life from my real aspirations.

A few short years ago, the Christmas season was so magical. Time with family, the spirit of giving, the songs, the smell of baked goods, and the warmth, despite the chill in the air. It was all lost that year.

Have you noticed how the beginning scenes of most holiday movies open to a person with a chaotic, bah-humbug, bad attitude leading a purposeless life? Have you mocked those magical moments stirring up permanent perspective change? As the Christmas season unfolded, buying into the belief behind cinematic grandeur did nothing to save me from myself.

No One / Cold

Driving my desperation a bit further, please accept this submission of a poem written during this timeframe, entitled "Re:"

Again
I re-enter my trance
Open up the past
Of the life that I despise

Again
I re-aggravate the wound
Peel back the skin way too soon
To make room for the flies

Again
I re-dress my pain
Drips down the rest of my vein
White wrap set to catch

Again
It re-heals over like before
Redness fades from the aching sore
Waiting for me to scratch

Until It Sleeps / Metallica

As my war with depression waged on, my enemy chose to ambush under the cover of night. Despite deep insomnia, I adopted an accidental ritual to coax myself to sleep.

Step One: Lie down at a reasonable time, then toss and turn for hours.

Step Two: Beg the unforgiving universe for respite to my situation.

Step Three: When my problems didn't resolve themselves, fantasize about various ways to die, ending the torment.

Step Four: Cry out of sheer hopelessness.

Fifth Step: Count rhythmic whimpers until sleep consumed me.

I followed this strict process every night from November well into the new college semester. I felt the noose tighten, constricting all rational thought into swirling paranoia. This was not my life's destiny.

Without a plan to attempt suicide, I fantasized about my exit constantly. What was the most convenient way to stage an accidental death? Some quick, unforeseen genetic disease? Mowing down guardrails in a high-speed vehicle accident? Criminal militance toward law enforcement? The demented ways were endless, but at least then, I'd never have to struggle with sleep again.

Smothered / Spineshank

After my girlfriend leveraged several breaks to avoid cheating, it all came to a head. While lying in the darkness of my room one evening, exercising my nightly ritual, the phone rang.

With hopeful jarring, the drunk girl on the other line invited me to a party. Declining despite a desperate need for human connection, I advised her she had the wrong number. She, and her friend howling in the background, insisted I come out.

Declining again, I told her I didn't drink with strangers. She persisted again by introducing herself. Wait a second, my stepmom said that name every time she talked about my brother Aaron's girlfriend. When I found out he was at the party, I reluctantly agreed.

When I got to said shindig, the whole crowd consisted of three girls and my brother. Pretty hoppin', but it'd been forever since I hung out with Aaron. As we chatted over a few beers, he shared the alarming news of his upcoming Iraq deployment. With odd morbidity, it became clear this conversation could be my last memory with him. For a moment, the tragedy of my situation escaped me.

Once upon a simpler time, cell phone ownership was uncommon. I returned to my dorm the next morning to several voicemails on my answering machine. It turns out, my girlfriend made out with some dude when she was drunk, which made her miss me. Through shaky tears, she vowed to abandon the party lifestyle in full commitment to us.

This was it, I guess. My last chance to make this life count. I either: 1) fixed us and things got better, 2) couldn't fix us and dumped her, or 3) couldn't fix us and killed myself to avoid witnessing her pain. The noose continued to tighten…

Sing / Dope

There comes a time when you decide to bite the bullet. To crap or get off the pot. You choose to either let the demons win again or kick them in the teeth. As things continued to spiral painfully downward, I was faced with the decision daily.

With hope my relationship could change, I had some decisions to make. Also, I had a one-hour drive to an orthodontist appointment to reflect on life, once again. Just my luck, Dope's newest release, *Group Therapy*, prepared me for the journey.

While scanning the album for potential hopefuls, I remember snickering at "Sing." Really, Dope?! You're experimenting with the hopeful song market? I chose to give the song a go. In a way, they ignited this fire; maybe they could extinguish it.

As "Sing" played over my system, I was hooked, repeating the track for most of the trip. I didn't want to die. Maybe life deserved a serious attempt before I further considered ending it.

Citizen/Soldier / Three Doors Down

What if I told you all I love music so much I accidentally joined the Army to snag a free download code from a local recruiter? That would be obnoxious. Proud to announce, this isn't what happened.

I did join the Army. I did get a free song, but it wasn't my chief motivator— just some added icing to the cake. For the first time, I didn't have to speculate if a song was about, or for, me. 3 Doors Down was commissioned to tell our story. However, the cart's miles ahead of the horse here; let me explain.

After September 11, I attempted to join the National Guard. At the time, I had no idea what the World Trade Center was, but media coverage of Iraqis celebrating in the streets, during American mourning, called me into action. This atrocity required justice, but the Army couldn't accept a young Soldier with braces.

A year later, my braceless face was incapacitated with a girlfriend who couldn't bear absence for basic training attendance, or worse, an inevitable deployment. Dropping my vendetta, we agreed to let others pursue justice.

Then, "the others"—namely, a few high school classmates and my brother—got activated. My philosophical contribution, safely debating war ethics from a college campus, was nowhere near equitable to my buddies. Mere moments from childhood, they provided direct solutions to real world problems.

While attending a Catholic school fundraiser, my girlfriend was enticed with tuition assistance by a recruiter. "Hey, we have a meeting with Staff Sergeant Decker tomorrow to join the National Guard!" she reported.

Taken aback by this demand, I snapped, "Listen, I'm not lying to him twice. Plus, Dad's still pissed I didn't sign up when I got my braces off. If I walk in that armory, I'm leaving a Soldier."

Grabbing my hand, she replied, "Me, too. We're joining the Guard together."

The next day started as scheduled: a few morning classes, a lunch shift at Hardee's, and my afternoon English Comp class. Then, back to the armory to rectify my wrongs from a few years ago. After some quick paperwork, I'd swear into the Army. No big deal. All in a day's work.

When I reported to Hardee's, my boss greeted me at the door. I expected normal break coverage instructions before she left to attend a funeral. Instead of directions, I got pink-slipped for giving an extra ounce of roast beef, valued at three cents on internal waste collection accounting sheets, to a regular customer. Three measly cents determined my destiny.

Pursuit of happiness shapeshifted into raw survival as I sped to campus to scour help wanted ads. Seeing an open position at the local Dairy Queen, I hopped in my car, in a Hardee's uniform, to apply. Lucky for me, DQ was once my life. If I could normalize my very recent termination, I'd seal the deal. After explaining my sudden unemployment, the owner called my first boss for a character reference. With just enough time to change clothes before my afternoon class, I was offered a job on the spot.

I wish the timeline was exaggerated, but let's recap the journey: I got to work at 11:00, was fired by 11:30, rehired at a new job by 1:00, attended my Comp class, then joined the North Dakota National Guard at 2:00. What a day! With that level of production, I even managed to snipe a download code for 3 Doors Down's "Citizen/Soldier." For the first time in quite a while, survival instincts pulled me away from my predictable productive rut.

One last thing: my girlfriend, you ask?

She didn't join. Within twenty-four hours, her mom convinced her joining the Guard would inevitably result in deployment. Not to be made a liar, twice, I signed the dotted line on my own. Me, my long black hair, claw ring, black nail polish, Hot Topic pants, and my most tasteful KoRn shirt were now Soldiers.

Love Song / Third Day

As positive momentum continued to build, soul searching reminded me of my small hometown Presbyterian church. Walking home from Sunday morning service was inexplicable. Despite January temperatures reflecting -24°F on the thermometer, I felt warmth.

For seventeen straight months, a traveling Bible study teacher invited me to his weekly fellowship group. I could conveniently sit in without any sense of Christian accountability. Go to the group, get the feel-goods, get on with life. If my will to live was a metaphorical gas tank, $5 worth of spiritual gas skirted the perfect line between torment avoidance and religious extremism.

I cleared my Thursday night to attend the study. As I approached the meeting room, I was greeted by darkness cast over empty chairs. No big deal. Sometimes, other scheduled meetings forced the study to move to the basement. I started down the steps. When I got to the secondary room, it was dark, and empty, yet again. The one night I gathered the courage to go, no one was there.

Waiting in the hall, I prayed sincerely for the first time in years. *I reached out to You and this is Your response? How dare You?! You have until I exit this building to show me a sign or I walk away forever.*

After a ten-minute wait, it became evident the study wasn't happening. Giving God time to act, I slowly made my way outside. *You heard the deal,* I thought as I crept the hallway at a sloth's pace. "Here we go," I whispered as I climbed the steps. At the top of the stairs, the usual meeting room was still dark.

My answer seemed clear, but a deal was a deal. He had until I got outside to do something. Anything. Without a soul in sight, I continued toward the exit. Tugging open the first set of double doors, "Ten feet left," I sighed. Nothing. Approaching the second set of doors, I shook my head and pulled.

The door opened easier than usual. As I peered into the darkness, I was greeted by the Bible study teacher. "You bug me for a year to come to your group and don't show when I decide to come? What's up with that?" I joked.

Gripping both of his backpack straps, he explained. "I'm so sorry! Some of my regular attendees had a basketball game tonight, so we went to support them. I stopped by to see if anyone else showed up. You wanna do a small study with me?"

Sitting in my dorm's lobby a few moments later, he detailed humanity's need for Christ. How sin separates us from God, from each other. Traveling down the Roman Road to Salvation, the warmth of my high school church participation returned. *You can't keep living life your way and expect things to work,* I thought. *Nope, that wasn't the deal. You're here to avoid torment, not chase religious zeal. Feel good and go.*

After starting my new job at DQ, I still attended his Thursday night group to receive temporary hope injections. They worked as prescribed, with conviction as an annoying side effect. Once per week, I had to consider trading my pursuit of happiness for a deeper sense of contentment. However, conviction's emotional charade was much easier to manage than dealing with the demons of suicidal ideation.

As my new internal war waged on, one of my dormmates invited me to a Saturday afternoon matinee for *Passion of the Christ.* We had history. For both years of our college experience, we lived in the same dorm. We even partied together as freshmen before I started dating my girlfriend. He was nowhere near a church dude. Admitting he'd seen the movie already, he wanted to catch another showing. Watching it with him would allow us an unbiased glimpse, separate from free showings scheduled by local churches and collegiate Christian organizations, to verify what we knew about Jesus.

Before the movie began, we stopped by Kmart to stuff my oversized JNCO back pockets with Mountain Dew and Snickers to sneak into the theatre. Walking the aisles, I asked him why he watched the movie so many times. "I dunno. It makes me feel weird: not good, not bad. Just weird." He confessed, "I saw you talking to the Bible study teacher a few weeks ago. He used to volunteer at Eastern Montana Bible Camp. Great dude. If you wanna meet Jesus, I think you'll find Him. While you're watching it, be open to what God would want for you."

During the previews, I ate a single Snickers bar. The movie was as accurate as my friend described. Instead of snacking on snuck-in treats, guilt and straight-up conviction consumed me. As Jesus was beaten, I felt the sharp barbs of cat o' nine tails dig into my flesh. The tension of each strand pulling away for the next lash. Those blows belonged to me. Why would Jesus ever volunteer to endure this torment? Since he's omniscient, didn't he expect my rejection?

The movie ended, as they do. What didn't fade was the nagging within my soul. As I polished napkin holders at DQ that evening, I wasn't ok with who I was becoming, not even the progress I'd made. "Why? Why would You want to die for me?" Driving home after my shift, I asked the question I'd been avoiding, "Now what?"

My answer was clear. An audible voice from inside my car announced, "You can't keep doing life your way. You have to change everything. You have to commit to Me."

Back in my room, I grabbed a bowl of ramen noodles and got to work. A year earlier, I'd read a *Rolling Stone* article about newly converted Christian kids gluing their CD collections to a youth group bulletin board. My life had amounted to this giant mountain of posters, guitar tabs, sheet music, and CDs. To redirect from endless pursuit of happiness, I had to reduce excess emotional baggage: no more KoRn, no more Manson, no more hatred, no more desire to die. Kneeling in the pile of my own filth, I prayed for the emptiness to go away. I prayed for the will to live. I prayed to truly follow Jesus, even if I lost everything.

After closing my prayer, I memorialized my decision to a Pandora contemporary Christian station. Like an Archer firing direct inspiration into the moment, Third Day's "Love Song" was first to play. A quick time check placed me in the beginning minutes of February 29th: Leap Day. God used the one day, occurring every four years, to save my life.

For one last time, I cried myself to sleep that night. Yet, this time, I cried tears of joy. The joy of being seen. The joy of feeling loved. For the first time in twenty years, the joy of feeling alive. I had no idea what the future held, but I was ready for the change.

Falls On Me / Fuel

Despite my actions suggesting an apparent demise, I didn't intend to end my relationship. Especially after becoming a Christian, I tried reshaping it into something more meaningful. These dramatic life changes, against her will, required normalization, and patience, for us to work. That was, if there was anything left to salvage.

Late one spring night, we went for a simple stroll, without destination, to hash things out. Our walk led us to a park near her house. Discussing our path forward, we laid in the grass, staring at the stars, listening to Fuel's

Natural Selection. Our frail connection symbolic to the thin headphone wire tethering us together between earbuds.

To be clear, my purge removed weapons I felt responsible for my demise. Weeding my CD collection from four hundred discs to about a hundred, I retained mix CDs for further purging and albums that still inspired me. Fuel's entire discography made the final cut.

Our conversation turned toward God. What was her experience with religion?

She went to a Catholic church as a child, but couldn't understand life with restrictions. She enjoyed attending parties and interpreting life through the lyrics I introduced her to. She couldn't fathom my choice to turn away from everything. Supporting my newfound faith, she wouldn't go with me, but also, was afraid of me meeting someone else.

How could we survive with completely different belief systems? Lying in the damp grass, I attempted one last emotional plea. "Do you ever feel like God's holding you? Like when you look at the stars, you know He's out there?"

"Umm, not since my grandpa died…"

"I need to do this but not without you. How's that gonna work?"

"I'm not sure. We'll find a way."

Closing our unproductive conversation, we returned to her room. Lying on her bed, I changed the topic of discussion to my plans to campaign for student government. Surprising enough, this fleeting comment led to a separate argument regarding my over-ambition. Her contradictory desires became increasingly difficult to honor.

"Do you even love me anymore?" I asked her. With my head on her chest, I felt her heart pause before racing to the pace of a death metal drummer.

No response.

Sensing our relationship was dangling by a thread, I left prior to causing any additional damage.

After I got fired, my girlfriend swapped jobs to McDonalds in a show of solidarity. She got off later than I did, but we committed to a nightly phone call to stay connected. When she called that evening, she was mad at how the shift went.

Falling into the classic male trap, I resorted to helping her fix the problem.

Not wanting to hear it, she hung up on me.

Anyone who truly knows me knows these phone-based storm-offs are amongst my greatest pet peeves. Can you imagine what hang-ups do to a person with a crippling fear of abandonment? I hate it but won't call back.

During her personal reflection while showering, her guilt forced a return apology call.

Not catching the original hint, I rationalized again and she hung up again.

I was LIVID. As George W. Bush would say, "Fool me once? Shame on you! Fool me twice? You can't fool me twice!"

When she called to issue her second apology, I dumped her over the phone. Sure, canceling a one-year relationship like an unwanted subscription is classless. To make myself feel better, I promised to meet up, aside from the tension of the situation, to discuss options.

When we met the next day, I had to break her heart for a second time. I couldn't avoid the mess; I had to let her go. Like others bailed on me, I had to bail on her. Most of my torment hinged upon this one necessary act; I felt like a hypocrite. Harboring resentment for departed souls while vicariously vanishing through the same swinging door. My choice was excruciating. It was either "stay together for the kids" or never smile with sincerity for the rest of my life.

So Cold / Breaking Benjamin

Although things were improving, I still felt the need to protect myself at all costs. After ending my one-year relationship, I possessed the courage to purge my remaining friend circles. Casting the baby out with the bathwater, I exited the party scene. Closed the Lost Cell chronicles by terminating my friendship with Stickel. Refused interactions with negative people.

Without an ounce of subtlety, I glared eyeball to eyeball with person after person and slashed friendship after friendship. In those moments, the push and pull, I erred with intention on safety's side. It felt selfish. It felt cold, yet the necessary evil required for my journey to total restoration.

I didn't consider these extractions as permanent. Maybe some friendships could be rekindled at a later date. Maybe someday a future junction would join our paths together again. In those moments, during the struggles between life and death, survival was paramount to relationship. Along with any other emergent situation, the required explanation would arrive when safety was attained.

Like the Sun / I Mother Earth

What does a music fan do when the busyness you put yourself into dissipates? When no one else is around? Most of my collection got the ax the night I became a Christian, but these other life clearing activities granted excess time to conduct a deep dive purge. Songs with cussing. Songs with obvious suicide/drug references. Songs without positive societal contribution. I leveraged a calculated algebraic equation to sift through the remaining rubble.

When I wasn't attending Christian events or praying through self-destructive behaviors, I spent hours ripping CDs to my computer. The onset of mp3 players required my entire music collection to digitize anyways.

When you have as many CDs as I did, you forget where you encountered this stuff in the first place. To be honest, my decision to write a book didn't begin when fingers danced across the keyboard for this project. It began while balancing song lyrics against my new belief system. I wasn't just cleaning my music collection, but assessing every aspect of my life.

I haven't completely reviewed the happenings of my circumstances since I thinned my collection during the spring of 2004. You see, music has a teleportive quality to it. Continuing on my journey through the opening notes to the songs I studied, every good, bad, and ugly life detail was being revealed.

Did I believe contentment was obtainable? Could I abandon the quest toward happiness? It wasn't clear. But, if you searched for me when I wasn't in the public eye, when I wasn't getting to know Jesus, I was elbows deep in CDs, liner notes, with a lyric search engine, trying to find myself again.

Frontline / Pillar

I had no problems giving up most stuff, but swapping hard rock for Christian contemporary, like I thought I was supposed to do, was my biggest hang-up to becoming a Christian. I can't put a finger on it, but the concept of CCM seems insincere to me.

Are you confused? Worship. Angry? Worship. Hurt? Worship. Sometimes, I felt those emotions, sometimes all at once. How is praise the only acceptable answer to the frailty of the human psyche? I needed confirmation I could be genuine with these dark thoughts. Maybe it should've, but worship didn't alleviate the tension.

While filtering my collection, I was shocked to find several Christian acts, from Thousand Foot Krutch to Blindside, 12 Stones to POD, hidden away in CD binder pages. Bands exploring the darkness I was trying to rectify in the world.

I began my new journey. What were my new friends listening to? "My dude, you know who rocks so hard? Jars of Clay, dc Talk, Audio Adrenaline. Check 'em out!"

Man, the disappointment I found in their cream of the crop. Then, I got a recommendation for a rap-rock act similar to POD called Pillar. Since Satellite's one of my favorite albums of all time, I started on my next mission.

If the stuff I consumed before was difficult to find, Christian rock bands like Pillar were even more challenging. Their first two public releases were only available on eBay. Since I'm in the business of beating dead horses, let's go ahead and take another whack: 1) I joined the National Guard, pending basic training, 2) I became a Christian, and 3) I needed better music than my recommendations were providing.

Pillar offered the subtle pivot point between awkward life chapters. With the benefit of military-type references, I got some rap, some rock, and some contemplative, slow tracks. They weren't angry, just honest about things they didn't like. While the traction I gained was minimal, it was more effective than waiting for four bands to release new albums.

Pitiful / Blindside

While listening to "Anything Right" one afternoon, a familiar voice taunted me from the background vocals. A voice unfamiliar to any other POD track. My research led me to Blindside's lead vocalist, Christian Lindskog.

I'd owned Blindside's *Silence* since the fall of 2003. At the time, a few songs from the album captivated me. Back into the abyss of my collection until I found out about this connection. Could it be? Was I on the verge of a breakthrough? After another listening session, it became evident I'd left gold quietly sitting amongst my CDs for over a year. How in the world did I miss this treasure?

While retracing my steps, Blindside, The Used, and my ex-girlfriend came into my life at the same time. Fate pulled me toward The Used and a relationship. A year later, a single guy jammed out to the other album I should've fallen harder for. You see, time has its way of rectifying things.

The best news yet, Blindside had three other CDs needing my review.

(*) Star / Project 86

What else had I overlooked? My brief love for "Me Against Me" caused me to pick up Project 86's *Drawing Black Lines*. After adding the track to a mix CD, the brand-new disc sat in my collection, untouched.

With other distractions out of the way, I gave Project 86 a much-needed second chance. Wading through the waters of Andrew Schwab's intrinsic lyrics, I came to two conclusions: 1) Holy Crap! Project 86 is a Christian band! and 2) This CD possessed similar depth to the music I'd given up a few short weeks prior.

Music is a large part of my identity. I didn't just apply reverse osmosis to purify my collection, I was familiarizing myself with God. Sure, I read the Bible, listened to sermons, prayed, and hung out with other good Christian people. I did those things, but if God wasn't present in my music, then what's this all been about?

As shallow as it may sound, I gave God a second ultimatum before becoming a Christian. If we're still tracking, the first was direct intervention the night I met with the Bible study teacher. The second one was I wouldn't commit to Christianity if I had to get rid of my music. When I became a Christian and cleaned my music collection, He remained faithful.

I don't intend to get preachy, but having the right music was so important that I prayed to receive good rock music. Yes, you read that correctly. "Lord, please provide me with equitable replacements for the music you asked me to give up. Amen."

I soon discovered this prayer was answered long before the first step of my Christian conversion.

Say Goodnight to the Bad Guy / Project 86

With a career spanning over six years at the time, Project 86 was a much bigger band than I realized. Yet my collection only contained the third of their four releases. As I dove further into their discography, they provided a substantial turning point to my music exploration process.

Andrew Schwab considered music creation a true calling, one he cared to do well. With great sounding songs at face value, *Songs to Burn Your Bridges By* became the unironic title I used to actively ignite life's unnecessary bridges. These songs rivaled, if not exceeded, the expectations I had for music quality in the past. All while meeting the excessive new standards I established to protect myself from darkness.

Ridiculous / POD (Ft. Eek-A-Mouse)

As luck would have it, the friend who invited me to *Passion of the Christ* also made the decision to become a committed Christian. Neither of us shared the details of our recent conversion with the other. Yet we basically became makeshift roommates, spending every free moment avoiding homework assignments, trading song recommendations, and engaging in heated political discussions.

As our bromance bloomed, and Christian belief clarified, we entered into a pact to stay single through the summer to focus on our faith. My best friend got the short end of the stick; he still had to exist in normal society for the duration of our commitment. With my pending basic training ship date, I just had to fare the semester. If movies are accurate, my summer would consist of assembling weapons blindfolded and buffing floors with a toothbrush.

Love enjoys feeding on the souls of the unsuspecting. Despite our rock-solid temporary vow of celibacy, we managed to simultaneously collect feelings for separate girls at Campus Crusade. How did we manage this predicament? Acting upon our emotions would be inappropriate. Crushing on them from a distance, however, was well within the parameters of our agreement.

If the actual relationships happened, they'd have to wait until fall. In the meantime, we converted negative energy into a juvenile parody about our love interests to the tune of POD's "Ridiculous." With Eek-A-Mouse dropping reggae scat similar in sound to their rhyming names, the song practically wrote itself.

SPOILER ALERT: Fall came and went. All that remains to commemorate the torment of a hopeful relationship is our poorly penned remix.

Collide / Skillet

Now, a quick hat-tip to a prevalent voice in my early Christian development. Club 3 Degrees was a premier Christian nightclub established in the heart of downtown Minneapolis. In a defiant stance against cultural norms, Club 3 challenged preconceived notions of Christian purists. You know, those King James comfort clingers, singing four-part harmonies over pipe organs. They provided us edgy Christian scene kids a safe place to experience life in.

Past concert rosters include the likes of Big Dismal, Grits, Falling Up, Pillar, Project 86, Disciple, Kutless, Skillet, 12 Stones, and many, many more. Stop by Three Degrees Church, where one visit may lead to a meaningful lifelong relationship with Jesus. They changed my life, and I believe, the same could be true for you.

With that out of the way, Club 3 Degrees was the venue that hosted my first ever rock concert. We came to be entertained, but smack-dab in the middle of a Skillet show, in the midst of a moshpit, I had my first casual encounter with The Holy Spirit. With arms to the sky, eyes slammed shut in purposeful prayer, and waist-to-waist in a jam-packed, sweat-drenched audience, "Collide's" gradual slow build set the scene.

I felt two cold hands grip my open palms, sending an icy surge through my fingertips, down my spine, then into my toes. With nowhere else to go, the current reversed course through my core before exiting through my skull. With the emotional stimulus of the New York Stock Exchange, I was left with a confusing sense of overwhelming admiration as love bartered within my soul in incremental, rapid-fire transactions.

Creeping back to reality, I was greeted by the jeers of my parent's *Hells Bells* documentary. If the premise they argued was true, how is it that rock music drew me closer to, not further from, The Almighty?

Infected / Demon Hunter

Have you ever been on a familiar road trip? With the route mapped out, rest stops planned, and eyes locked on your destination, you begin your travels. Garth's retirement already forced one unintentional musical redirection in my life. The journey into Christian music was no different. Mile markers flew by to mark my journey's progression through a firm foundation of hard rock favorites. My exit, the point of no return, required a viable, TALENTED Christian metal band.

I can't recall exactly how I found out about Demon Hunter. However, when I trace my desire to abandon old musical tendencies to a specific source, I always land on the afternoon I first heard their self-titled album. In my quest for reassurance, I needed a definitive sign that I hadn't left quality music dwelling in the rearview mirror. Via the weird way of "Infected," Demon Hunter hand-delivered the cease-and-desist order through the factory speakers of a Ford Taurus. There was no need in glancing back; my best experiences were still facing forward.

The Reason / Hoobastank

If I were to stick a label on this story, it would be this: I am not a Hoobastank hater. I've chosen to dislike this song for mere circumstances surrounding the music. Disclaimer concluded, onward we go.

A month after ending my relationship, the guilt set in. To be clear, dumping her was my idea. She was the fatted calf I sacrificed to save myself. Through months of mentorship, most mature Christians I spoke with shared the complications spiritual imbalance causes on romantic relationships. To appease the ceaseless nagging, I reasoned with a trusted mentor for hours to attempt reconciliation. Avoiding the finality of a definite yes, he cracked, "You need to pray about it. God'll tell you what to do."

Fantastic! I HAD prayed about it; guilt had to equate to God's nudging for fast action.

Like some weird accountability bouncer, I begged my friend to escort me to her house. Arriving completely unannounced after midnight, she entertained my strange thirty-minute soliloquy. I apologized for breaking her heart. Maybe I was a little hasty in ending things. I wasn't pursuing her, but God intends His people to exist in peaceful relationship. If she could forgive me, maybe we'd be friends again someday. Like a high-powered tornado, I touched down with a whirlwind of ideas, then left.

My best friend rarely has a thought without communicating it. For years, our friendship has relied upon our ability to share bitter truths with each other. As we returned to our dorm, he provided unsolicited advice, "I think you're making a huge mistake. It's over. Shouldn't you leave well enough alone?"

"Probably," I admitted. "I've never seen a couple get back together and be happy. Have you ever noticed how old habits force them to fall apart all over again? You've heard me say that before. She knows I just wanna be friends."

"Really?" He chuckled. "It's after midnight. What else should she think? It's like Romeo and Juliet or some chick flick. Your actions can only be construed as romantic interest. I think you screwed up."

"Nah, man," I argued. "There's no way she could confuse my intentions. I made it pretty clear."

Tucked behind a smug grin, he replied, "I hope you're right."

The next afternoon, I received a call from the ex-girlfriend. She hadn't slept well. If I was free, could we cruise around in her new car to chat some more? Of course, friends sometimes go for car rides. Sliding into the passenger seat, she shushed me, "I don't wanna talk yet. Can you listen for a minute?"

As she drove, Hoobastank's "The Reason" blared over her stereo speakers while we awkwardly held hands. With precise intention toward my greatest weakness, this chick was weaponizing music as an accelerant to the previous night's discussion. My friend was right; I screwed up.

"What do you think?" she asked over the last lingering note.

This simple song left little to the imagination, and I, the music connoisseur, had never heard it. I wasn't prepared for this. I shot back, "What're you trying to tell me?"

After a pause, she began her explanation, "Listen, even if we're being pulled in different directions, I'm willing to make it work. I can change for you."

I was livid. I had to protect my exposed jugular from direct attack. "Yep, just like I thought. We're separate people now. I never asked you to do anything FOR ME. You need to do what's best for YOU. I'm staying single until after basic training, anyway. We'll have to talk about it then."

The exact moment I entered my room after this awkward interaction, my phone rang. "Guess who I talked to?" my mom quizzed.

Still seething, I made a lame attempt at sarcasm, "Who is my ex-girlfriend? I'll take other questions I don't want to answer for $100, Alex."

"Yep. She said you were getting back together? You know your father and I don't like her. I could care less if she's gonna try harder this time. You need to find someone else," she ordered.

"Fine, Ma. I'll fix it." I hung up the phone. Staring at the receiver, I knew what I had to do. In short, I had to break her heart for the third time in two months. What kind of special jerk generates this level of destruction? Through active sobbing on the other line, I apologized for instilling false hope toward reconciliation. I admitted guilt for how things turned out. Maybe it was best if we stayed separated.

Jumping way out of chronological order, basic training isolated me from most of society for ten weeks. My sole source of music was locked behind the vault door of my imagination. That was it. With the exception of Army cadences, the void of normal music was filled with three civilian songs: Toby Keith's "American Soldier," Creed's "My Sacrifice," and a little mystery ditty.

Have you guessed it? Yep, as my company marched past the post fire station, firefighters hosed down their trucks to the ironic backdrop of Hoobastank's "The Reason." Let me let you in on a little secret: drill sergeants may seem like heartless monsters, but on rare occasions, they display a shred of empathy. Marching in silence, they allowed us one small, fleeting reminder of civilian life.

Imagine my place in this military formation. Miles from home. Our comfortable cadences gone. The sound of freshly polished boots stomping in time to "The Reason," echoing off the brick walls of historical buildings.

Now, imagine this: my girlfriend, or worse, ex-girlfriend, almost joined with me. She would've been in this formation. Getting caught in the undertow of inertia, my potential consequences clarified for the first time. With genuine gratitude, I'm forever grateful my lack of impulse control didn't impede my destiny.

Mad World / Gary Jules

Donnie Darko was an instantaneous cult classic amongst us emotionally tormented 2000s kids. Prior to my Christian conversion, a few friends had it playing at a party. What a horrible venue to take in such a complicated movie. The extrovert in me wanted to socialize while the artist longed to explore the film's expressive depth. Depth requiring microscopic inspection of every scene for full understanding. To not be bested in intellectual debate with other tortured artists, I had to watch it again.

Time advanced several months, as it does, to a slow afternoon working at the DQ drive-thru. To pass the boredom, my co-worker Matt and I conducted a scientific experiment based upon a theory we had: can female attractiveness be depicted by voice alone? A rating would be assigned, Matt collected the money, I'd hand their order out, then we'd compare results.

Our first subject was a senior citizen, a little too mature for this juvenile game. The second customer sounded adorable, but I cast a vote of seven in an act of scientific defiance. Putting her money in the till, he confirmed my wager, "Seven's about right."

As I handed out her Hawaiian Blizzard, her sparkling brown eyes locked with mine as a perfect smile warmly greeted me. Science was wrong; pretty girls can have pretty voices. Racing back to Matt, I changed my rating to a nine.

The after-school ice cream surge sped business up, forcing us to abandon our game. As I made change for a later customer, I remember promising myself I would marry that girl if I ever got the chance.

You see, anyone can build confident plans without accountability. How can a person act upon such a wild fantasy? Was I supposed to canvas all twenty-seven thousand Dickinson residents in a door-to-door campaign to find her? What would I say if I tracked her down? As quick as she entered my life, my grand plans for our future faded into a disappointing pipe dream.

After Campus Crusade later that evening, our group packed away tables and chairs into a storage closet. If regular flirting isn't awkward enough, Christian flirting's worse. My best friend, with me flying wingman, used an aggressive table moving game as an avenue for interaction with his secret crush. In short, he/she who moves the most tables, who serves with the most efficient love, wins. In the haste of competition, one of the round tables railed over the top of my foot, causing an immediate charley horse.

As I stooped over to nurture the piercing pain, a pair of black-and-blue DC shoes parked a few feet in front of me, almost as if awaiting acknowledgement. Rising to address the shoe owner, my drive-thru experiment's familiar face reignited my matrimonial delusions of grandeur into a well-hidden emotional cocktail.

It turns out, her kindness from that afternoon stemmed from attending this group together. In our brief discussion, we agreed to meet the following week at game night. With a few weeks left before basic training, I had enough time to leave a lingering interest without fear of being locked forever in the friend-zone.

The next week, we met up again, but spent the entirety of the night chatting in the lounge. After the event, she offered me a ride in her new Chevy Blazer. With a dorm less than two blocks away, I didn't need a ride; I needed more time with her. Firing up her vehicle, a punk rock mix CD, packed to the rafters with Rancid and NOFX tracks, blared over her speakers. I used the extra five minutes together to insult her taste in music. "Slap drumming? Nasal, whiny vocals? That's what you're into?! Nice."

Not a strong end to the evening, but this fatal flaw was enough to make me doubt our future together. I had to say something.

The next morning, she stopped by for a quick visit after her last final. Not even my vocalized hatred for punk rock could slow the wheels of motion. Not even her careless comment to my best friend, who was dozing off in my room when she arrived, about how college guys wear the same hooded sweatshirt every day. Not even the skirmish that ensued as my outspoken best friend defended his West Point hoodie's honor. Even after all this momentary drama, she still wanted to make plans for later in the week.

"How 'bout a movie? I've been meaning to watch *Donnie Darko* for months," I recommended.

She flashed her trademark smile. "Sure, that'd be nice."

In one last attempt to smooth things over, my word vomit continued. "To be clear: it's not a date. Just a movie amongst friends. I promised the guy you met upstairs to stay single through the summer. Again, I'm sorry he was a jerk to you. You have to know him, I guess. I think he's tired or something."

I didn't really watch *Donnie Darko* that Friday evening, either. For a second time, the movie served as background noise to another conversation: music and movies, the Christian dating scene, the desolation of college, finding yourself amidst parental expectations. Conversation so natural, it became easy to project into the exact situation I hoped to avoid: a budding relationship left to whither, and die, due to neglect during my time away at basic training.

The cadences, alone, taunted me, "Oh, I wonder what she's doing now…"

How in the world would we ever replicate that innocent, carefree evening? Even worse, why did I explicitly grant her freedom to pursue other romantic interests during my absence? My famous last words, "Be free; we aren't dating. Let's write each other over the summer and see where this goes," echoed in my head. None of that mattered: I was gone; she was home. I had no other option than to wait out the drought.

Falling Further / Spoken

Descending into the St. Louis airport that June, I had no way of knowing Spoken's *Imperfect Moment of Clarity* would bookmark my summer music listening experience. Little was I to know, I'd have to sleep to the sound of other dudes snoring. Only sing along with cadences called out in formation. My sole music source was committed to memory, with zero time to cram for the exam.

I was okay with physical punishments, waking up before the sun, blistering butt-chewings, and structured schedules. I wasn't ok with having to involuntarily quit music cold turkey. How was I supposed to thrive in a challenging environment without my medicine? What if I needed a certain musical experience, but couldn't recall it? WHAT WAS I GONNA DO?!

This shouldn't be a spoiler, but I lived to tell the tale of a world void of music. Please allow my time off the musical map to serve as encouragement to you audiophiles who don't believe a world without music is possible. I'm here to tell you: it is. I did the heavy lifting. You get the blessed assurance to know it's dark, unnecessary, and pointless. Avoid that world if you can.

Bring Me Down / Pillar

The Army has an apparent need to break new recruits of any preconceived notions, personality quirks, and bad habits. I know. I've received several lectures about my desire to express individuality. Oddly enough, the first few weeks is chock-full of down time used for intense character reshaping exercises.

I'm not exactly sure what we did, or didn't do, but they marched my entire unit to a miniature mountain behind our barracks one humid summer afternoon. As we stood in formation, peering down its crest, rumors from other training units confirmed our impending doom. Here she was: San Juan Hill, the legendary location where the souls of belligerent Soldiers were crushed into the fine powder of submission.

For the better part of an hour, we swapped exercises to the shrill swelling of sharp whistle blasts. Tweet: FRONT! Tweet, Tweet: BACK! Tweet, Tweet, Tweeeet: GO! Even for me, a guy who prides himself in astounding work ethic, this was the hardest I've ever had to work.

My trick to stay motivated during these smoke sessions was to play my favorite songs in my head. I also sought the meaning of these pointless, soul-breaking exercises. What if I faced a situation where people counted on my ability to persevere? I had a frame of reference to draw from. You sleep when you die. If you lose the will to fight, that moment may be sooner than you'd like.

As I ran past my buddies, their desperation was visibly apparent as hell on earth roamed amongst us. Little were we to know, our hour-long physical torment held nothing in comparison to the dawning emotional anguish. Lined up in perfect military formation, our drill sergeants made us take turns announcing our rationale for joining the Army, complete with a list of people we'd disappoint if we failed.

As I waited for my chance to speak, I listened to my buddies' heartbreaking stories about how they needed the Army as deliverance: provide for young children at home, join the Army or go to jail, or departures from abuse, addiction, and desolate upbringings. They had no other option than to forge on.

You can't feel as miserable as I did knowing my enlistment into the Army was a choice. With high school buddies in Iraq, my Vietnam veteran father, and grandparents who served in Korea and World War 2, I joined because defense of this nation is passed down to the next able-bodied generation. Yet some of my buddies couldn't quit. Too much was hanging in the balance, and in some cases, without a support system to cheer them on in this new endeavor.

After this character development exercise concluded, we were sent to shower. I used those few moments to take a personal inventory. For the first time, I realized I was covered from head to toe in sweat. Sweat I wasn't entirely sure was mine. As I looked around, I noticed there wasn't a clean, dry uniform in the room. With passionate motivation, we entered into a verbal contract to look out for each other, as family would. "If one of us fails, we all fail! We win when we have each other's back!" my buddy pleaded.

Let our common enemy, the drill sergeants, try, but we were unbreakable. We were becoming Soldiers.

Rain / Erase the Grey

If you've seen *Forrest Gump*, you may recall the scene where Lieutenant Dan battles with God on Forrest's shrimp boat after losing his legs in Vietnam. He understood his fate, the fate of his fathers: become an officer, serve in a war, die for his country. It was his destiny, only it didn't happen that way. Through the pounding hurricane rain, Lieutenant Dan makes peace with living life as a disabled veteran.

I had a similar come-to-Jesus conversation at basic training.

Before I proceed, it's important to note we burn an obnoxious amount of time in lines in the Army. We line up for food. We line up to shave. We line up to get shots and see doctors. We line up to draw equipment, wait for transportation, and receive uniform inspections. We line up alphabetically. We line up in reverse alphabetical order for line experience diversity. Sometimes, we even stand in lines to get into OTHER lines. Of my fifteen years in the National Guard, I'd venture to guess I've waited in lines for approximately 5% of that time. You're welcome for my service.

While waiting in one of these aforementioned lines to depart the firing range, it was my platoon's turn to board the cattle cars first. Which still meant waiting in line, but for less time—a small, yet meaningful, victory basic training Soldiers cling to. One of my buddies decided to interject his opinion into their instructions.

Our senior drill sergeant screamed, as loose saliva sprayed from his mouth, "First Platoon, back of the line! Half right, face! The military press!" Imagine how a barbecue grill's ignitor switch sends a spark into an immediate surge of flame. That tiny flame burst within his eyes.

We parroted his command, "The military press, Drill Sergeant!"

If your platoon got moved to the back of the line, you were last the next time like we went first this time. We knew this rule. We also knew our return to camp wasn't a pleasant, calming vacation, but a sleepless night waking up every other hour to keep the site secure from potential attack.

Every face in the formation twisted in anguish as the ball of physical exercise bounced around the spinning roulette: bench presses, one-handed chest flies, flutter kicks. Creativity finds no end with a drill sergeant scorned. The impatient civilian laying on the horn of the last cattle car couldn't save us from ourselves. While boarding, our senior drill sergeant glared through each desperate soul as he promised, "Oh, you think we're done?! Wait 'til we get to bivouac. It's on, privates!"

The ride's overwhelming silence made sonic space for the drizzling rain. Treacherous grey clouds lingered above us, threatening the onset of a Missouri flash flood. Silent pleas for compassion intertwined with the stench of body odor as we awaited our fate.

It's not physically impossible to bench press a ten-pound weapon a hundred times. What is difficult is doing it under the branches of a tree while getting waterboarded by Mother Nature. Time stands still in periods of trauma, so I can't tell you how long we were punished. My best guess is over two hours. We really screwed up.

Correction, one of my peers screwed up, dragging us along for communal punishment.

In my infantile faith, suffering seemed like penance for past transgressions. I'm not sure why I picked this event, but in my head, Lady Justice's eternal scale tipped in my favor as life's unfair punishments exceeded my number of perceived sins. Through nature's systemic game of Chinese water torture, I shrieked the most honest prayer in my life, "Why is this happening? These idiots don't know You! They don't follow the drills! How long will I have to suffer for them?"

Even the lyrics to Erase the Grey's "Rain," the song I tried to inspire myself with, couldn't bring comfort, "Let Your rain fall down on me? Stop this stupidity now!"

The swirling, atmospheric sound of wind, rain, and thunder intercepted my prayer, rendering it seemingly ineffective. My cosmic sign wasn't conclusion to the torment, but an exercise change to push-ups. While balancing my weapon on my hands to keep it out of the mud, dim light reflected off a shiny object in the darkness. The streaming water uncovered a cross from someone's necklace, probably the last sorry group of suckers in my position.

It may not be profound to you, but this was the exact message I needed. How long did Christ Himself have to suffer for me? How long did He wait for my return? The endless weight of my past, present, and future sins were paid for on that symbolic two-inch metal cross. Life's a remaining byproduct, a simple chance to display the grace we've received.

At the exact moment of my self-realization, cattle car headlights pierced the darkness. Our company first sergeant's shadow created a hopeful flicker as he barked over the rattling engine, "Load 'em up, Colón! Lightning was spotted on base. You can finish this tomorrow."

Like the flip of a light switch, a sleepless night disappeared. We were gifted with a warm bed and shower to return fresh for weapon qualification in the morning. With the same peace Lieutenant Dan possessed while hoisting himself off the side of the U.S.S. Jenny, I still wrestled with my peer's childish behavior. After that night, I did it with a renewed sense of my own ignorance.

Wild World / Cat Stevens

Eventually, what my best friend called the "Summer of Darkness" had to end.

After my successful indoctrination to the Soldier lifestyle, I returned to the freedom of college campus. I was relieved of drill sergeant criticisms to fulfill the desires of my heart. Sure, I still marked time while marching around, "Left, left, left, right." Sure, I still frantically searched for my weapon and battle buddy, both mechanisms I'd never needed prior to basic training. However, the comfortable, carefree society I once knew felt foreign as I transitioned back to academia.

Since my best friend and I spent all our free time together, we decided to cut the middle man and become roommates. The conclusion of our Summer of Darkness left time, and space, to engage in new shenanigans. With so much time off the musical map, I relied on his attendance at Sonshine, the largest Christian music festival in our area, for new band recommendations.

Instead of new tunes, our room seemed to favor the musical stylings of Cat Stevens. While unpacking, we sifted through our nice things to wear to "Wild World." Returning to our dorm after exposure to said "Wild World," Cat Stevens provided us a comfortable place to reflect on the treachery of college politics. Our junior year started off, not with the hot singles from the summer, but with refamiliarization to a song from our childhood.

I can't ponder my relationship with my best friend without "Wild World" taking center stage. There aren't many times when the song doesn't sneak into the conversation. I also think of Fox News, the other murmur in our room. I'm not sure how Cat Stevens, now known as Yousef, or a conservative news outlet feel about being lumped together. They don't have a choice, though.

Without their expressed written consent, I'll remember my memories how I'd like.

Nobody's Home / Avril Lavigne

My greatest fear of summer severing the flowers off my budding romance never materialized. After a few failed dates on her end, weekly pen pal exchanges kept our spring conversation alive. Now, our trajectory was solely dependent upon us.

Moving on from my first relationship, I found a happier, drama-free partner. Although I served in the National Guard, returned to college with my best friend as a roommate, and got more involved in campus life, my happiness created a conundrum of conscience. I chose to do what Shaun Morgan declares in "Betray and Degrade:" "Yeah, I'm guessing that I should be kind of happy. It's a fault of mine." Since *Poison the Parish* wasn't released until 2017, I hadn't learned that lesson yet.

My primary source of unrest was accidental run-ins with my ex-girlfriend. When most normal people break up, they beg for opportunities to show their ex how happy they are without them. I was terrified of these chance encounters. While I finally understood our relationship wouldn't work out, I couldn't be at peace with leaving her in the wreckage that nearly consumed me. Maybe if she found whatever she was looking for, I could stop being an additional source of pain for her.

Eye of the Storm / Blindside

I'm not sure how we discovered it, but imagine one of your favorite bands was playing a free show the next day. What's a college kid to do? Yep, for my group of friends, that meant packing eight people into two cars for an impromptu road trip. Thursday morning, no idea this was happening. Friday morning, enroute to a free concert, sponsored by Budweiser, with one of our favorite Christian artists. A concept so far-fetched, we had to mentally prepare for potential let down. Half the hype was we were either getting punked, or we were gonna see Sweden's finest, Blindside, playing FOR FREE at a venue three hundred miles from home.

During a pit stop from our last concert, my best friend bought a stuffed wolf hat. In essence, it was a stuffed animal wolf face designed to sit on the wearers head, like a coonskin cap. That hat was a crowd favorite at the last concert.

Where the audience sought rock n' roll acceptance through wristbands and chain wallets, my best friend evaded normal fashion by sporting a goofy-lookin' hat on top of his trademark white bandana. Imagine a twelve-year-old kid impersonating a gangster. A hat so ridiculous, bands asked to sign it and fans posed in pictures with my best friend to capture the moment. He wore the same get-up to this show: grey West Point hoodie, white bandana, and wolf hat. We had to test the theory of its fame.

Arriving at the baseball diamond the concert was held at, we were surprised to find a small crowd forming around the stage for the night's festivities. Our crazy risk paid off! While most people were there for the two free beers, provided by Budweiser, my group was there to jam out.

The intoxicated crowd's short attention span fixated on my friend's wolf hat. Tucked somewhere in my photo collection, I have this picture of an unknown drunk lady following my friend around pleading to wear his hat. Try as she may, she never won the battle.

As the Summer of Darkness ended, so did our temporary vow to remain single. Using this concert to get to know his new crush better, my best friend invited her along for the ride. Somewhere along the way, he gained her attention. Maybe her heart backflipped in her chest, as Simon did off guitar amps, or she fell for him, as Christian nearly did off a tower of monitors, as we watched the concert. Maybe she found our playful negotiations with the band for a hopeful "Liberty" performance during the meet-and-greet charming. Maybe it happened during the accidental incarceration of an eight-hour car ride. We couldn't pinpoint the exact moment, but somewhere along the way, their relationship took root.

As they became an item, the three of us hung out so much we weren't considered individual people anymore, but a collective three-headed force of impulsivity. This musical experience was the glue that bound our friendship. As simple as that, and without warning, what our other friends affectionately coined "The Trio" was born.

Torches Together / mewithoutYOU

I purposefully left out a large chunk of my story from the Blindside concert. It's a shaping experience of its own. Allow me the opportunity to tell you how I met Aaron Weiss.

Holding our usual spot on the rail, some local battle of the bands winner took the stage as opener. Behind us, a weird group of people, sending off some serious Pennsylvania Mennonite vibes, played soccer barefoot. Imagine fathers from 1970s photos reanimating into a heated soccer game at the family reunion. With their beanies and beards, aviator sunglasses and mustard yellow/brown sweaters, they weren't dressed for the late summer heat. They were dressed to impress—for who, we weren't sure. This group of people was so out of place they drew attention. Honestly, who plays soccer at a concert?

Apparently, the members of mewithoutYOU, the openers for Blindside's tour, play soccer before concerts. They were rock stars who refused to act like rock stars. Just a few musicians, posing as regular dudes, hosting potlucks and pick-up soccer games before concerts. Their music was unlike anything I'd ever listened to. Poetic rants screamed over distorted guitars. None of my friends heard of them, but here we were. Front and center, staring at the band. I enjoyed them, but not enough to seek them out again.

Then, I met Aaron Weiss. Sure, we'd met him earlier kicking the ball around while the rest of our group held our stage-front spot. The short interaction lacked the necessary depth to make an accurate personality assessment.

While on stage playing "Torches Together," a song about coming together and working in community, two drunk dudes got into a knock-down drag-out in the pit. Aaron dropped the mic, ended the fight, and pulled them back to talk. The band performed an extended instrumental while Aaron resolved the problem. Once he worked the issue out, he took a seat next to the kick drum, meekly massaging his beanie in disbelief as the band finished the song. Addressing the crowd, he delivered a passionate speech about humanity's need to love each other. Then, the concert forged forward as if nothing happened.

I'm sure my silly face is amongst a million little blurs throughout his career, but I'd venture to guess I got to know Aaron Weiss pretty well by this one simple act. You see, this concert, like all others I've attended, had security guards. No other band, much less its voice, would've left the stage to stop a fight.

For the first time in my life, I chose to listen to a band I would've dismissed had I heard them in any other setting. My reason's this: preaching love and acceptance is a sweet sentiment to bring awareness to world problems. If an actual performance of your song about community is interrupted by violence, your awareness campaign already failed. While Aaron didn't generate world peace over the course of one evening, he paved an avenue for co-existence and basic understanding, even if for a moment.

Anyone can write a song. Few artists are willing to live their music's content out in real life.

My Throat Is an Open Grave / Demon Hunter

Imagine finding an eighty-five-inch flat screen TV at Black Friday pricing—let's say, 70% off. Wouldn't you feel a civic responsibility to share this deal with your friends, even without details on their current home entertainment needs? You deliver the great news; they make the decision.

Lacking formal training on how to share my path to Christianity, I told my tale whenever I could, wherever I could. My life was absolute trash before Jesus, a catastrophic collision course destined for definite destruction. Then, Jesus generated a life-altering change in perspective. What kind of jerk stays silent on such good news?

After speaking to a youth group one evening, a parent asked if I'd been baptized. The truth is, I checked this once-in-a-lifetime achievement block twice, once as an infant and again prior to my Presbyterian confirmation in high school. He continued with loving instruction, "Baptism shouldn't be taken lightly. It's a commandment, a public declaration of commitment to Christ. It's not necessary for salvation, but faithful entrance into ministry."

In other words, my other baptisms weren't completed with correct intention.

As I scheduled my third, and final, baptism, the pastor encouraged me to share a Bible verse or Christian quote to proclaim my newfound faith to the world. How was I, a lifelong music fan, supposed to provide new insight on two millenia of biblical wisdom? Easy, tack on unconventional source material from the Demon Hunter catalog: "It feels good to be alive, cause I've been dead for so long." All I knew, thoughts of death and suicide once consumed me. One day later, I was transformed by Jesus. Wading in the waters of a baptismal font one last time, I could finally say I was there for the right reason.

American Love / Haste the Day

After being out of normal civilization for three months, the concept of burrowing through new music became overwhelming. Normal people challenged my lyrical search engine reviews as an insane chore, but being lax with musical messaging was nearly my demise. Let's be clear: musicians aren't irresponsible in their artistic choices; I wasn't mature enough to leverage it to my benefit. Back then, I had no other choice than to be meticulous about what music I took in.

As the accompanying playlist suggests, I favored nu-metal prior to my conversion. Although dark, the genre's aggression dances on the balance beam with softer elements. Sifting through my friend's CDs from Sonshine Music Festival, I stumbled upon Haste the Day's *Burning Bridges*.

Imagine the metal mayhem of Zao prancing through peaceful pastures in perfect tension. Once the first blood droplet begins seeping from your ear canal, a different dude serenades you over melodic rhythm guitar. Even better, a thorough content review using darklyrics.com showed exploration of American excess, good vs. evil, addiction, and darkness. A little heavy metal infused with positive introspection.

On a separate but related note, I cannot tell you how many times I've heard the outro to *Burning Bridges*. My roommate had it on loop at all times. Some weird metal song was the peaceful ambient noise to our often-chaotic lifestyle. Sometimes, the run-around rigamarole of the academic environment leaves you in a place where a little instrumetal only makes sense.

New Medicines / Dead Poetic

As I struggled with my sense of musical identity, I sought the icon to highlight the fall of 2004. My quest for a new, talented, hard rock/heavy metal band with a positive message began. It couldn't come through recommendation; I wanted to hand-carry this new gem to my peer group. A symbolic album, with a little screaming, to depict metaphorical momentum. Lastly, it didn't have to derive from Christian sources, but if it was, it couldn't be blatant, worship-styled music.

Reading that description, I may seem like a monarch demanding the first-fruits from the finest music in all the land. Let me point out how fragile these times felt. Any unintentional, wrong move carried the burden of burying me knee-deep in the filth I worked so hard to escape.

Further, non-Christians may accuse the church, my peers, or some pastor of lingering in the backdrop to slap careless, straying fingers back into submission. Please remember, I embarked on this oddly specific journey all alone. Is needing a musical act to fuel my chilly, late-night prayer walks too much to ask for?

Stay / 12 Stones

If finding purchase worthy CDs was difficult, try finding guitar tabs for these obscure releases. I measured creative process progress through the inch of mounting dust on my hibernating, jet-black Ibanez. Do you dare to establish your own voice while critically combing other artist's messages? What if I scribbled something that sent someone, like my former shell of self, into the same desperate tailspin?

Despite hesitation to write new material, I exploited the lull to improve my guitar playing. After Paul's feature in "Bring Me to Life," official 12 Stones tab booklets became easier to buy. Refreshing the results of nail-biting eBay auctions, I noodled along with high-ranking Ultimate Guitar tabs for accuracy. Unable to find specific versions a second time, I wrestled through printed pages, chicken scratch in the margins, now forever immortalized in a four-inch, three-ring binder.

Still nervous about contributing to someone's psychological demise, I determined producing anything had to be better than wasting potential talent. After a quick sticker swap from Korn to Jonah33 on my Ibanez's beautiful body, my long hiatus from music creation was over.

My Heartstrings Come Undone / Demon Hunter

At face value, The Trio may seem like my best friend, his chick, and a wobbly, third wheel. That's not true at all. The atomic impetus birthed at the Blindside concert never lost momentum, like the expansion of the universe or incessant car warranty robocalls.

We were musical: impromptu worship session coordinators and sing-songy, Gregorian chant Ong language applicators. Tong-O-Nong-Yong! At meals, we nourished the body, and soul, by facilitating cafeteria-wide eating contests. For the record, Trix, when paired with blue raspberry lemonade, will bless your palate in a blissful, exquisite kiss. We enforced societal order by dishing push-ups out to classmates critical of elected officials. We were the respectful, responsible mayhem integral to collegiate life.

One of our trademark midnight romps for snacks led us to the local Walmart. My selection of a two-ounce cotton candy container left carrying capacity for my best friend's weighty announcement. "Just letting you know, we're pursuing youth ministry degrees next year."

"What?! You're leaving me? In May, right?" I asked.

With his gaze locked on the soda display, he explained, "Nope, like a few weeks from now. We need extra cash for the wedding and move to Knoxville. You wanna be my best man?"

"I guess," I accepted. "What'll we do until then?"

"We'll visit you a ton," he promised. "I'll call, too. It'll be fine."

If the gallon challenge taught us anything, the human stomach has hourly lactose digestion limitations. Pushing the envelope too far, too fast, turns the whole ordeal into a barfing contest. The same's true with the human heart. Disassembling the mystery behind The Trio, the most meaningful relationship of my academic career, required every spare moment remaining in fall semester.

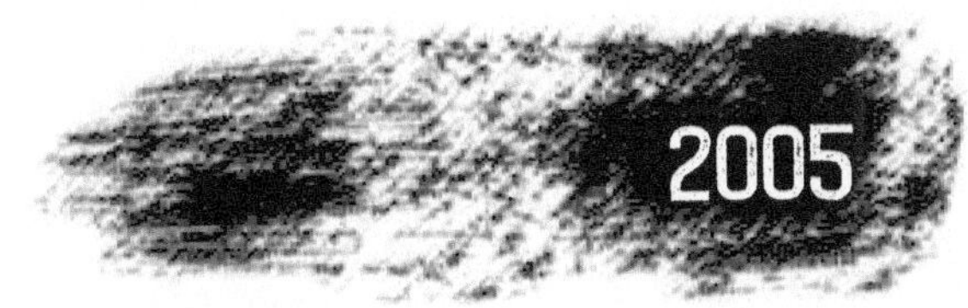

Autumn / Modern Day John

While enlisting in the National Guard, I signed a contract to attend basic training one year with an option to attend advanced training the following summer. As summer approached again, I knew enough to be comfortable. Stuff the mp3 player in the forgotten wasteland of a padlocked military container for six more weeks. Letters, three-minute calls from a phone booth, smoke sessions, ruck marches, and sleepless Army nights lorded over my life.

Lying in a dark, shared hotel room, my bunkmate added lumber-shredding percussive elements to the music blaring in my headphones. The poor sucker was clueless about the chaos surrounding the next few days. Even my previous summer's experience did little to calm my nerves. Yet this dude was sleeping?

One tiny error would derail my entire summer: serving in two wedding parties, proposing to my girlfriend, beginning my senior year of college. If I could only complete my training, real life lingered in full-force on the other side. With one last chance to breathe, I hit the play button on my mp3 player, signaling the start of another summer away.

Tongue / Seether

The day after my last final, I was on a plane to Missouri to complete my training. Nervously fidgeting in my window seat, everyone's advice echoed in my head. "Listen to the drill sergeants. Don't volunteer for anything. Fake it 'til you make it. Don't be first, but don't be last." Sound words of wisdom, but were they enough to carry me through the horror of war? With conflicts raging in Iraq and Afghanistan, training established the muscle memory necessary to maintain clarity during catastrophe.

My buddies despised simple Soldier tasks like polishing boots or pulling fireguard. I found solace in both. I guess I'm twisted. There's a certain therapy behind applying the flawless, high-gloss sheen of a mountain lake to the worn exterior of combat boots. There's also therapy in pacing the halls after lights out, mapping out actions on objectives in wartime scenarios. Somewhere in the darkness, I found casual confidence in performing life-threatening tasks under direct assault.

Thus began my side hustle. For six weeks, I exploited their laziness to tap into a second income stream. To reward myself, my back-alley barracks business funded a massive, life-altering CD haul. My peers called me crazy, but I believe they projected self-hatred onto me for their own stupidity.

I mean, I shelled out $400 for twelve CDs and a new mp3 player. My bank account didn't feel the difference. Like a child collecting candy on Halloween, I shoved Alter Bridge's *One Day Remains*, Edgewater's *South of Sideways*, Dark New Day's *Five-Year Silence*, Seether's *Karma and Effect*, and seven other forgettable CDs into a shopping basket. I have yet to meet another normal adult who has dropped such a large sum of money in a casual, hasty manner. But hey, when you exceed life's expectations, you must treat yourself.

Most of that CD binge drowned in the wake of Seether's *Karma and Effect*. To this day, it's still my favorite Seether album. First, it cost me a buttload of lost free time and sleep. One night alone, I pulled five hours of fireguard. You should've seen the drill sergeant on duty question his sanity after repeated Kessel sightings. Second, without use of a single expletive, *Karma and Effect* harvested the rawest form of emotional intensity. When you combine my hard work with this album's perfection, it imprinted a commemorative seal directly to the fibers of my heart.

On Fire / Switchfoot

A few weeks after my Army training, The Trio reunion episode featured a bride, groom, and his best man. Being best man seems insignificant sitting next to the maid of honor's miracles. My fraternal appointment consisted of a bachelor party and dumping the tuxedo afterward.

Aside from that, the gang journeyed through five distinct plotlines: 1) My best friend asking me to build an entire wedding dance playlist with less than a twenty-four-hour notice. 2) Per the groom's request, trolling the wedding party by handing out an obnoxious amount of mints. 3) The wind changing direction in the eleventh hour, avoiding an outdoor wedding plagued by the faint scent of a nearby horse farm. 4) Gifting an unpractical, creepy lawn gnome to celebrate the union and travels of my two best friends. 5) My best friend sliding me a note— *"The trio is splitsville"*—as they departed for their honeymoon in a black limousine. His iconic, italic-styled handwriting formalized the end of an era.

Between this experience and my own engagement, I creatively took to the notepad for the first time in forever. My mission was clear: capture these raw moments in lyric form as they occurred. What else could I do? The Trio was splitsville. With my own wedding to plan, senior year of college, and student body presidency awaiting, our shenanigans would have to stop. Real adulthood was right around the corner.

Studying Politics / Emery

I have a degree in Political Science—your run-of-the-mill social science program where students spin Enlightenment era wisdom into the modern pottery of governmental application. Long before hasty, faceless Twitter attacks, we tackled opponents in treacherous in-class discussion. Our daily actions weighed against deep-seated beliefs in classy character assassination. I was studying politics.

These lessons came to a dramatic head as Bill Ayers (yes, THE Bill Ayers) coached my class of young, formidable adults toward non-peaceful protest during a guest lecture circuit. "Aren't you tired of the senseless killing in Iraq?" he barked. "Do what my friends and I did to express discontent about Vietnam!"

My shock must've been obvious, because he reprimanded me with a dirty old finger and an icy stare. "Don't like it, you snot-nosed punk? What's your solution? How much life have you lived?"

Thoughts of detaining my classmates in an involuntary National Guard activation flashed through my mind. With a general gesture behind me, I asked, "Should you really be telling THESE people THIS?" Donning a uniform to remove the rubble of a building, the mere ramification of his recommendation, freaked me out. Yet here he was. I didn't have to agree, but I had to allow him space to talk. I was studying politics.

Seize every opportunity for potential gain. Say the correct thing, in correct timing, with correct inflection. Never say the wrong thing. Stand on principle. Emotion is weakness, yet a weapon. Be a jack-of-all-trades, all while mastering none. Walk the tightrope. It ain't that easy, but it's not that hard. You, my friend, are studying politics.

The Nobodies / Marilyn Manson

There's an ongoing Christian discussion about the evils of secular music. The two basic camps include Christians who refuse to listen to secular stuff and those who embrace it as another function of the world. Despite preconceived notions from years of conditioning, I have come to learn that music is a tool.

Take a hammer, for example. Hammers can be used to build houses, communities, and improve the quality of human life. That same hammer can be used to bash someone's skull in. It isn't the tool that's inherently evil. It's the intention of the user, NOT THE CREATOR, that defines the purpose of any particular instrument.

During trying times of tragedy, people storm the nation's streets in a passionate witch hunt to find the culprit. Blame the school system, the parents, the media, violent video games, musicians, pop culture, the lack of morality, or the church. As long as we can justify why it isn't our fault, we allow ourselves to move on without meaningful resolution.

What would happen if we owned our shortcomings to correct our version of the story? What if we take personal responsibility for the music/media we ingest? It's perfectly normal to be angry. It's perfectly normal to be sad. It's perfectly normal to be contemplative. What tangible action do we take with these emotions once we have them? The power remains in our hands.

The Bleeding / Five Finger Death Punch

In the deepest recesses of my soul, a confused child still wanders. For years, I've tried to ease personal pain by finding similar spirits in need of capture. One of my earliest attempts resulted in volunteering with the Best Friends program. With music as a universal language, my junior friend and I spent several weeks playing *Tony Hawk Pro Skater* with popularized party country blasting in the background. Dusting my old collection off, we settled for the only guy around, Tim McGraw, who still seemed to know what was going on.

In time, it became apparent my junior friend's love for Tony Hawk pushed him into full-fledged skater trash. While watching an afternoon marathon of Bam Margera's mistreatment of his poor parents, he asked, "CKY's pretty good, right? What about H.I.M.?"

"Huh? Sure." I replied. "Hey, man. Don't try to punch your dad when he's taking a dump. That won't end well in real life."

"I won't," he promised. "Should I ask for DCs for my birthday? Bam wears 'em."

"Seriously," I warned. "Don't punch your dad on the john. Or, like, ever." No, he didn't need another parent, but my opinion seemed to matter.

Allow me to submit this as a tangible life lesson for you all. Keep vulnerable restroom positioning free of violence.

Oh, I still encouraged him to explore his personal music tastes. Adults in my life gave me that gift when I was young. Despite my frustration, I owed the same to him.

Take it from me, his accidental discovery of Five Finger Death Punch was a much-needed palate cleanser. Finally! My useless knowledge of Ivan Moody's origin story in Motograter became relevant. My struggle learning "The Bleeding" on guitar gave us something else to do between *Way of the Fist* listening sessions. I mean, if you're in a position to mentor other confused children, you have to do it right. Take hold, little buddy. Your journey through life's gonna require some better tunes.

Pointing Fingers / Justifide

An atheist Army buddy once jokingly told me, "You Christians see Satan everywhere. You like thinking the world's after you."

I would've loved to argue with him. Arguing is, after all, amongst my favorite pastimes. However, he exposed a flaw I couldn't acknowledge until he pointed it out. The thing is, when you start the argument behind the eight-ball, you have no other option than concession.

For a short time, life became about persecution or spiritual warfare. Someone, or something, had to resist earth's true purpose. If it was a person, they had to be against the goals I had. They attacked to persecute. If it wasn't another human, it was spiritual warfare. Problem solved. I'd have to become more resilient, more patient, and move faithfully forward.

Can't a Christian just cling to some face in the cloud experiences? You know the type. Morning toast etched with the image of Jesus. Oranges and purples hand-painted in a vast skyline at sunset to offset all that holy war. A few signs/miracles to validate a belief system. Is a little spiritual fuel too much to ask for—regardless of the world's willingness to being conquered?

Not Ready to Die / Demon Hunter

At the height of my 2004 depression, one of my late-night pity parties was interrupted by a phone call from an older woman named Anne. She claimed we met at the post office, where I agreed to type a manuscript for her. Nope, never happened. "Sorry, ma'am," I reported. "I think you have the wrong number."

"Oh, dear. I called the number the young man gave me. Are you sure?" she pleaded.

Her next request was pretty obvious. I had to cut it off. "Listen, lady. It wasn't me. Plus, I'm really busy."

"Can you help me?" she asked. "My book's due to the publisher soon. I can't see well enough to type anymore. I'll pay five cents a line for your trouble."

Wait, there's money involved? Quick math put me over a hundred lines per hour just to meet minimum wage. Not very lucrative to obtaining riches, but her desperation made me cave.

A few days later, a handwritten draft full of Christian child-rearing advice appeared in my campus mailbox. As you may recall, I was agnostic at the time. God represented a vengeful father frying His creation with a magnifying glass as we scurried for safety. A principled artist couldn't accept money to peddle a lie. Sure enough, she called back. I rejected her book; she pled for a second time; I accepted again.

For the next two years, we exchanged manuscript pages through strange scavenger hunts around town. Believe it or not, I only met with this eccentric female author in person twice: once to help her install ceiling tiles on a Saturday afternoon and the other to hand the project off a final time. After my graduation and wedding, I wouldn't have time to help her anymore.

The last time I ever saw Anne was during our final manuscript exchange in the Walmart parking lot. Through the open windows of my 98 Ford, the beautiful spring air was complimented with the sporadic infusion of lilacs in bloom. Our interaction was supposed to be brief. I left the keys in the ignition with Demon Hunter's *Summer of Darkness* blaring in the background. Before forking over my hard-earned dough, she dished out professional, marital, and life advice. Since our belief systems somewhat aligned, I was more receptive to her guidance.

As the conversation ended, she called me back one more time. She whispered, "Don't let others know you listen to that music. They won't believe you're a Christian."

I wanted to say, "Hold up, lady. I didn't insult your neck-to-ankle floral pattern dress, old lady head scarf, or sensible, gout-combatting shoes. Leave my boys in Demon Hunter alone." Instead, I thanked her and walked away. For the second time in my life, my music offended another human being. This time, my Christian music wasn't Christian enough for another Christian.

Breathe Today / Flyleaf

Most people can tell you exactly where they were during historical events. The assassination of JFK. The Oklahoma City bombing. The collapse of the Twin Towers. Occurrences so astronomical that time freezes. I'd hate to compare tragedy to obsession, but I can tell you the exact moment, with precision, when I met Lacey Mosley.

During my last supper in the college cafeteria, poor time management leading to four long years of all-nighters sat in the rearview mirror. Somehow, someway, I managed to navigate the unchartered territory of collegiate life to graduation. My last final rested in my advisor's dusty briefcase.

Rather than trade nostalgic stories, I sought new band recommendations from the Campus Crusade worship leader. The musical itch I couldn't seem to scratch: a female-fronted band that wasn't symphonic metal, poppy bull crap, or stereotypical chick rock. "Like, imagine Kittie dropping albums today," I coached. "Wouldn't that be awesome?!"

"You heard Flyleaf yet? She screams like Kittie. Best part, they're Christian."

You see, we didn't have smart phones to conveniently peruse internet sites on the spot. As we continued talking, I had to keep their name fresh in my mind. "Flyleaf, Flyleaf, Flyleaf…" It was a lot of work to look into this recommendation. Once my stuff was in my temporary room, I had to set up my computer, connect to the internet, and still remember who they were. Kids these days will never know the trouble.

My shower kit wasn't even unpacked yet. "Flyleaf," I whispered while typing in Rhapsody's search bar, relieved I still remembered. "'Breathe Today?' Sure." I mumbled to myself. An angelic voice floated perfectly over distorted guitars, settling into a guttural, ear-piercing shriek. My temporary workspace became home for all five of the EP's tracks.

"Who hurt you, Lacey Mosley?" I said aloud. No answer. Opening a web browser, I spent hours assembling the puzzle of her past. Isolation. Torment. Suicidal ideation. Damage as deep as I once felt. Still, I couldn't shake the nagging guilt of a missed deadline. It was fine, though. College didn't own me anymore. I had breathing room to pursue the studies of my heart.

Collide / Howie Day

One week after college graduation, I got married. I haven't spoken much about it because I didn't give it much thought. That is correct. A child of divorce, terrified of making the same mistakes. The weight of my pending nuptials never occurred to me until an afternoon shopping trip for my remaining groomsmen gifts. Wandering past the local mall's quarter kiddie machines, the intro chords to Howie Day's "Collide" distorted over the loudspeaker. A song meant to reassure Rose during brisk mall walks took me out at the knees. I was getting married.

My thoughts raced. *How am I different than my parents? Can we even make this intricate institution work? Is our relationship somehow a fluke? When will she quit on me like everyone else?*

I shook my head, hoping to flick dangerous doubts through my ear canal. My fiancée wasn't cold like my mom. More importantly, if fear existed, it was natural. I had to use it to repel the vicious cycle from my youth. With gifts to buy, I took a deep breath and stepped into the first store.

In Memory / April Sixth

Wandering into the last store for groomsmen gifts, I ran into my cousin. Her normally joyous demeanor was buried beneath unfamiliar burden. Tired, bloodshot eyes glistened from recent tears of torment. "Are you OK? What's going on?" I quizzed.

She barely pulled the words together to answer, "Nate's being put on Hospice. If you want to see him before he passes, you need to stop by soon."

I visited Nate often when I lived at home. Witnessing someone your age writhe in pain puts perfect perspective on the frailty of human life. I used to care enough to pray while his mom delivered medication to alleviate the pressure from his spinal tumor. Then, through selfish ambition, I left him to suffer alone. In one chance interaction, it all came flooding back. The smoldering fire soon to expire.

I sped to the hospital to rectify my wrongs. His room swirled in chaos: Nate shrieking in pain, staff scurrying around, hospital machinery lamenting the tense atmosphere. I had one minute to say something impactful. Thumbing through my Bible, I declared, "Nate, John 10:10 says the enemy comes to steal, kill, and destroy. Jesus came to give abundant life. It may not feel like it now, but you're almost home. Can I stop by in the next few days to visit?"

In classic Nate fashion, he quipped, "My priest… just stopped by… to give my last rights. You may want… to come sooner." Always the joker, but laughter didn't seem right. They loaded him onto a gurney, carted him down the hallway, and tucked him into the back of an ambulance. The siren blared as they pulled away like a highlight reel playing in reverse. People come to the hospital to live, not leave to die.

There I stood, adrenaline streaming through my veins. A mere twenty minutes ago, I was groomsmen shopping. Only one place could address the weight of my predicament: a road outside town we kids called "The Boob."

If you drove fast enough, your vehicle would catch air. Sitting under the stars two years ago, adrenaline was the necessary sign of life to counterpoint suicidal ideation dancing within my skull. Oh, The Boob knew the balance between life and death. Maybe this all-too-familiar field would work its magic again.

Reflecting on old times, I prayed for Nate to find peace. He was my first friend when I moved to Belfield after Kindergarten. Baseball cards and bottle rockets. Staying after school with our names on the board. Starting a minor brush fire with improvised explosives. Walking together at graduation. Listening to 80s rock in his 1957 Chevy on cool summer evenings before college. A young life ceased at the source. How does the world move on from such a tragedy?

Grace Like Rain / Todd Agnew

I never saw Nate alive again. He passed away shortly after returning home. As I left for his funeral on June 2, the day before my wedding, my mom called. "Hey, you know that version of 'Amazing Grace?' You should play it at the funeral."

"Mom," I argued, "I'm performing for my wedding tomorrow. Plus, I haven't practiced it. Plus, no one asked me."

"I asked his mom," she interrupted. "Problem solved. It would mean a lot to the family."

"Ok, Ma. I'll bring my guitar." I wasn't ready for three emotionally-charged performances in two days. Even if I "forgot" it, she'd find a way to get one. She always got what she wanted.

Nate was the first to convince me of Garth Brooks' talent. It was only fitting that his memorial video was set to "The Thunder Rolls." As I reached for my guitar, the whole experience felt like a cruel joke. Although I'd just watched the casket lower into his grave, I still prayed Nate, sporting his black Garth Brooks shirt, would stagger through the reception hall's double doors.

It wasn't fair. The moment I finished performing I'd have to leave for my wedding rehearsal. Playing foolish games, like *How Well Do You Know Your Bride,* at the bachelor party. Greeting some of the same people from the memorial video, and the funeral, in the receiving line. Opportunities no longer available to Nate. Life experience taught me to play the part, but morbidity robbed every step along the way.

At the same time, Nate's death intensified these moments. How much life do we shuffle through without knowing our fortune? We're supposed to go to college and become professionals. Most of us will get married. Most of us will have children. It's the circle of life, yet we bear blindfolds to the lotteries we win. Until our complacency's shaken. Then, and only then, we begin realizing that life, in its simplest form, is somehow still incredible.

Silence / Blindside

I'm not a man of few words. The Army teaches three Bs of verbal communication: be brief; be brilliant; be gone. On rare occasions, I'm one of those things. To me, there's nothing worse than careless misunderstandings or hurting someone's feelings. To decrease discomfort, I line silence with an increased word count. Under tight timelines, the artist in me pitches a quick song reference. Please accept this pretty prose as evidential inspiration from the drive-thru of a fast-paced society. Let's go forward and do great things.

For a wedding, though? My bride-to-be and I sought a masterpiece blending her classically trained vocal chops with the torment of my dark artistry. A piece demonstrating love rooted in greater purpose, without the cliché mutterings of Shakespeare-like soliloquy. Subtle, yet precise. Intimate, yet elegant.

Under these firm guidelines, I shuffled a full mp3 player during a two-hour trip with my National Guard unit. Song after song representative of the momentary illumination of passing headlights piercing the darkness through dirty bus windows. Brief brilliance before being disqualified for missing the mark. Next.

At first, the intro rumble to Blindside's "Silence" tricked me for a blown tire or sleepy driver veering from his lane. *That's the song?* I thought, inhaling deeply to slow my racing heart.

I pressed the back button to reset the experience. The simplistic arrangement was reminiscent of a butterfly emerging from the wake of a thunderstorm. Closing my eyes, I sunk into the bus seat. A haunting harmony, sung by my fiancée, superimposed with perfect character into the track. One practice confirmed my wild imagination. Brief, brilliant, gone in five minutes. Love defined the precise way my fiancée and I cared to depict it.

Our cover of "Silence" was the last hurdle before every twisted possibility: lost love, divorce, custody, an unending life of loneliness. All dangling on a balance beam the width of a wedding ring. Innocence to marital fratricide was no longer an option. This time, I carried negligence in any future failures. On the other hand, the same slight odds allowed me to denounce repetition of my familial curse. Ready or not, the courageous journey began as the last note resonated. Out of the Silence, the full force of my opportunity for lifelong love began.

When Will I Wake Up / TaKen

"When Will I Wake Up" was penned on a plane as a wedding gift for my wife. After leaving the love song market in high school, I made exception for her. You see, our union felt like a surreal fever dream. How else could I, a goofy-lookin' dude with a broken past, land a chick of her caliber? Life as I knew it didn't glide on positive trajectories. Nonetheless, I was willing to stay asleep, to fib a bit, if it prolonged my unfamiliar euphoria.

Other than my best man, no one knew a thing. The morning of the wedding, I played the song for him and made final arrangements. The wedding dance was held at my hometown American Legion post. Before leaving for the evening, he'd secure a chair and seat my wife while I grabbed my guitar from its secret location. He provided words of wisdom as I confirmed tuning. Near the end of his speech, I'd approach the dance floor and perform. Then, our guests would send us off on our honeymoon–handkerchiefs and happy tears.

Before that night, I'd never played my music in public. Every potential piece of critique kept my work private. Despite the crowd, I locked in on a single soul. I meant every word. As I wrote them. As I rehearsed them. As I gave the gift of music. Although seething with insecurity, I truly meant it. Real dreams take effort. Fortune requires acknowledgment. Promises endure pain.

Several months after my wedding, my best friend called to ask for a recording of the song. "I've had the melody in my head all day, but I don't remember the words. It's driving me crazy."

"Dude, I don't have the right gear for that," I argued. "Producing studio quality music's difficult."

Laying on theatrics, he coaxed, "It'd be cool if you did. It's really good. Don't you feel my pain, Tong-O-Nong-Yong?! I have a mystery song stuck in my head!"

If I, a meager rocker without a band, were to record, I needed a reputable identity to capture the correct target audience. Dropping tracks under my given name could peg me as a singer/songwriter. I titled my independent project TaKen, a versatile rock moniker with subtle inclusion of my initials.

My new nuptials and traditional career path diminished my dreams of stardom. I couldn't even call music production a hobby at that point. For years, an old three-subject notebook filled with lyric fragments, incomplete riffs, and a two-song catalog told my story. Lack of knowledge always eclipsed the allure of writing. My best friend's simple request jumpstarted my home studio aspirations. Stop overthinking; get to work. After recording the song with an M-Audio Fast Track, I dropped a low-quality version of "When Will I Wake Up" on myspace.

The track sat on a forgotten playlist until 2008 when I received a DM from Quickstar Productions. They offered to remaster it for an acoustic compilation CD. For $200, I got a hundred physical copies, publication to streaming services, and profits from online sales outlets. If this was real, it was a lifelong dream realized. To have my song in physical form? To see my name in print like that?

After another quick trip to Music Mart for a Peavey microphone and Boss Micro BR, I worked on recording a better version of the song. My knowledge of the process was inspired by the Blue Oyster Cult Behind the Music skit on SNL. The band members play the piece in one room, capturing every instrument in one flawless take. When legendary rock producer Bruce Dickinson finds fault, everyone starts over. Although archaic, this method seemed pure to me.

Three all-nighters and fifty-two takes later, I appeased the finicky needs of my inner Bruce Dickinson. Packing my submission, I sent it certified mail to confirm receipt prior to the deadline.

My plan to set and forget the project was interrupted with unexpected updates: cover artwork design, final master approval, pictures of palletized boxes, tracking numbers. After what felt like a year, I received undeniable confirmation of my status as a recording artist. Even better, my song followed the highest rated track from the album on iTunes. Hundreds of unsuspecting listeners would catch my music while listening to the song they actually bought the CD for. If a spark hit the primordial soup just right, my shot at superstardom resided inside the ooze.

My home studio has morphed quite a bit since then. I've upgraded the Peavey microphone, Boss Micro BR, and cheap Johnson acoustic guitar. The plastic rolling cart, filling space most places I've ever lived, still holds accessories, tabs, notepads, cables, *Zen of Screaming* DVDs, and training videos.

My lonely telephone remains open for my shot at the big time. So far, I've only accrued interest in extending my car's warranty. Maybe one day, a serious inquiry will jumpstart my career. Until then, I cling to the humble beginnings of my home studio origin story.

Breathe Into Me / Red

Red's debut album, *End of Silence*, released on June 6, 2006. How on earth would I know that? A Google search? Nope. I remember the date because I remember what I was doing. My wedding was June 3. On June 4, my new wife and I left on our honeymoon. Imagine an action-packed week filled with zoo visits, amusement park rides, and home essential shopping interrupted by some prima donna searching for an obscure album release.

Could I have ordered it online to review when we returned? Yep, I could've done that, but I wanted it ON release date. Could I have purchased it on iTunes? Yep, I could've done that, but this band was new. I NEEDED the whole musical experience. One doesn't get album artwork and liner notes with a digital copy. However, they can digitize a physical CD. It's simple: physical art receives greater appreciation.

I'd hate to cast the impression I sidetracked a seven-day romantic rendezvous searching for a CD. I might be an idiot, but not an absolute idiot. My album quest led us to places near our natural destinations. *End of Silence* and Day of Fire's *Cut and Move* was purchased at our fifth stop on June 6. May my conscience rest a little clearer with this confession: I spent a portion of my own honeymoon fanning the flames of my New Release Tuesday addiction.

Bayonetwork: Vultures in Vivid Color / Norma Jean

My first job after college was door-to-door supplemental insurance sales. I had a trip to Chicago scheduled to receive company training to learn about our coverage, memorize the sales pitch, and handle objections. First, I had to become licensed. After a five-day intensive prep course pouring over North Dakota insurance law and ethics, my employment was contingent upon passing a hundred-question test.

At night, I crammed for the exam in a hotel room while listening to Norma Jean's *O God: The Aftermath*. I can't explain the psychology behind it, but aggressive music soothes me. The chaotic audio converts a complex torrent of emotion into something I can process sensually.

Is it a useful study aid? I passed, so I'd have to say yes. I mean, barely, though—a one question cushion to the minimum passing grade. So, I'd also have to say no. Like the medical student who graduates last in their class still gets to practice medicine, I was licensed to sell insurance.

I'm still splitting hairs on Norma Jean's role in my early professional life. No matter how I look at it, they were responsible. I passed because they helped me. In potential failure, they were terrible employment-blocking acquaintances. If Norma Jean hindered me in any way, I would've cut them out of my life. Can you imagine the travesty of missing their later catalog? I could care less. How else should a young man, the classic protector/provider, conduct their personal business?

Wasteland / 10 Years

If you asked me what aspiring political scientists did for employment in 2006, I'd tell you they sold supplemental insurance door-to-door. After completing my training, I took up my tie collection and company binder to pound pavement in endless cold calls. My immediate supervisor, a dude I had several classes with, defined my sales territory. With 10% of Dickinson State University's political science graduates peddling the product, I have to believe it's true.

The thin in-town population of southwestern North Dakota communities put us in remote, rural areas. We took turns driving as I settled into my new occupation. The space between places we could cold call left room for hours of unintentional music review sessions. My manager loved listening to punk records. If I was lucky, he'd settle on Less Than Jake, Say Anything, or a teen dude soundtrack with a Blink 182 song. That was rare, though.

When I took up driving responsibilities, I'd "accidentally" leave my CD binder at home to bask in the complexity of 10 Years' first album all day. The struggle for stereo control was real.

If you shadowed me that summer, you'd find me cruising country roads in a 98 Ford decorated with flaming warrior head stickers, jamming to 10 Years, enroute to my next insurance sales stop. Taking the rejections personally. Not selling much of anything, but learning more about music than I ever thought possible.

The Tide Began to Rise / Demon Hunter

You know what else dudes with political science degrees do? They become officers in the military. The way I saw it, the Army helped me achieve first-generation college graduate status. They should reap the benefits of my advanced education. Submitting my application packet, I was accepted into Officer Candidate School.

After spending twenty-seven days doing regular civilian stuff, like going to work and paying bills, I'd have to report to an aggressive basic training-like environment. The former basketball player in me knew exactly what to do. One weekend a month, I had a 250-mile pregame commute to find the right mindset.

With so many great tracks, Demon Hunter's *The Triptych* was my go-to drive CD. If I made it through Officer Candidate School, the reins of the National Guard's future rested in my palms. A type of leadership that requires unifying Soldiers, across all walks of life, to complete complex missions. Also, it requires confidence and competence: the innate ability to look your Soldiers eyeball to eyeball, deliver a solid plan to take the hill—without breaking laws or getting people killed, and defending the American way of life.

Aside from combat, the average Guardsman/Guardswoman joins to serve our community. When disaster strikes, we use these same skill sets to bring relief to the homeland. Fires and floods, tornados and tragedy, we answer the call. We don't salivate at the concept of war; we serve from a genuine place of love. For our families, for our friends, for our neighbors, for our communities. This type of leadership requires strength, but without utter callousness to the point of lost compassion.

When I call curtains on my military career, retrospect should reflect, if I didn't lead with heart, there was no meaning to my service.

3x3 We Carried Your Body / Living Sacrifice

Once I left college, my free time was spent researching new Christian metal bands to bring to the masses. Great success with Demon Hunter, Haste the Day, and Norma Jean left me foraging the family tree of the Christian metal scene. Who was the undeniable source, the godfather—if you will, to where my music found its market?

All signs pointed to Living Sacrifice. As I discovered, many bands built off the limited success they achieved. Wading through the filthy resistance of Christian and secular markets for twelve years, they hit stride with *Conceived in Fire*.

I spent several months listening to any Christian metal band I could find, testing thousands of albums against the magic of *Conceived in Fire*. Without a clue to the end game, I knew what I was looking for had to exist. No matter how daunting a thousand-mile journey may be, you have to be willing to put cold feet to the floor. I would urge you to never neglect where that journey started, the location of your first steps.

Mausoleum / Karnivool

My pilgrimage into Christian metal began with a borrowed hard drive chocked full of over a thousand unfiltered albums. Scandinavian, black, death, speed, hair, metalcore, doom, and every other subgenre. First, I bit the symbolic jugular owned by Living Sacrifice. After that, rhyme and reason dictated visiting the remaining bands in alphabetical order. I stumbled across Comeback Kid, Extol, fewleftstanding, Figure Four, Gryp, Nodes of Ranvier, Officer Negative, Still Breathing, Stretch Armstrong, Strongarm, early-era Underoath, Zao, and many other bands I could keep listing all day.

On the other hand, most bands weren't worth another listen. The way I saw it, if you want to find hidden treasure, you have to be willing to wade through murky waters. Believe me when I tell you I did.

Hiding somewhere near the middle of the hard drive, a weird bookmark of sorts, was Karnivool's *Themata*. I still can't fathom why it was there. It isn't Christian, nor metal by most metalhead's definition. Yet, each song had impact, even the eleven-second silent track entitled "Omitted for Clarity." Let's put it this way: after several hours of reading lyrics along with screaming vocals, a dude's frontal lobe starts throbbing.

I hate to be the person to say it, and hopefully, metal purists forgive me, but Karnivool provided me with much-needed headache relief. Let the pretentious gatekeepers snatch my metalhead status. In my defense, my genuine love for music transcends their need to keep people in blemish-free boxes.

Grave / Nodes of Ranvier

When I tell people I'm from North Dakota, I get two responses: "How's the Sturgis Bike Rally?" or "Sweet! My family went to Mount Rushmore when I was a kid." Maybe I'm dissecting microscopic hairs, but I can only conclude: 1) people assume North Dakota is a fictional land OR 2) people find my home state so boring that we have to travel elsewhere for entertainment. Since North Dakota's represented by one of the fifty stars on our nation's flag, I have to conclude the latter.

No matter the level of truth, I don't appreciate facts being hurled at my face. Can you imagine loading up the covered wagon for treacherous twelve-hour journeys to catch the latest sensation in concert? The struggle is very real. Until we start talking music, I take offense being associated with the other Dakota. Sure, North Dakotans can claim Johnny Lang's "Lie to Me" and Wiz Khalifa's "Black and Yellow," but neither song satisfies my fix for furious music.

While poking around the heavy metal hard drive, I found Nodes of Ranvier. The stars aligned for them in several ways. A metal band signed by

Victory Records, these South Dakota boys launched from where others didn't dare to leave. A musical concoction earning Nodes of Ranvier one new fan during my Thousand Album March. With half a hard drive left to sift through, I slowed down for one solid evening to reflect upon *The Years to Come*.

Paralyzing Kings / 10 Years

My gift to the world is amateur analysis of complicated song lyrics. I investigate these things so you don't have to. Sometimes, I even project Christian themes onto secular acts. My own writing grapples with denying desires of the flesh to feed spiritual needs. Why wouldn't other artists feel the crushing weight of being truly human?

On two different occasions, my best friend and I engaged in heated debate on the topic. After I found Flaw's *Endangered Species* in 2005, "You've Changed" got me thinking: what personality shift caused Chris Volz' frustration? My friend and I both knew "Whole" explored his devout Catholic mother's suicide. To me, if Chris saw ending your life as blatant disrespect to the Holy Trinity, he maintained some sort of belief system. "You've Changed" was a clear lamentation of watching one of his friends circle the drain. My friend wasn't convinced.

I revived the argument when five.bolt.main's *Venting* came out. The same guy, a few short years later, wrote about navigating stormy weather with a broken compass. You're telling me a strict religious upbringing doesn't feed artistic interpretation of spiritual quandaries? Despite clear proven parallels, my friend still wasn't convinced.

That's why I love 10 Years. Their name alone is cloaked in ambiguity. I started a separate hour-long argument over the lyrical content in "Paralyzing Kings." "Righteous Pharisees befriending silent movements? Absent-minded actions outweigh forgiveness? Come on! It's all right there!"

My friend shot back, "You're reaching! They're just pretty words."

"What about the crowd surrounding Jesus during the crucifixion?" I continued. "'Father, forgive them, for they know not what they do?' They're pretty similar pretty words."

"10 Years isn't Christian!" He chuckled, almost mocking me.

It was the closest I ever got to winning an argument with him. Part of me knew he maintained argumentative charades to get a rise from people. If he didn't concede defeat, I couldn't win. Despite cross-referenced exhibits and rock-solid logic, my friend still wasn't convinced.

A Cross and a Girl Named Blessed / Evans Blue

A few months after college graduation, I landed a Saturday morning side hustle as a rural route carrier. If it's not common knowledge, mailboxes perch on the opposite side of normal traffic flow. Rural carriers weren't assigned European-styled LLVs people associate with the United States Postal Service; we drove our own vehicles. For easy access, we coasted the span between mail receptacles from the passenger side. To add unnecessary pressure, retired farmers would impatiently pace at the mere mention of a one-minute mail call delay.

CD swapping became an unsafe luxury. I gravitated to reputable albums with solid track lists: Red's *End of Silence*, Project 86's *Songs to Burn Your Bridges By*, five.bolt.main's *Venting*, and Evans Blue's *The Melody and the Energetic Nature of Volume*. Imagine, if you will, Kevin Matisyn serenading the routine of a humdrum job. I could hardly discern the real weight of work, but this was as close to perfect as I could get.

The Ending of Autumn / Hundredfold

That fall, I accepted a third part-time job as Ministry Director for Youth for Christ. The musician in me delivered the Gospel through gratuitous use of song lyrics. Ministry's much more than preaching, though. It's Bible studies. It's conversing with hurting, confused kids. For my wife and me, it was volunteering at a local youth club when concerts came through town.

That's right—my musical journey drilled so underground, it struck the weak veins of rural, Southwest North Dakota. We're talking bands like Noise Union (RIP), This Is Luke (RIP), and Hundredfold (RIP). If my own high school experience was true, keeping idle teen hands busy was necessary to avoid potential crises.

Void of formal training, I hurled experimental handfuls of inspirational spaghetti to see what stuck. Adolescent life's fragile enough. What if my educated guesses created more questions than answers? If one careless misstep caused them to stumble? How does one convey a message they've barely figured out for themself? All I knew to do was point them toward Jesus. Then, we would mosh. On second thought, I guess I knew how to do two things.

Headspin / Lukas Rossi

At the start of our marriage, my wife was a loyal reality TV fan. Despite her mild-mannered demeanor, she found outlet in *Big Brother* house guests provoking controversy, rooting for underdogs to thrive in cruel environments. She didn't need drama in her actual life. Tucked behind the protection of a fourth wall, she received safe minimal doses of emotional tension. While I never understood the concept of reality TV, I watched with her to unite interests. I guess great marriages require basic compromise.

During a commercial break for *Big Brother*, I was introduced to *Rock Star: Supernova*. Imagine a rock-styled *American Idol* where judges Jason Newsted, Tommy Lee, and Gilby Clarke award a record deal and supporting tour. Talent reality TV shows all work the same. Some famous host—in this case, Dave Navarro—announces contestants for their chance at recognition. Some are horrendous; some talented; some promising with appropriate mentorship. The show hosts a callback and eliminates singers every week until a champion is crowned. Like I said, *American Idol* with one key difference: hidden rock gems jammed into an hour of live performance.

My Thousand Album March distracted interest from the dull allure of prescribed television. Why watch the man's ramblings when I so clearly controlled my entertainment needs?

Rock Star: Supernova was different. From the moment Lukas Rossi graced the stage, I needed to validate my ability to recognize artistic potential. We couldn't afford a TiVo, but never missed an episode. I even recall skipping social events to catch the show in broadcast. Sure enough, his passionate performances and Rise Electric discography was the perfect concoction for reality TV victory.

Let's talk about the real winner, though. If you ask me, I won. My quick romp through the endless maze of reality TV was complete. Where others have tried and failed, I retired from a desolate institution with an undefeated record. My prize: a lifetime supply of affirmation in my ability to gauge raw talent.

Impossible / Manafest

I am not a rap fan. The six tracks in the book playlist, depending on how loose we cling to a definition, can vouch for that. Let's admit my musical fabric includes miniscule threads of the genre. The occasional, glaring social commentary on the pressures of poverty fades to parties. Clubs. Money. Girls. Grow up. It gets old to me.

Enters Manafest, a Canadian rapper discovered by Thousand Foot Krutch's Trevor McNevan. His dad died by suicide and he shared freely. The residual aftermath, the abandonment, the depression found a home in his lyrical content. Like me, he wanted to use personal tragedy as a means to serve others.

You see, there are two versions of people who exist: the inner torment and the outward projection. Social media was new back then, but the hologram of plastic perfection was not. Especially in youth ministry, I thought about the concept every day. How many kids faked performance for appearance? Harbored dark secrets needing a shoulder? Oh, the stuff I hid, that terrorized me or drove insignificance, in my own fragile teenage years. Maybe that's why, around this time, my dreams of stardom waned. It doesn't take a rock star to change the world; my sphere of influence required a grassroots movement.

Adrenaline / 12 Stones

For our second 12 Stones show, I assembled my wife and faithful concert buddy, Jesse, to watch them with Chris Daughtry at the North Dakota State Fair. Keep in mind, I don't hate Daughtry. My Absent Element CD would declare different—a special piece of merch history his tear-streamed fans wouldn't even recognize. Catching him was added icing on the cake.

12 Stones opened with a humble set from their three-album discography. Now, I'm usually the pit peacekeeper, preventing injuries and handsy perverts since 2004. In a strange twist, I was the maniac amongst

American Idol fans. I guess music never moved them before. Sometimes, the institution calls for some respectful rowdiness to make the crowd bounce.

"What's HE doing, Mom?" I overheard a teenage girl whisper to her mother.

"Don't worry about him, babe," her middle-aged mom replied back, emphasizing every syllable to ensure we heard her. "Daughtry's not like THIS," pointing toward us with a trembling finger.

From the stage, Paul shouted, "Y'all ready to get some adrenaline pumping? All right! We got one last song, then come chill with us at our merch booth. We'd love to meet you!"

"Are you serious?!" I screamed. "Let's go!"

We stirred the pit one last time before calling for an encore. "One more song… One more song…" Our cries denied as Daughtry's crew began set-up.

Rounding up my entourage, we left our usual front-of-center spot to meet my boys. Approaching the band wearing shirts circa 2003—my wife's with an image when Kevin Dorr was still bassist—turned heads amidst the Daughtry-accrued, fair-weather fans. It was our job to portray how the legend, that is 12 Stones, journeyed to rural North Dakota. We traded stories about the *Scorpion King/Daredevil* soundtracks, "Bring Me to Life," and an early bootleg concert DVD from Mandeville, LA after their first album.

The band packed up; we moved to the outer edge of the crowd to catch Daughtry. Although different from our usual concert experience, it was nice to watch a show from that far back. Cloud nine's haze was interrupted by a quick shoulder tap. Turning around, I was face-to-face with Aaron Gainer. "Can I join you?" he asked.

"Absolutely!" I said, presenting the vacant space next to me. "I meant to ask, Paul's Finger Eleven shirt—you guys ever tour with them?"

"Nope, just huge fans," Aaron replied. "What's your favorite album?"

"Dude! *Greyest of Blue Skies*, for sure. It's so good."

In all the commotion, Eric Weaver and Justin Rimer joined us. "What're we talking about?" Eric asked. "Finger Eleven albums? Yeah, *Tip's* where it's at."

"I'll give it another listen. Have you guys heard Daughtry's Absent Element record?" I asked, before being interrupted by autograph-seeking blonde girls in red halter tops. We traded album recommendations for ten minutes straight, never once mentioning 12 Stones.

Autographs and pictures are nice, but try describing moments they've given me through media players over the years. "I was sad. I listened to 12 Stones. I got better." That story's boring. You know what isn't? Being fangirls with the dudes from 12 Stones at a Daughtry concert. People will listen to that one.

Storm the Gates of Hell / Demon Hunter

I have two tattoos. I got my first when I graduated from college. It's Galatians 2:20 with a shaded image of Jesus behind it. The verse is my contractual agreement with God: "It is no longer I who live, but Christ who lives in me; and the life I now live in the flesh I live for the Son of God who loved and gave Himself for me." In my constant state of identity crisis, sometimes, I need a reminder.

I got my second to commemorate graduation from Officer Candidate School. To date, this course is my proudest professional achievement. If I'm honest, I didn't know whether I'd graduate until those coveted gold bars were pinned to my chest. The tattoo's a Demon Hunter logo on a Full Metal Jacket helmet arranged into a military coin. A circular inscription around the edge reads: "Wake the lifeless; die to fight this; stand beside me; Storm the Gates of Hell." In a fallen world, warfare, both spiritual and actual, is a harsh reality. In either instance, war requires vigor and unbridled intensity. Sometimes, I need a reminder.

I knew the expectation while swearing into the Army. Scanning garbage piles for roadside bombs on slow crawling convoys. Dodging stray rockets launched in fiery trails from distant hilltops. The increasing shriek of artillery rounds before exploding into their final resting place. Indiscriminate bullets delivering death sentences in pursuit of the enemy.

It wasn't about me anymore. My fears became the very problems I dutifully solved. Every frantic situation—these stressful, violent puzzles—concluded only when my Soldiers returned to their families.

Few lyricists can pen inspiration to such a lofty realization. Similar to the day of my baptism, it was, once again, Ryan Clark. If I'm expected to lead Soldiers into the pits of Hell, I have to instill confidence for them to follow me there. So, I say again, "Wake the lifeless. Die to fight this. Stand beside me. STORM THE GATES OF HELL."

Failure / Unloco

That summer, I secured my first professional job as a Resident Director. Was that enough to make me happy? Sure, sort of. Yet with every significant change,

I need a corresponding identity crisis looming in counterpoint. I epitomized the American Dream: a meaningful career with benefits, an officer position in the National Guard, a youth group, a framed college diploma, a picket fence princess. Every bootstrap tug paid massive dividends, almost with an unrealistic return rate.

As a child, a life of failure signaled eternal loneliness. What if my friend circle only expanded due to my fortune? Would the same be true if my newfound success was stripped from me? Would people associate with me, then? Classic over-analysis eclipsed my level of limited success.

Falls Apart / Hurt

Even worse, what if I jeopardized good fortune with a careless mistake? My lousy track record almost mandated a critical slip. It's silly to ignore the wet floor signs, right? Those same fair-weather friends leaving me sprawled out in the mess I'd made. All it would take was one mistake and my entire empire would come crashing down.

The Bird and the Worm / The Used

My first officer assignment was platoon leader in a horizontal construction company. With all of life's crazy meandering, my right-hand man was the first squad leader I reported to as a young private. Remember the National Guard Soldier's wedding I attended at nine years old? The guy who inspired my G.I. Joe purchase? He was my partner in crime. More ironically, he still worked with my dad at Stark County Social Services.

I'll never forget Dad's stern warning as we exchanged my first salute: "Take care of your Soldiers. Listen to your NCOs. If I ever find out that you mistreat them, don't worry about UCMJ; I'll find you." His dress uniform's pristine condition, seventeen years past his own retirement, said everything. Father/son relationship aside, never mess with the United States Army.

"Dad, don't talk through your salute," I ordered. "Troop care is cutting time in formation."

"Keep it up," he smirked. "We'll see what your platoon sergeant says after drill."

Platoon leadership was a great experience. The training. Equipment maintenance. Interpersonal communications. Professional development. Ordering beans, bullets, and band-aids. Most nights, I crawled to my room at a small hunting lodge after dark. With physical fitness in the morning, I had just enough time to nuke a meal and call home. Nodding off mere moments later, The Used's *Lies for the Liars* documentary blared in the background. It took me three months to watch the whole twenty-minute video. Despite my deep infatuation with Bert McCracken's creative process, my eyelids were too heavy to hold open.

An old Army commercial boasted higher productivity before nine a.m. than the rest of America. Some may remember the claim. Long and short, the early bird gets the worm. Ironic lesson to learn while exploring the *Lies for the Liars* backstory, eh?

In Vain / Mad at Gravity

Back to the quandary. Sometimes, leadership feels like a fruitless endeavor. Whether guiding my residents, Soldiers, or youth group, every avenue took months to generate tangible results. Let's say, a student was struggling in the college environment. My staff and I counseled them, consoled their fears, and resourced their concerns. If they moved into the next semester, we obtained first proof of success. Since leadership's about influence, not control, all we could do is mentor them toward the next imaginary line.

The ultimate goal is graduation, right? Were these little conversations impactful enough to nudge students toward a magical date FIVE YEARS into the future? Try identifying evidential momentum in real-time.

I'd often field phone calls from helicopter parents. "Yes, ma'am. I'll have your daughter call you. No, ma'am. She seems to be doing well. Yes, ma'am. Sometimes, college kids need space. It's hard not to hover, but I promise our staff does everything we can to prepare them for the world." Those were my comments by day. Then, I committed hypocrisy by night, making the very mistakes I nagged parents about.

Loyalty / American Head Charge

Chad Gray wore an American Head Charge hoodie during a Mudvayne concert in Minneapolis. The clown from *The Feeding* album artwork gawked at me throughout their whole hour-long set. Didn't my brother Chad's girlfriend have a cousin from Minneapolis who toured with American Head Charge? Smooth move, Mr. Gray, pander to the local crowd.

You could almost sense the judgment in the clown's eyes. "Ha, ha-ha, ha-ha, ha! I know an album you don't!" Both Chads, Chad Gray and my brother, suggested I check it out. Take it from me, Chads know their way around a good time. I had no other option than to be a sheeple.

Vices Like Vipers / Oh, Sleeper

Heavy Christian music experienced a massive awakening in the mid-2000s. For the first time, us scene kids didn't need to sacrifice quality for messaging. With releases from bands like Oh, Sleeper, Inhale/Exhale, Staple, Dead Poetic, and Red, we found solace with topics taboo to church attendance. Our secular counterparts even noted positive shifts in lyrical content, overall musicianship, and production quality. The sun set on corny Christian music.

In turn, the gap between Christian and secular metalheads narrowed. Our metal scene credibility opened more honest, respectful dialogue evangelical Christians didn't dare to drum up: suicide and addiction, death and destruction, heaven and hell. Oh, the judgment-free discussions artistry afforded us. Conversations void of persuasive pretense. Conversations shifting seamlessly from guitar tone to the human condition. Sure, Jesus stated we are not of this world, but doesn't our temporary residence on this pale blue orb call for some capital improvements?

Wounds / InMe

I can't recall when I came across InMe's *Overgrown Eden*. I do remember when I fell in love with it, though. My first significant project as an officer was a border road construction mission in Yuma, AZ. We had two weeks to patch up potholes in an existing road and place the base for a new trail.

Arriving on site before dawn to shoo snoozing rattlesnakes from our equipment, we worked in the sweltering, late-June heat until the sun peaked, then packed up early to repeat the process. My battle-tested Soldiers often compared the 115-degree temperatures, and trash-covered sand dunes, to Iraqi deserts. At mission completion, we tacked on a two-mile stretch of new road, cranking out 1/3 of a mile per day. Not bad for a rag-tag group of North Dakota boys.

Since my Soldiers were true professionals, I aspired to be an even better leader. After sending them off for the afternoon, I completed my reports, prepared the next morning's safety brief, calculated stockpiled materials, and wrote performance evaluations. I preferred completing these administrative tasks later to observe road construction in real time. If I behaved, my troops even let me operate the vibe roller (I'm guessing to minimize project site damage), but still, heavy machinery was involved. Grabbing a chilled strawberry lemonade, I'd throw *Overgrown Eden* on and knock out some spreadsheets from the air-conditioned comfort of my room.

Vices / Dead Poetic

Addiction takes the forefront of everything, forcing all other priorities. It's widely seen and vastly judged. We all have disgusting flaws that strangle us despite our best efforts to pry them away. While it may be difficult to expose these shortcomings, everyone has them. Everyone has an internal spiritual conflict. Everyone harbors unmentionable dirty deeds, seething with the shameful seeds of robotic response. When will we realize these imperfections unify us more than we'd care to admit?

Sixteen / Demon Hunter (Ft. Bruce Fitzhugh)

Why don't rock/metal collaborations happen as often as they do in rap? Where some rap songs have several guest vocalists per track, you're lucky to grab one feature on a metal disc. Industry newcomers require trusted henchmen to inch the gate open. "C'mon through, little buddy! If you break anything, your escort is responsible. Further access to our coveted kingdom shall be granted if you prove yourself on the supporting tour." Card-carrying members control access to our community.

Demon Hunter didn't need Bruce Fitzhugh's buy-in on their fourth album. Without a consistent touring schedule, my boys were already staples to the metal community. You see, this collaboration was never meant to establish credibility. "Sixteen" warns with a Surgeon General's seriousness: unprotected exposure to fame can cause soul decay. Given my addictive nature, what on earth would I do with fifteen minutes in the spotlight? Better yet, was I prepared for the golden thread of terminal consequence presenting itself in minute sixteen?

Stitches / Haste the Day

In my young professional life, I wasn't equipped to deal with conflict. I needed to be liked. I needed to be a stone-chiseled hero. Oh, I said a lot of words to tiptoe through daily interactions. Carefully selected words to present the least offensive, abrasive, critical concepts. Then, and only then, I donned my needle and thread. Sew the lip with surgical precision to avoid further conflict. I believed people would sense my wisdom, ask for further guidance, and repent when necessary. I allowed destiny to dictate how I developed people.

Meanwhile, I received financial compensation from three different organizations to lead others. My residents were hurting. They wrestled with identity apart from their family of origin, interpersonal relationships, unfamiliar freedom, and careers. Members of my youth group were hurting. They wrestled with managing parental expectations, budding identities, peer pressure, and maintaining purity amidst teenage rebellion. My Soldiers were hurting. They wrestled with the weight of warfare, using alcohol to stomp out survivor's guilt, depressive thoughts spinning into suicidal ideation, and juggling Army requirements with civilian career aspirations and demanding home lives.

Still, I sewed my mouth shut—not to offend, appear judgmental, or stress them out. Excuses always come easier than solutions. The truth remains, I felt rejection of my ideas was blatant, open rejection of me as a person. If I played the part, I could avoid the hurt. Nothing could change until I learned to speak a challenging five-word sentence. Gripping the bathroom sink after my daily shave, I'd stare into the depths of my soul in the mirror and whisper, "You're worth more than this." Once this truth became clear to me, maybe I could persuade others of their potential.

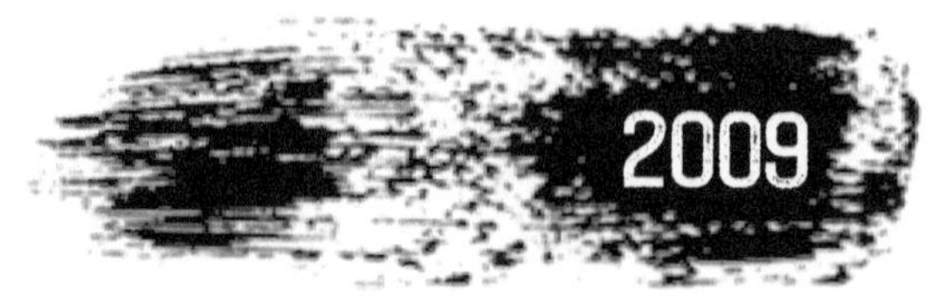

Deliverance / We as Human

North Dakotans are a resilient people. If you need proof, I want you to imagine living in a place where January temperatures frequent -20°F. Pretty cold, right? Now, imagine the fortitude required to inhabit this frozen tundra year after year. You'd almost expect the brutality of a Viking. That's where you'd be wrong. In all my cool-guy Army travels, Canadians are the only other group of people I've met who could rival a North Dakotan in kindness.

You need further proof? A blizzard dumped ten inches of snow on us the morning my National Guard unit reported to support flood relief. While mother nature hurled insults at already existing injuries, I couldn't get my car out of the parking lot. Duty called, so I took the last remaining mode of transportation available. With two duffel bags and a rucksack filled with cold weather gear, I started the one-mile journey via leathered personnel carrier. Not because I'm fantastic, but because I'd witnessed countless other people do it.

At the halfway point, a tractor operator offered me a ride to the armory. This Good Samaritan left his warm, cozy bed to help people clear their driveways, FOR FREE. He interrupted one random act of kindness to commit another. So, yeah, we're tough, friendly people.

Boy, the North Dakota floodwaters raged in 2009. So much so, my unit was activated for a second mobilization that concluded the day after my brother Matthew's graduation. My Commander granted me leave to attend the ceremony. After thirty whole days supporting the state, on two occasions, I paid my dues.

Grabbing We as Human's *Until We're Dead*, I headed back home. The four-hour drive gave me time to think. *How are these dudes still independent? How did they write and record this alone? Maybe there's hope for me, yet.*

I might've been speeding. I might've only made one pit stop. I might've had a bathroom related near-miss upon my arrival. However, I slid into an empty chair as an old lady banged out "Pomp and Circumstance" from a stage-side upright piano. My renewed dreams of rock stardom would have to wait; it was someone else's time to shine.

My Alibi / Blindside

Most young professionals want to believe they're offered jobs based upon credentials. They're young enough, and naïve enough, to believe they're unique, magical snowflakes. The reality continually remains, it's not WHAT you know, but WHO you know. Until recently, I used to believe my experiences set me apart from the rest of the blizzard. Yet most of my professional assignments were a direct result of someone knowing who I was, what I was good at, and where I needed improvement.

Even as a Christian, I maintain a belief system hinged upon the need for a righteous Savior to stand on my behalf on Judgment Day. Nothing I could ever say, or do, on my own would grant me keys to the Kingdom. At the end of my life, all I can do is point toward Jesus and let him corroborate my alibi. It's never been about what I know, but Who I know.

Basking in youthful ignorance, I believed my encyclopedic knowledge of the music industry set me apart, too. Humor me as I sift the dirt from this rabbit hole. Let's say somebody with industry relevance approaches me. As per usual, I gift them from the memory bank of random band factoids or acknowledge subtle lyrics from some obscure release. Kinda like the time I tried discussing Josh Brown's discography with Fireflight's Dawn Michele. I expected this poor girl to respond with: "You're familiar with his work in Day of Fire and Full Devil Jacket? That's awesome! Tell you what, void of any tangible musical ability, I'll have our agent call you."

For what?! An album full of rhythmic, spoken-word research over djenty breakdowns? Get your pen ready; you just witnessed the live birth of Wikipediacore.

World So Cold / 12 Stones

Studying mass shootings is amongst my greatest guilty pleasures. The stark contrast between differing dynamics is intriguing. Take Columbine, for example. I dissected every piece of media surrounding Dylan Klebold and Eric Harris in twisted, back-alley assessment. What delusion drove these tormented psychos to kill?

On the other hand, I poured over the courageous actions of Rachel Scott and Cassie Bernall. These girls glared death in the face to defend their beliefs. Feats of greatness are as interesting as society's decays. For every evil person, I need reassurance many more potential heroes exist.

When the Virginia Tech shooting happened, I researched Seung-Hui Cho and the victims. Some YouTuber even set the day's news footage to 12 Stones' "World So Cold." Paul and I spent an entire afternoon trying to crack the complex algebraic equation of devastating loss. Answers in hand, I scrawled the flow chart on a dry-erase board for my youth group. "You see, pain morphs into hate that churns endless, unanswerable questions. These lonely questions fester into a permanent stain of cancerous growth stealing so many young lives. Don't suffer in silence. Reach out if you need help. If you're well, be available for someone else's outstretched hand."

Maybe that's why we take to social media when tragedy strikes. Somehow, we need acknowledgment in the chaos. Even after a lengthy sensing session with my youth group, I still had the bitter taste of humanity's true condition clinging to my palate. I recorded and posted a spoken word poetry piece entitled "Our Lives Are Like Knives" to myspace. Point being, our lives are a tool—providing help or dishing out harm on a treacherous collision course. We get a vote on how we live. Mahatma Gandhi said, and my misguided youthful zeal would echo the concept, we must be the change we wish to see in the world.

Kingdom of the Blind / Dry Kill Logic

Oh, my bleeding heart! Amidst the confusion of the Virginia Tech shootings, I got my first glimpse of potential hate crimes. The college I worked at had a large international student population. Another ignorant student spraypainted "Free Tibet" on another student's car simply due to their coincidental citizenship. We never located the coward.

You could sense the tension around campus while I made my rounds later that evening. My phone rang as I passed between buildings to console concerned students. "This is Tony. Where? Altringer Apartments? I'm on my way."

One of my California residents called to report an attempted burglary, which local police ruled out. With nothing missing, the young officer narrowed motives down to a heartless prank or race-related crime.

"Wait," the student whispered. "They think this happened because I'm black? What if they do it again?"

"I'll have campus security watch your place a little closer," I said. "Would you like me to call someone to stay with you?"

"No, thanks. This just sucks, you know?"

An hour later, I returned to my office. My pulse knocked within my neck, causing confusing cranial surges, as I wrote up the report. Throughout my life, and studies, I'd read of occasional racism. Before that evening, they were unfamiliar fairy tales from historical faraway lands.

With Dry Kill Logic's "Kingdom of the Blind" repeating on my iPod, the rage subsided. My poor residents shouldn't have to creep around uncertain corners because we failed to keep them safe. Regardless of this travesty, I couldn't allow others to redefine North Dakota Nice. My people are respectful and loving—not perpetrators of hate. Say what you want, but if you cauterize the heart, you kill the kindness.

Deathbed / Relient K (Ft. Jon Foreman)

Logging life's details isn't foreign to me. In Christian circles, sharing your story's a big deal. I was once owned by depression, suicidal ideation, and a crippling past. Jesus came into my life and dramatically transformed me. Since then, I served as student body president, graduated from college, and stormed the workforce with three leadership positions. Jesus saved me from self-imposed disaster.

After accepting Christ, nothing terrible ever happened to me again. I adopted the coveted Christian Poker Face. Practice at home with me. First, grab your Bible from your bedside nightstand. Using your left hand, pin it symbolically to your ribcage just below your heart. An unbelieving public should know you believe the Bible to be accurate. So accurate, your life is based upon it.

Keep your right hand free for handshakes, high fives, pats on the back, and the widely-popularized Christian side hug. Trust me, temptation decreases when the space between private parts increases.

Next, work on your smile. Pastors, other Christians, and mainly, non-believers need to know you want nothing more than what God has gifted you. You're too blessed to be stressed. Not only do you understand it all, but you're ecstatic about it.

If you must, perfect your pose in the mirror. Don't force your smile. Bible tucked. Right hand extended. Perfected sincerity shows the joy you've obtained to a fallen world.

It's pretty obvious; I still struggled with stuff. When asked to share my testimony on Easter Sunday, I felt the church needed profound transparency. How else would God use me? Not wanting to just regurgitate past details, I anticipated God would help me overcome my biggest struggles: divorce, abandoning my children, and addiction.

Using Relient K's "Deathbed" as inspiration, my speech summarized one key point: broken people need constant support to avoid repeating their personal history. Was I doing all I could to stop letting my past define my future? No matter how futile the fight, another day of life means another volley for the war. Someday, Jesus will validate the authenticity of my faith. Until then, true sincerity was achieved between Freudian slips of my Christian Poker Face.

Never Too Late / Three Days Grace

Nearing the end of another academic year, I glanced down the barrel of my departure from North Dakota. After six months of officer training, I'd leave home forever for the vast sunshine of an unknown world. In my personal farewell tour of sorts, I attended every concert available to create lasting memories with close friends and family. I'd venture to guess we saw over fifty bands during my last seven months in North Dakota. You can't mourn losing the familiarities of home from the euphoria of a moshpit.

The greatest concert line-up I've ever witnessed was so huge, bands like Skillet and Red shared opening responsibilities. The second band on the bill was Three Days Grace. I loved their self-titled album, but hadn't given much attention to *One-X*. To appreciate the whole concert experience, I had to wade through the unknown portions of their discography. By show time, *One-X* snuck into my list of favorite albums.

Let's be honest, my last few months at home were kind of tragic. One of my Soldiers died in a fatal car crash. Some of the buddies I joined the Army with suffered untimely deaths. Casualties of war and suicide plagued the headlines of my attention. The natural progression of tracks like "Never Too Late," "Get Out Alive," and "One-X" lent inspiration to tough times. The lyrics became elixir to the constant stream of obituaries surrounding me. Somehow, preparing to see Three Days Grace was hopeful catharsis to an uncertain world.

No Jesus Christ / Seether

As co-headliners, the third band on the tour remained a nightly mystery. After Three Days Grace performed, a backdrop unraveled from the rafters. An animated Japanese girl tore open a kimono, exposing a hollow ribcage. Seether was next in the chute.

I've christened two different stereo installations with Seether's *Finding Beauty in Negative Spaces*. That's a weird thing to say, so allow me to expound. First, I use well-known albums to correctly balance the bass, mids, and treble. Using familiar music to equalize a new stereo installation makes technical sense.

Second, I'm a sentimental fool. With new installs, I remember, and boast about, the first CD I listened to on that stereo. For my then state-of-the-art Alpine deck with in-dash navigation and iPod docking capabilities, *Finding Beauty in Negative Spaces* was my maiden voyage. Seether holds that honor.

You see, catching Seether live was an important landmark. From late-night walks the summer before college to the fields of Fort Leonard Wood, Seether served as soundtrack to most of my adult life. I guarantee it'll be the tall tale I tell my grandkids. "Hey! Bring it in. Have you heard of Seether? Have I told you about the time I saw them in their prime?" There's no way of knowing Seether's historical impact the exact moment I reach geezerhood. Regardless, I earned bragging rights that night.

Change (In the House of Flies) / Deftones

Who was the closer? Breaking Benjamin, still touring in support of *Phobia*, prepared for their fourth album release. To this day, *Phobia's* still my favorite BB album. With every soaring anthem, to include the intro and outro, they found ways to capture a lyricist's attention, without saying a word.

During Breaking Benjamin's set, Shaun Morgan assumed front man responsibilities for a cover of Deftone's "Change." Meanwhile, Benjamin Burnley threw bottles of water to the audience.

Rapid ticket sales forced us off the floor. Although we had to enjoy this memorable event from the first few rows of seats, Ben took a leisurely stroll to spray the nosebleed section. He doused us for the showmanship while handing out bottled water to combat dehydration and high concession stand prices. With this level of kindness, you have to wonder why people cast judgment on the metal community.

There I was, witness to the blessed union of two great bands, performing an amazing cover. At this point in history, both Breaking Benjamin and Seether headline their own tours. Let the record show, one night in 2009, two of my greatest heroes merged talents in a memorable way. That, my friends, is the power of collaboration.

Surrender Your Sons / Norma Jean

Speaking of Deftones-related collaborations, I drove around drinking in Norma Jean's *The Anti-Mother* one beautiful spring day. The sunlight radiated gentle heat on my scalp through an open sunroof.

Despite my considerable time on the musical map, I received Norma Jean's newest album with my first order from Columbia House's subscription service. Eight CDs for a penny? Sure!

The precise drum work pounding in my chest distracted me from the lyrics. Around the middle of my Norma Jean listening experience, I sensed Chino Moreno's lingering presence. My sneaking suspicions could be confirmed by the liner notes, riding shotgun in the jewel case.

Parking in front of some unsuspecting citizen's house, I began my research. With the liner in one hand and my phone in the other, studies confirmed my hypothesis: Chino provided writing credits, vocals, and guitar for several of the album's tracks. I wasn't just hearing a Deftones influence; I was hearing the Deftones.

The pretentious grin of a Cheshire cat spanned across my face as I put my research away. Dang, dude! Sometimes, when you got it, you got it.

Where Are You / Manafest

The Red Barn was a Christian rock venue in Williston, North Dakota. The owners must've recognized North Dakota's lacking entertainment options, since they converted an old barn into a concert venue. I'm not sure how, but they scheduled tour stops with bands like Fireflight, Disciple, Dizmas, Brian Welch, and Write This Down.

Manafest was the first act we caught at The Red Barn. When I arrived with my youth group, we were surprised to find a real show. Manafest's tour schedule didn't mention a stop in Williston. Even though the venue didn't have an elevated stage, I was in my usual spot, screaming along to the songs.

"A'ight. Imma need a volunteer for this next one," Mana announced.

Giving elbows of encouragement to kids in my youth group, I didn't even raise my hand. Amidst a sea of enthusiastic palms, his condemning finger pointed firmly in my direction. "Nah, you feel me." He commanded, "I want you up here! You know 'Droppin' Hammers?'"

"Me?" I muttered. "Uh… yeah." If I was honest, I skipped it every time. The lyrics are pretty easy, though. "(Name a city) droppin' hammers, like what?" I starred as male lead in my senior play. This should be fine.

Like a flash from a camera, I rap-chopped from the "stage" with Mana. At first, my contributions were minimal. He rapped, "Williston droppin' hammers, like," and I chimed in, "What?" I crossed my fingers, hoping he didn't ask for more. No such luck. With Mana's arm around my shoulder and a mic in my face, I bombed. Realizing I didn't know the song, he yanked the mic away and demoted me back to the "what?" guy.

After the concert, my group had to drag me to Manafest's merch booth for autographs. I couldn't show fraudulent face there after my poor performance. "How'd you hear about me?" he asked.

"Trevor McNevan. I love your music. Well, not 'Droppin' Hammers.' Sorry 'bout that," I mumbled, allowing myself to make shy eye contact with him.

He offered forgiveness with a firm handshake. "It's cool. Glad you're a fan." Pulling me in for a hug, I could sense the exchange of gratitude. At some rinky-dink venue, I watched Manafest, for $5, less than a hundred miles from home. Like a floating dandelion plume, did Mana ever anticipate his art would take root in some forgettable farm town?

1992 / Spoken

The Red Barn also hosted the last concert I attended in North Dakota. Inhale/Exhale was supposed to open for Spoken. With a smoking tour van on some distant highway, Inhale/Exhale never made it.

I had tickets to see Spoken in 2006 with August Burns Red, Living Sacrifice, and Demon Hunter in Minneapolis while attending insurance training. At the last second, my company sent me to Chicago. To avenge my injustice, I vowed to catch all four bands in concert. Spoken, with loving support from The Red Barn, provided my first shot at redemption.

During the concert, we encountered a strange new phenomenon scene kids called emo dancing. If you'd like, try it out at home. This dance requires practice and a great imagination to perfect.

First, imagine Dad won't take you to Hot Topic until your suburban lawn matches everyone else's. You're already pissed off when the sputtering lawnmower decides not to cooperate. Lacking mechanical expertise to solve the situation, desperation morphs into aggression as you rip the cord harder from the starter assembly. Now, remove the mower, keep the mentality, and dance your sorrows away. For added pageantry, I recommend alternating arms in aggressive attempts to start your imaginary mower.

Once again, my group was in the front row, screaming our hearts out. At the back of the room, emo kids danced sadness into oblivion. Two opposing scenes collided at The Red Barn that evening. To pay homage to our mullet-of-a-crowd, business in the front (my group) and party in the back (the emo dancers), Spoken dedicated "1992" to Billy Ray Cyrus.

I share The Red Barn concert stories, not to brag, but to plead with aspiring musical acts. Manafest and Spoken aren't chart-topping artists by any means. Most people have no idea who they are, but through the internet, music can travel to the world's most remote corners. Yet these bands came through, not knowing exactly what to expect. Remember, for this one dude, seeing two respected acts near my hometown was momentous to my musical journey. Never forget the little guy. He knows and loves what you do.

A Glass Can Only Spill What It Contains / mewithoutYOU

Michael W. Smith founded a Christian rock/metal venue and indoor skatepark called Rocketown in downtown Nashville. This may not surprise other people, but I always thought he was a stuffed shirt. Yet CCM's biggest name paid dues to the 2000s metal scene. I still don't listen to his music, but let's be clear: I was premature in casting unnecessary judgment. Maybe I'm the stuffed shirt.

At the time, my best friend and his wife attended Bible college in Tennessee. Once a year, my wife and I took a spring break pilgrimage to enjoy concerts from their robust music scene. That year, we chased mewithoutYou down at Rocketown. Like I've said before, mewithoutYou aren't typical rock stars. First, they set up their own gear and stage props during soundcheck. Sure, it was a couple cardboard cutouts of a sun and moon dangling from household rope, but I've never seen a band do it themselves.

Second, during set-up, Aaron came to center stage to tune his acoustic guitar. Again, my group was front and center in the pit. We earned our spot with a half-decade of continued dedication. A young hipster couple fidgeted with anticipation next to us. As he tuned up, the female blurted out, "I love you, Aaron!"

Without batting an eye or straying from the task at hand, Aaron responded, "I've wrestled my whole life with the concept that Christ Himself could love me. Why would I take your word after a few moments in my presence?"

That was cold. After snapping a quick picture, we glanced over to gauge this mega-fan's feelings. You could almost visualize his words germinate realization as confusion bloomed into intrigue. On stage, Aaron had already disappeared behind a stack of guitar cabinets. From empty words to life lessons in two sentences. That, ladies and gentlemen, was a pure act of rock star defiance.

My Last Serenade / Killswitch Engage

It'd been years since I last saw Stickel. In a chance encounter in a Taco Johns' lobby, we reminisced about the good ol' days: party-hopping and Hardees, fart CDs and shenanigans, shopping cart bumper cars and Lost Cell. In two short months, he'd be married and I'd move away, maybe forever. While eating burritos from brown bags intended for takeout, we stayed to explore the concept of a Lost Cell reunion. Neither of us mentioned the bitter betrayal of previous life changes, but we both knew our story needed a better ending.

For several days, we built a setlist over text messages from old favorites: Tool's "Sober," Chevelle's "Get Some," and Godsmack's "Awake." Cruising down memory lane, we swapped Marilyn Manson and KoRn lyrics, just like old times. You've heard my musical journey, but Stickel drifted away from Manson to Mudvayne and Lamb of God. After hours of exploring YouTube footage, we got into wild card selections: Mudvayne's "Happy?" and 10 Years' "Wasteland." His interest in technical playing intersected with my need for positive lyrics somewhere near Killswitch Engage. Plus, it only seemed fitting to close out our literal "End of Heartache" with one "Last Serenade."

We met up for our first official jam session with a drummer Stickel knew. Halfway through the first song, "Awake," a guest percussionist banged the breakdown on the garage door, "DUN, DUN, DUN-DUN!" The band played on as I rolled the door open to a dimly lit driveway, revealing a proud Dickinson Police Department officer. "Sounds great, gents!" He grinned. "The neighbors don't think so, though."

"Screw it!" Stickel screamed as the officer drove off. "It's not even late!"

I tried reasoning with them, "C'mon, guys. My Commander'd be pissed if I got a civil disturbance charge. It's kinda opposite of what Soldiers do." We celebrated having our set shut down and called it a night.

A few days later, we found another jam space. After a quick romp through "Smells Like Teen Spirit," Stickel dropped a bomb. Lost Cell wasn't just jamming; he brought us together for an actual gig during his wedding dance. We spent that first session planning the four-track setlist, practicing The Beastie Boys' "You Gotta Fight (For Your Right To Party)," picking costume components, and assigning awkward back-up dancers.

If Lost Cell was this focused years ago, we could've possibly stood the test of time. Life has a crazy way of rectifying broken things. We couldn't think about that, though. Momentum momentarily gained toward our reunion, even if for a short while.

Iris / The Goo Goo Dolls

As we continued wedding preparations, I pulled double duty: Lost Cell rhythm guitarist/singer and Best Man. To be honest, most of our energy went into grand plans for the four-song set. A large part of great art resides in presentation. For costumes, we stuck with rented tuxedos and top hats, adding class with aviator sunglasses and prestigious fake mustaches.

On stage right, the wedding ushers threw down some of the worst moves of all time. You know the type: the monkey, the picky shopper, the disco finger, the uptight white guy, and many more.

Next, Stickel and I demonstrated versatility by playing three different instruments, apiece, throughout the four-song setlist. Like a weird game of musical chairs, we traded electric, bass, and acoustic guitars with every track change. After picking up bass for The Beastie Boys' "You Gotta Fight," and Marilyn Manson's "Coma White," I switched to Stickel's seafoam-green Jackson for Staind's "Outside." We closed our strange concert with The Goo Goo Dolls' "Iris"—his dedication to his new wife. People, that's an acoustic piece with a crazy alternate tuning, featuring my first public guitar solo.

Even though the entire set was videotaped, I'll never watch it. We can't allow reality to taint our performance that evening. We stepped off and killed it, period.

As non-touring performers, this was an aggressive vocal performance to pull off. Let me recap the setlist: one about partying, one about the dangers of drug abuse, one about insincere people, and one about love. Four entirely different songs meant to display the diversity of Lost Cell.

As the curtain dropped on our reunion concert, the bitter reality of goodbye set in. Lost Cell never delivered upon our promise to dominate the rock world, but for one night, we flew higher than we ever could've imagined.

The Transitive Deficiency / As Skies Revolt

Atop our leaving North Dakota bucket list, my wife and I locked our gaze on the Lifelight Music Festival. The Army had already taught me how to cope with porta potty usage and shower droughts. For a chance to catch fifty+ bands, I'd fight off dehydration with friends and family. For unseen big-ticket acts, like: As I Lay Dying, John Reuben, Seventh Day Slumber, Brooke Barrettsmith, and Showbread? Taking in half a concert on one stage before waddling, sweat-soaked and sunburnt, to watch another great band? To have actual options? Yes, please. I was willing to apply Soldier skills to three days of field concerts.

Festivals happen to host performances from reasonably local, unsigned acts on the rise. Over one short weekend, bands like The Skies Revolt, Write This Down, and The Clocktower Showdown went from perfect strangers to frequent flyers on my iPod playlists.

The Skies Revolt could've just played a normal set. Instead, some renegade in a cardboard box robot costume graced the stage the whole time. Like with wind energy, live music and audience interaction recharged his dance battery. The crazier we were, the more he danced.

What we suspected to be a hype-man from the street team turned out to be a pay-rolled The Skies Revolt employee. When we stopped by their merch booth, Mr. Cardboard Box Robot trolled the sales floor. Believe me when I tell you, his entrepreneurial prowess far exceeded his stage performance. We walked away with their whole discography and the companion comic book for *Is Alive and Well*. These dudes were either clinically insane or artistic geniuses that transcend comprehension. I've chosen to accept the latter.

Once in a Lifetime / 12 Stones

I'll never forget June 25, 2009—not just because it was my last day as a North Dakota resident. While loading our belongings onto a moving truck, one of my RAs delivered the disturbing blow that plagued the entire summer: Michael Jackson, age fifty, was dead. His cause of death was pending a toxicology report. Newscasters predicted people would remember where they received this historic news. A decade later, they're still correct. With a dolly full of boxes near Woods Halls' main entry, I consoled a music major's sadness about the King of Pop's passing.

Life is short and brutal. You see, most of mine was spent confined to the corners of The Great Plains. Every angle against the vast horizon presented unchartered territories. A giant world few are willing to evade comfort to fly into. Armed with my deluxe edition of 12 Stones' *Anthem for the Underdog*, I took my seat in the Penske. Skipping to "Once in A Lifetime," I wiped away a solitary tear as I slid the key into the ignition. Truthfully, history can't change without the occasional, haphazard dice toss. Win or lose, there was no going back; my bet was already on the table. I could only hope we chose the correct destiny.

Alien / Dead Letter Circus

At this point in time, North Dakota was all I'd ever known. Sure, I'd taken temporary residence in other states for military training. Never tarred with the sticky residue of permanence, though. While traveling to Fort Benning, I had thirty-nine total hours to ponder the devastating burden of adjustment. Windshield time, better yet: stereo time, gave license to high-stakes ping-pong between the pros and cons of leaving home. For the first time, my safety blanket to life's burdens, my woobie—if you will—was in the rearview mirror. For all intents and purposes, I was an alien.

Nightmares / Simplistic Urge

Can you smell that? The faint scent of a distant storm brewing? Please admit you can sense the dark clouds rolling in? Dramatic life change lending to another identity crisis? I don't have a prize to give you, but outside observers should easily spot this excruciating pattern. All my life changes carry the added benefit of over-analysis and intense personal reflection.

At this point, I'd been an officer for over a year. Then, I found myself in the trenches of Fort Benning—one of the greatest testosterone-producing factories on the planet—with other young officers. Our commissioning source taught us a lot, but this is where rubber grazed the pavement. I'd like to claim the competitive games didn't affect me. I mean, I'd been an engineer platoon leader for sixteen months. I already knew more about real Army leadership than my peers.

Yet, my immaturity sucked me into the undertow of arrogance. I aimed to be the best warrior: smarter, more confident, and more capable than all others. I'd be the weapon our enemies couldn't outgun. Forget the humility guiding me to this career path. Forget I accomplished nothing on my own. Forget my Soldiers carried the actual burden. Forget all of that. The day of reckoning was nigh; I now lurked the proving grounds to personal greatness.

I hadn't assessed myself for several years. Sometimes, you just ride the euphoric tides of life's ebbs and flows. You can't search your soul from a wave's crest. It's much easier to assess performance from the crushing roll of the undertow. After abandoning three leadership positions, after leaving my wife in New Mexico, my over-inflated ego no longer had a stage. It wasn't my name that was muttered to address the problems we faced—and I hated it. From ringmaster to passive audience participant in two weeks' time.

Late one night, caked in dirt and sweat, I sat in a hard barracks chair in full battle rattle. I'm told the equipment a Soldier carries into combat weighs about eighty pounds. That's a lot of weight for one person, especially since I weigh a buck-fifty. As the air conditioner provided comfort from the unbearable Georgia humidity, my soul search commenced. Who was I becoming? The ultimate warrior? The competitor? The jerk?

Eighty pounds is harder to haul when you're toting around a massive ego. Can anyone tell me how much one of those weighs?

Instead Laugh / Onesidezero

After alienating my peers with a know-it-all attitude, I spent most of my time alone. On our days off, they made plans and I was always left out. It turns out, people avoid jerks.

For safety's sake, the Army imposes a 150-mile limit for weekend travels. I yanked this restrictive chain to explore every local used music store/pawn shop within the area. One morning, I even visited a hip-hop shop in downtown Atlanta. "We don't have what you want here, son," an older gentleman said from behind the counter. Thumbing through their selection, he was right. I guess my heavy metal t-shirt was a dead giveaway.

Next stop, I discovered a massive music store with every type of media imaginable: CDs, tapes, records, and eight-tracks. With endless free time, I invested the entire day there, to include a lunch break and a few employee shift changes. Although arrogance has several downsides, not having people around to dictate my desires is a win. To be honest, though, the allure of these trips comes from sharing cheap finds with friends. At the end of the day, all I had was a dusty pile of albums no one else cared about anymore.

All Falls Down / Adelitas Way

I'll never forget the first time I heard Adelitas Way's "All Falls Down." Driving back from the music superstore that evening, the lights of Atlanta were in my rearview mirror. The lights of Columbus ahead. In total darkness, I explored my fresh-picked treasures. With a smile, I recalled the frantic employee escorting me to the register to close the sale. Hopefully, they didn't think I was crazy, or worse, a shoplifter. Who spends an entire day at one store?

Without distractions, the empty interstate called my attention to my wife in New Mexico. Over the past five years, I'd abandoned this poor girl for a year due to military training. For the mathematicians, that's a 20% absentee rate.

Then, it hit me. After becoming qualified, I was destined to be away even more: more training, more activations, more separations. Most likely,

I'd deploy during one of the most inopportune times. This line of work doesn't grant much immunity.

"What am I doing to her?" I whispered. "When will I commit the fatal flaw of being over-extended to my job or military career? Be real with yourself, to avoid poverty, you put her last." Meanwhile, "All Falls Down" blared in the background. I was caught in a psychological tailspin.

"How am I supposed to juggle all of this?" I continued. "No matter how hard I try, something's gonna fail. I can't win." I could feel myself sliding down a complex rabbit hole. With the burden of failure pressing on, the only relief from tension came from listening to this song on repeat. At least, until I drowned my attention in another meaningless task.

Your Hands / Uriah

The moment I realized my arrogance, I tried making amends with people I'd wronged. It was too late; the damage was done. I couldn't blame anyone, but me. People keep respectful distance between themselves and self-serving serpents. I had to acknowledge my ego got in the way of lasting friendships. Then, writhe alone in the painful bed I made.

In three short weeks, I'd travel back to Missouri with a chance to transform myself into a less deplorable person. Oddly enough, I had to relearn the key qualities of my success thus far. Four weeks prior, I was a malleable student with humble roots. A confident coach driving results for the team, unconcerned with personal victory. A trusted confidant encouraging safe spaces for growth. An enthusiastic cheerleader motivating impossible feats of greatness. My professional success could only be attributed to these traits. I needed to toss-and-turn in my temporary bed, then, never act that way again.

My Funeral / Dope

As I made the trek from Fort Benning to Leonard Wood, memories of my immaturity lingered behind me. With my first visit to the Army Engineer School as an officer, I couldn't help but reminisce about basic training. Five short years ago, I pulled fire guard and buffed floors as a young private. Maybe I'd perch atop San Juan Hill to revisit my physical/emotional humility exercise. Maybe I'd exchange salutes with an old drill sergeant to symbolize my progression. Officer Candidate School, the border mission, fighting floods.

As I navigated the winding Missouri backroad rollercoaster, I reviewed who I was, where I came from, and the harsh lesson from Benning when I lost focus. Holding on for dear life, I sang along with my car stereo. I was back where my military journey began.

John Wayne Gacy, Jr. / Sufjan Stevens

During my training, I met another political scientist, hailing from the home of Paramore: Franklin, TN. Between music, politics, and engineer estimates, we got to know each other well.

One particular evening, we linked up to record an original piece on his beautiful Martin acoustic guitar. It was our first musical exchange; I had no idea what to expect. Waiting for the final note to fade, my fingers hovered over the Boss Micro BR's stop button. It took several moments to process what he played. "Wow. Dark, yet so approachably hopeful," I asserted. "What inspired you to write it?"

"You heard of Elliott Smith or Sufjan Stevens? Pull up 'John Wayne Gacy, Jr,'" he coached over the music video. "Hear those lyrics? Wait 'til the end. Did you catch that? A gut punch to judgment, eh?"

Sufjan Stevens or Elliott Smith would've never graced my playlists without this recommendation. Their songs were far softer than what I listen to. However, I do appreciate skillful lyricists. The turn of phrase. The self-awareness. The meticulous honing of craft. From Garth Brooks to Ryan Clark, Jesse Hasek to Kevin Matisyn. Storied musicians draw me in, and these gentlemen told great tales.

Waltz #2 / Elliott Smith

Being an officer forces you to embrace the finer things. You will frequent golf courses. You'll give, and receive, putting advice. Driving advice. You'll invest in every aspect of your golf game. Even if you've never played in your life, you will eventually end up on a golf course.

You'll study political ideologies, explore the economic implications to war, and reflect upon history. There's a lot of reading, writing, and arithmetic to being an officer. We're expected to discuss, and prepare for, ethical dilemmas. To be clear, we're politically agnostic. However, we need to understand how certain world events impact daily operations. We embrace the victories we've seen in the past. We explore missteps to incorporate them into our long-range planning.

Even my musical tastes were impacted by going to officer training. Make no mistake, I still listened to hard rock. It just expanded to new areas I would've never embraced any other way. Take Frank Sinatra, for example.

Sure, I'd heard "Fly Me to the Moon" before, but can anything be more American? It's hard to explain, but his music instantly transports you back to World War 2. In one smooth take, you feel empowered to win complicated wars, end economic depression, and put Americans back to prosperity. Pinkies out, ladies and gentlemen; Frankie's singing.

Several weeks in, I produced an operations order with one of my classmates. After shuffling my Top-Rated iTunes playlist, we got to work. We were thrown some Frank Sinatra, a song from Paramore's *Brand New Eyes*, followed by Uriah. Later, an Elliott Smith deep track played, calling my attention to "Waltz #2." Queue it up next. Then, Breaking Benjamin's *Dear Agony* in its entirety. Pointing out my weird taste in music, my classmate asked, "You're all over the place, huh?" With a quick nod, I kept typing. My eclectic Washingtonian friend had no further questions.

The Poisoning / Living Sacrifice

Believe it or not, I used time away from normalcy to binge-watch *The Wonder Years*. As a kid, a crush on Winnie Cooper captured my attention. The series required a review aside from my childish daydreams of improbable love. Instead of getting into trouble, I got into *The Wonder Years*.

In one episode, the gang spends an entire evening hunting down a Rolling Stones secret show at a small venue. Since leaving home, I'd attended ONE concert. Hinder made a stop at Benning while I was there; live music too close to miss. The aching itch sent me jonesing for another concert. After some quick research, I found a Living Sacrifice show near our 150-mile travel radius.

"When is it?" I whispered, pulling up a calendar. "Today?! On a weeknight? We have PT tomorrow. Where, though?" I pulled up MapQuest. "A backwoods venue, 147 miles away?" I grabbed my keys and iPod from the desk, sprinting toward my car.

If *The Wonder Years* taught me anything, shenanigans will ensue while looking for a secret concert. If I stayed the course, I'd pull in right after the doors opened. A few problems: 1) the dark, moonless evening made navigating windy backroads difficult, 2) overgrown trees hid half of the road signs, and 3) my Alpine GPS didn't work well on state roads.

Along the drive, I missed a turn somewhere, landing in a neighboring town. I pulled over to check a map and rerun the GPS. 163 miles from base. My heart skipped. Rule breaker! Plus, precisely no one knew about my magical quest through the forest. What if I got lost? Or hurt? How would the search party know where to look for my missing carcass? *Hey, idiot!* I thought. *You're violating commands for a Christian metal band? Head home, oxymoron! Now!*

On my way back to base, a city sign sang its siren song, "Over here! None shall know!" Solid logic, onward we go! My tires screeched as I turned toward the concert venue. Back on track!

"You're crazy, but you did it!" I shrieked to myself. My heart continued to race as panic slipped into ecstasy. Time check: the show started twenty minutes ago. Foot to the floor, I sped to the next highway distance sign. Mile check: I'd pull in during the encore. Not worth it.

One last time, I decided to return home. Like I missed them in 2006, seeing Living Sacrifice live just wasn't in my deck of cards.

"Oh, well." I sighed. "If I can't go to Living Sacrifice, they're coming to me." Using the shoulder to turn around, I cranked the volume to *Conceived in Fire*. My three-hour drive gave time and space for a private performance. Ironically, like my *Wonder Years* gang, I never made my concert, either.

Ignorance / Paramore

Military training held me in purgatory from late-June to early-December. Not wanting to lose both Halloween and Thanksgiving, my wife flew out for a visit. Like most Christians, Halloween wasn't a big deal to us. However, distance from familiarity causes a greater longing toward time-honored tradition.

We spent the evening eating pizza, waiting for trick-or-treaters with our small bowl of candy. A concert on MTV2 teased performances from Paramore and Dead By Sunrise all evening. Void the laughter of kids in costumes, we abandoned hope and snacked on Laffy Taffies to the soulful stylings of Hayley Williams.

Make It Real / Tread

Welcome to Sapper Stakes! An eight-hour, all-out engineering mission intended to make us beam with regimental pride. Armed with blanks, gear, extra water, some maps, and the trusty iPod, my team took off into the sunset. In a race against the clock, we measured bridges, determined river flow rates, identified mines, and stormed a small village to detain an IED maker. The faster we completed the test, the faster we got evacuated to warm beds.

After a full day of in-class learning, our intellectual capabilities were pushed beyond their limit. Physical exhaustion lingering with intoxicating strength. Spinal lesions from rucksacks cursing the burden of preparation. The quiet darkness of 0330 taunting the world's slumber. In written form, this may sound like complaining. I assure you; we live for these moments of real-world application. The Super Bowl of Army engineering.

Before the metaphorical blast from a starting pistol, our instructors gathered us around a map to point out a wastewater drainage pond.

"Check the fences for signs!" the crusty sergeant barked. "Should be obvious, but we get 'em every cycle. Don't be that group."

Got it. Blast through the missions with accuracy, speed, and lethality. Avoid the wastewater. Easy, right?

An hour later, our group ducked behind trees in a fierce fire fight. As we bound toward the source of the attack, mortar rounds whistled overhead. I'm up, he sees me, I'm down.

"Cover me while I move!" I yelled.

"Got you covered!" my buddy declared from a patch of brush ahead. I could hear his weapon laying down suppressive fire. Each shot rang out to the beat of my racing feet.

"The road! They're shooting from the ditch by the road!" our team leader shouted.

Dropping to my side, my rucksack hit the ground with a thud. I rolled onto my elbows into the prone position. BANG! BANG! BANG!

Flashes from my weapon barrel signaled my buddy to move. A flare rocketed overhead, better illuminating our enemy's location. The poor sucker was pinned down. We had him surrounded, and he knew it. His hands shot into the air, lowering his weapon in surrender.

"How's the wastewater?" our instructor asked through muffled laughter.

"What?!" my team leader whined. "We checked for signs like you said!"

Guiding us to the fence line, the demented sergeant tapped the top of a sign. "NOTICE: Reclaimed waste water unfit for drinking or body contact." Upon closer examination, our uniforms reeked with the faint scent of human excrement.

Sometimes, leadership means choking down some humble pie to move the mission forward. Imagine being mocked with laughter and the soft soundtrack playing on your iPod. You wanna make it real, Tread? How's about a synchronized swim through human waste? Is that real enough for you?

Blue Letter / Seven Mary Three

Marriage causes a person to drift away from their family of origin to the new one they created in holy matrimony. It's the circle of life, but the abandoned kid in me takes these things to extremes. If I sense a painful departure, I drive it into existence. Add to that, I'm horrible at communicating with people outside my immediate peripheral vision.

It turns out, people like it when others strike up conversation. Also, communication works two ways. You have to speak to be heard; you have to listen if you want people to talk.

My officer course culminated with a weeklong field training exercise. Aside from the iPod, my technology was limited to butcher block mission trackers and ol' fashioned military radios. No phones, no computers. Returning to several missed calls from my adoptive mom, I dialed her up after the last weapon was safely stashed in the vault.

"Where've you been?" she prodded.

"I was training, Mom."

"That woulda been nice to know before you left. You never call. We always call you. When we do talk, it's The Tony Show. You never ask about us."

"Ma, we were in the field. I do ask about you guys. It's always the same. 'Not much goin' on here.' What do you want me to do?"

"You know what?" Her tone shifted. All anger dissolved to defeat. With a sigh, she said, "I can't do this. I don't have the energy or health to keep up with you anymore. Maybe, it'd be best if we just didn't talk." Then, she hung up on me.

Once again, in full military gear, I assessed my life. Staring at the BlackBerry in my hand, a thousand questions streamed through my mind. *Am I a bad son? I show gratitude, right? What about my feelings? Where's the middle ground? Why do people keep leaving my life?* Once again, answers escaped me. My equipment couldn't protect me from the mental war I waged.

I wouldn't have gotten to this proud moment in my life without their help. They taught me how to be courageous, to challenge myself. I did the work, but without their strong boot in my teenage years, I would've stagnated. Everything I'd accomplished, I accomplished for them. For crying out loud, their name was stitched into my uniform.

I just longed to hear affirmations from them, but they weren't the type to use feel-good terminology. "I'm proud of you, Tony. I love you." They didn't mutter compliments. They made corrections.

In the midst of uncertainty, I typed an unaddressed email. It divulged my disappointments and failures. Pled for any prideful display of my accomplishments. Showed gratitude for their contributions to my life.

Acknowledged their sacrifice. Promised a more equitable relationship. Begged for reconsideration to their stance.

The reread moved me to tears. This message could've fixed everything, or at least nudged us in the right direction. All it needed was their email address and a quick punch at the send button, but my pride took over. Ma always admitted old dogs don't learn new tricks. My emotional plea only delayed the inevitable. A man of my stature couldn't win as a doormat. No more tear-filled bargaining. If another soul never saw my value, I did.

Wiping away my weakness, I deleted the email, never to see the light of day.

Life Is Beautiful / Sixx A.M.

After officer training wrapped up in Missouri, I made a final trip to North Dakota to out-process from my National Guard unit. With job applications submitted across the United States, we had no idea where we'd end up. Without my parents, a home, or an income, I sought temporary relocation to New Mexico to figure things out.

It's hard to change direction when you're free-falling in failed flight. Sometimes, you have no other option than to embrace the chaos. Senseless optimism stemming from the thrill of risk. With little left to lose, the clear choice was to crawl back to the top. Isn't that what life's all about?

Descending Upon Us / Demon Hunter

Amidst the New Year's bells, a buddy put me in contact with the Tennessee National Guard officer strength manager. With plenty of Army opportunities within their engineer brigade, I aimed all attention at my civilian career.

After piles of ignored applications, I landed a gig as a satellite dish technician. It seemed like the perfect job: hours of driving, two installs a day, rocking the iPod while running cable. As an independent contractor, they weren't concerned with military duty. The more I worked, the more I earned. It all seemed so easy. After three weeks shadowing a seasoned employee and buying equipment, I'd be ready to go.

Where did I find motivation for outdoor labor in the guaranteed Tennessee spring rain? Demon Hunter. Tons of Demon Hunter. The slow build of "Descending Upon Us" prepared me to conquer my wet new world every time.

I'd love to say the experience went swimmingly. My first installation took me twelve hours over two separate days. No joke; the customer begged me to leave and come back the next day. Less than a week later, I got my wife's SUV high-centered on a washed-out dirt road. I spent my entire birthday trying to dig myself out—to no avail—before paying for a tow.

This cash siphon they called a job was losing me more money than I was making. Demon Hunter wasn't even enough to lift my broken spirit. Let's face it—some people aren't cut out to dabble with satellite dishes. I quickly proved to be one of them.

Fix Me / 10 Years

Whether I wanted to admit it, my parent's rejection lurked quietly behind everything I did. Keep in mind, I knew the fault I carried in the conflict. However, the steps my wife and I took were bold. Did they understand the audacity required to move across the country? The fear of breaking all you've built?

Yet, somehow, my pride was in full swing. I love adversity. Doubt me, and I'll win. Watch me hoist the trophy—with or without you.

Tucked in 10 Years' hometown, I dug deep into *Feeding the Wolves*. I'm not sure who pissed them off, but like-minded birds flock together. Let that anger swell into something beautiful. Let these intense tests of character continue. Like usual, let the pressure of discomfort dictate the path to peace.

Disappear / 12 Stones

Let's be real for a minute—part of me chose Knoxville residence for music exposure. The local scene included bands like 10 Years, Disciple, and Copper. Travis Wyrick produced several of my favorite albums from his studio in town. Red, 12 Stones, Living Sacrifice, Fuel, and Spoken all hailed from within a six-hundred-mile radius.

If I played my cards right, I'd network with the correct people for access to studio time. If not, at least I'd catch some great concerts.

My first show in Tennessee was 12 Stones opening for Red at a motocross event. Bands provided live music from a stage near the track. A quarter of the audience watched impressive dirt bike stunts from the bleachers. Half of us straddled the stage and track, attempting to watch both. The last quarter were my people: filthy rockers headbanging from the pit.

12 Stones' upcoming release at the time, *The Only Easy Day Was Yesterday*, was available on pre-order. I ripped it from the internet to prepare for the concert. Song by song, I typed the lyrics in a Word document to commit all five to memory. By show time, I was self-conscious the band would notice me singing along and connect the dots.

"Hey!" Paul would shout from the pages of my wild imagination. "Yeah, you! You like stealing from starving artists?"

"I just wanted to know the new songs. You know, for a better experience," I would plead. "I pre-ordered the album! Check out my order confirmation!" Presenting a computer print-out, the whole crowd would glare at me as Paul verified my purchase. Once complete, the band could resume their set.

Although this scenario was highly improbable, it consumed me. I've purchased 12 Stones' albums several times, either as replacements for worn-out copies or as gifts for friends. I've heavily invested in CDs, concert tickets, and memorabilia. If they deemed me a fake fan based on ripping an album—ahead of delivery, might I add—I was ready to state my case.

All this pent-up catastrophizing resulted in exactly nothing. 12 Stones played; Red played. Show complete without incident.

However, in a separate improbable twist, we couldn't help but notice one of Red's roadies. Wasn't he Spoken's rhythm guitarist for our last Red Barn concert in North Dakota? Flagging him down, I croaked through a concert's toll on my torn vocal cords, "Sir! Hey, sir! Remember us?"

Setting down a stack of microphone cables, he responded, "No way! It's the dude married to my mom's doppelganger!"

After a brief exchange and another picture for his archives, we parted ways once again. If I was in Tennessee to network, this was a great first step. In one chance interaction, our old acquaintance from North Dakota reminded us of music's binding power.

Only a Year or So / 36 Crazyfists

The day I was promoted to First Lieutenant will be forever embedded in my memory. Not because it was long overdue. Not because of the work ethic required for more responsibility. My promotion was memorable on its own. I could finally silence the playful jabs toward my starry-eyed inexperience. "LT Kessel, what's the difference between a Private First Class and a Second Lieutenant?"

"I'm aware," I'd answer. "They've been promoted one more time than me. You want me to spell lost without LT now, too?"

My promotion ceremony was significant enough. Tucked at the end of a five-day staff training exercise, my battalion commander called me forward. After upgrading my rank, he began: more responsibility, more trust. Pretty standard promotion speech content.

Then, the plot twist.

"We need leaders like 1LT Kessel here, for our next mission," he said, patting me on the shoulder. "Our battalion has received deployment notification; departure date and location are forthcoming. The training we just concluded is entirely relevant. With this news, I need three things from my leaders: take care of yourself and your families, look out for your peers, and prepare your subordinates. Be ready. This is what we train for."

Great careers require putting money behind your mouth. Give them what they paid for. One small reservation: our Tennessee residence had begun six short months ago. With a four-hour drive home, I had the daunting task of selling mobilization to my wife and job.

Don't Fight It / 10 Years

After a few listens through 36 Crazyfist's "Only a Year or So," I debated calling my wife to get the news off my chest. The four-hour drive would eat me alive.

I began rehearsing my speech to make sure I got it right. "I've got some news, but you gotta promise not to get mad…" What a perfect way to break the tension! It's like tagging an offensive statement with, "No offense." If she already promised to evade anger, I had a golden ticket to bad news admission.

A few practice runs later, I dialed home. "Hey, I've got some news, but you gotta promise not to get mad…"

Silence. "I have some news, too," she admitted. "But you have to promise not to get mad."

Nice! The field was level. What could it be? She had vehicle problems? Got a good scolding at work? Nothing she could say would top what I was about to tell her. New plan: let her take the edge off like a true gentleman.

"Ok, I won't get mad," I promised, hoping my offer would be reciprocated.

"Well." She sighed. "There's no easy way to say this, so I'll get to the point. I took several pregnancy tests while you've been gone. They all came out positive."

"What?! We're having a baby?! Why would I be mad about that?"

Like Elton John suggested, it's the circle of life: college, career, marriage, kids. We did everything in the correct order. Why would I be angry?

Then, the realization hit me: you get married and have children. Next, you raise them.

Quick math put our child at about six months old when my unit left. Most of that first year, without me. My worst nightmare materialized. I was about to become a vacant father, through no fault of my own. Significant milestones like: first steps, first words, first foods, the cute developments—all missed. Even worse, what if I never returned home?

As we explored parenthood, I realized my wife only held half the story. "Well, you promised not to get mad, but your news makes mine a lot harder," I transitioned. "I got promoted today, and my unit's deploying. We don't know where to yet, or when, but we'll be leaving for a year or so. We need to pray about your support system while I'm gone. Staying in Tennessee doesn't make much sense now."

We had a lot to ponder, but at least my conscience was clear. After several moments of uncertain conversation, we agreed to think about options and discuss it later.

If we're keeping track, I gained three new titles that day: First Lieutenant, soon-to-be Veteran, and father. It was reminiscent of the day I joined the Army. Getting fired from Hardees, rehired at Dairy Queen, and swearing in was bush league, though. Back then, it was just me. Now, people's lives teetered in my palms.

As I continued home, my head started spinning. Every potential possibility laid out like a demented choose your own adventure story. In desperation, I reached for the first fear I could think clearly about. All my failures as a son and here I was. A distant dad contributing nothing to my child's development.

After a few more romps through "Only a Year or So," I switched to 10 Years' *Feeding the Wolves* for some deep introspection. What have we learned? I'm better than my biological parents; I feed on the friction. Rounding the bases of the album, "Don't Fight It" caught different light under these new circumstances. Tomorrow doesn't have to hold onto yesterday.

My life's lessons, right or wrong, hold the formula to be a great father. Don't be scared; lean in. I wanted the chance to forge a better way forward. Here it was. With time ticking, all I could do was invest in my child while I still had the chance.

Faceless / Red

For a moment, imagine strolling through the doors to your favorite restaurant. The hostess seats you at your regular table. While you wait for the waitress, you thumb through the menu. It's all for show, though. You're gonna get your regular.

After hearing this much of my story, you know mine: an extra-large plate of identity crisis. This time, I wasn't even through my first serving. It's like the waitress offering dessert during the main course. That's how I enjoyed my identity crises in those days—a fat cat gorging from the limitless spread sprawled out before me.

Scared, excited, and clueless, we alerted the press right away of our pending parenthood. "Guess what?!" I quizzed my best friend over the phone one evening. "We're expecting!"

"That's awesome! When's she due?"

"Umm…like, seven months?" I guessed, taken aback by the question. "When do they tell us?"

"Have you had the first ultrasound? There's an unspoken rule that you announce pregnancies after the first trimester. You know, in case you lose the baby. Not to steal your thunder, but we're expecting, too. We're telling our family next month."

"Welp," I admitted. "Irreversible damage in our first act as parents. Congrats, man! I'm happy for you guys!"

We were a pair of brothers navigating life's phases together. From Christian dating to marriage, college to careers, and now the fears of fatherhood. How do you fade from the fine art of people-pleasing to firmly establishing one little human? How do you make such a large identity shift in nine short months? I'm not sure how other people do it, but we traded lyric fragments from Red's "Faceless."

My kid wasn't born yet, but this thing was already a financial leech. To avoid anticipated poverty, I entered into one of the most aggressive work binges in my life. At my full-time medical technology job, I scheduled ten to fifteen overtime hours a week handling physician's call routing. Military training ramped up in preparation for deployment: field training exercises, longer weekends, extra courses.

After extensive research, I turned my recording studio into a home office to take Xbox inbound customer service calls. Not only had I never owned a console, I'd never even played one. Rest assured; my charming voice provided subject matter expertise to the antagonized gamer's plight through ring-of-death issues.

For three months, I worked nineteen hours a day. You see, if haters gonna hate and players gonna play, then providers must provide. After making all essential baby purchases, I set my panic aside to balance our budget. That precious analytical hour, elbows-deep in spreadsheet calculators and checkbook ledgers, declared the opposite of my empty emotions. In the fear-filled world of fight or flight, I somehow accomplished both at the same time.

Careless Whisper / Seether

My son entered the world one day after my seventh anniversary in the Army. He was the hairiest, most beautiful baby I'd ever seen. Our nurse assured us his thick blanket of back hair, used for warmth in the womb, would fall out after a few weeks.

When I saw his ears, this little dude owned my heart. One of Will Smith's love interests on the *Fresh Prince of Bel-Air* mocked him for resembling "a car driving down the freeway with both doors open." Males in my family have ears that stick out like that. Miniature satellite dishes serving as a constant source of insecurity for me until I saw them on my son.

The formerly abandoned baby in me refused to put him down. Oh, I made excuses. "Look! He's holding my hoodie drawstring! He doesn't want to leave me."

His first night on the planet, we fell asleep cuddled on the hospital couch. Without a doubt, the last time I felt that totally whole was when my own father sang to me when I was three years old. Destiny's shrill calling never wailed so clearly: if I was supposed to be a father, I was gonna be a good one.

Like every other area of my life, music became an immediate staple to fatherhood. Where other people's babies slept a lot, our son was a reverse-cycling rock star. Even after keeping him awake all day, like baby books instructed, he still fussed in failed twenty-hour benders. No matter which song I sang to him, Lifehouse's "Breathing," The Calling's "Stigmatized," or Staind's "Excess Baggage," he still whined between fifteen-minute catnaps.

That's when I clamped onto the jugular. Judge if you must, but Seether's "Careless Whisper" put him right to sleep every time. Think about how wrong the lyrical content is for a newborn baby. You know what isn't wrong? Finding a surefire lullaby as an exhausted new parent.

Bulletproof / 12 Stones

We all divert to default positions during periods of discomfort. Our own factory reset, of sorts. While I was at a six-week Army school, 12 Stones announced "Bulletproof's" exclusive release to some internet radio station. Rather than waiting for the song like an adult, I attempted recording it live while in class.

To mitigate potential issues, I test-recorded several hours of internet radio from my hotel room for three straight days prior to release, skimming recordings, tweaking settings, and improving the process until the debut. I'd still have to manipulate the audio a bit afterward, but at least, I'd have it. You know, in case my deployment led me to an austere environment void of a year's worth of new releases.

On debut day, I rushed back to my room to preview the new song. Scouring the four-hour recording, one song at a time, I dug up a heavy song with screaming, great riffs, and a surprise breakdown. My boys in 12 Stones delivered on the hype.

Now, to snip it from the broadcast. I had mastered this process with tapes as a kid. 1) From the Tape A side, pause the captured recording before the intro. 2) Insert a blank cassette into the Tape B deck. 3) Measure available mixtape time with a stopwatch (or guess, I won't judge). 4) Rewind the tape back to where you want to record. 5) Press record/play together on the Tape B side. 6) Count three seconds for adequate silence between tracks. 7) Push play to start the captured song. 8) Wait it out. 9) Stop both tapes. Mission complete.

Whether I planned it or not, I accidentally wandered into the world of digital audio production. You see, songs can't be cropped like a picture. An editing program's required. Through extensive research, Audacity provided me a free solution for my predicament.

After carving "Bulletproof" out of the broadcast, I still wasn't satisfied with the quality of my recording. I detailed my new masterpiece through reckless application of compressor and EQ settings, trimmed additional reverb, and boosted the volume through brickwall limiters. If something didn't work, I reversed it until it sounded right.

It wasn't perfect, but no longer sounded like a recording captured by holding a microphone to a speaker inside a toilet bowl. Without an editing process for my own music, I'd just finalized my first mix.

Eyes Wide Open / Staind

Although it may not be apparent, I was concerned about leaving my family for a year. Why worry about things you can't control? When Staind dropped "Eyes Wide Open," my music collection was clearly the only aspect of my life with direct manipulation. The world would continue spinning without me, but the music I left with was all I had.

To prepare for a year from the scene, I converted my entire collection to a lower bitrate to maximize my iPod's 30GB storage capacity. Then, I fixed the audio tags to find any artist/song/album with ease. Rather than facing real feelings, I used music to distract myself from life's brutal reality, just like every other junkie.

While some Soldiers worried about our deployment's alcohol-free policy, I worried about New Release Tuesday. How was I supposed to get new music in a foreign country? Was my family supposed to slip new CDs into care packages? I began my last hurrah, my final binge, at least until I came home on leave. Time was ticking. With less than two months left, I hoarded every album I could fit onto my 2TB external hard drive.

Fade Out / Seether

From the moment we gasp for our first breath, we begin the march toward impending death. It's inevitable, but young people rarely reflect upon their mortality. Wading waist-deep through life insurance coverage, living wills, and morbid conversations about end-of-life intentions, the frailty of life locks cold jaws into mortal flesh. Even after flirting with suicide, after begging for permanent release from temporary problems, death remained a distant force.

Maybe Garth said it best in the lyrics to "If Tomorrow Never Comes." What would you do differently with today if you believed life could cease tomorrow? Yet, the Soldier in me still required gentle nudging from my battalion commander, "Celebrate with your friends and family. Tell 'em you love 'em. Even if it's uncomfortable, make your intentions known."

Looking back now, those tough conversations were foolish. It shouldn't come as a surprise; I'm still very alive. Dead people can't tell tall tales. However, reflecting on my history since these conversations, Soldiers I served with have passed away. Some in combat, some due to illness, others due to suicide. Life is truly fragile, folks. Even the minute stuff: commutes to work, genetic predisposition to disease, or fatal injury.

We know not when our number shall be called. How careless could we be to leave vital words unspoken? Crucial tasks left undone? What would it take to pursue our life's purpose with fiery passion?

Something to Remind You / Staind

Staind's most recent album, released in 2011, lingers with a strange sense of finality. In my state of mind, imagine how I processed "Something to Remind You." I had a thousand theories: artistic expression of mortality, reflections of an ominous medical prognosis, OR worse yet, a silent memorial to the Staind institution. Their last track tucked away on their last album.

Without guiding anyone to a specific conclusion, I must've sent the song to a dozen people. After a quick playthrough, my friends would say, "Wow! Great song!"

"Yeah, I know," I'd message back. "What do you think it's about?"

"Not sure. It's a great song, though." Apparently, normal people don't think about music the way I do. With countless musical conversations ending like this, I should've drawn this conclusion much sooner.

I obsessed over the concept of Staind calling curtains on their career, although their social media never indicated an end. With such a strong exit song, it only seemed logical. The symbol to my own goodbye tour: a trip to North Dakota, a trip to my best friend's place, a trip to visit my in-laws. Leaving no loose ends, I had every date and location planned out. At least, I was more transparent about my own departure.

There Must Be Something in the Wind / Blindside

Can you imagine America's top military officials receiving top-secret briefs from dark Pentagon vaults to plan my assignments around potential album releases? Analytics and charts, prepared by some junior officer schmuck (like myself) layering the walls like a Charlie Day meme.

"Gentlemen," a full-bird colonel briefs, "Blindside's *With Shivering Hearts We Wait* released this week. With *The Black Rose* EP hitting the market in 2007, we anticipate them to fall silent until 2015," his laser pointer tracing dates along a timeline. "The past eighteen months produced results from Seether's *Holding onto Strings Better Left to Fray*, Red's *Until We Have Faces*, and

10 Years' *Feeding the Wolves*. Intelligence shows 12 Stones in the studio as we speak, recording their upcoming album. For next quarter's update, we'll keep monitoring that project, Kevin Matisyn's work in Parabelle, Demon Hunter, and We as Human's pending record deal."

Why wouldn't the same people who taught me Soldier care show the same concern for my morale? My calculations, based upon previous release dates (no doubt, the nerdiest comment strung together for this project), had me focused on four potential releases during deployment. I'm really not asking for much: food, water, sleep, and the occasional new CD. If you noticed, I don't even need a place to live. I'll camp out for a year, if needed; just don't mess with New Release Tuesday.

This World Is Not My Home / Onward to Olympas

After saying goodbye to family and friends, I made my final pilgrimage from New Mexico to Tennessee for deployment. Make no mistake—this was a somber business trip. The tension of an uncertain future circulated through the air conditioning vents; HOWEVER, when your route runs through Garth Brooks' proud hometown, you seize your last chance to accomplish a childhood dream, even if an unplanned stop seems impulsive. Even if your black Living Sacrifice shirt (with death metal lettering) scares the residents of Yukon, you're gonna wanna wander down Garth Brooks Boulevard.

Driving at night is therapeutic. Keep the vehicle in nearly empty lanes, stay awake, and let your mind search the contents of your heart. My path, dare I say destiny, went through a deployment.

With Onward to Olympas' "This World Is Not My Home" on repeat, I reviewed my checklist one more time. My immediate circle knew how I felt about them. They all knew what to do if I didn't come home. Even if I didn't (a far-cry for a noncombat mobilization), my soul rested in a much higher purpose. Every perceivable box, checked. With eyes on the road, hands on the wheel, and an energy drink in the cup holder, I was ready to roll.

Landing in London / 3 Doors Down

My flight into country was the first time I'd ever flown anywhere overseas. Before that morning, I must admit drowning out every in-flight safety brief to the music blaring in my headphones. That flight, I searched overhead for the air mask drop-down, tapped the plastic door under my seat to identify my lifejacket, and plotted my path to the nearest exit row.

Did you know sitting twenty consecutive hours increases your odds for deep vein thrombosis—a medical condition causing blood clots in your legs? I did not. I guess what they say's true: everything, when not enjoyed in moderation, can be potentially dangerous.

I already felt small for leaving my family. Staring out the window across the perpetually blue ocean with some scattered clouds below me, I found ways to feel smaller.

From inside my metal vessel, I dutifully held my head high, which isn't difficult when you've received training. When you're stripped of responsibilities–like cooking, dishes, and yardwork–to focus on your Army job. When you have constant support from Soldiers to your left and right. Leaving's a lot easier for us than it is for them. Pooling somewhere behind us, we generated emotional, energy, and time debt with our families. They're the ones who had to drive away from a bus with minimal support.

With the trusty iPod and a backup charger, I guaranteed my music lasted the whole twenty-hour flight. As embarrassing as it is, I couldn't allow the shuffle function to dictate our descent. Floating above the lights of our arrival city, I queued up 3 Doors Down's "Landing in London." The city name's immaterial, but the sentiment is spot on. We were hailed as heroes, rockstars receiving standing ovations everywhere we went.

Minus a few honorable mentions, my wife and son didn't get the same accolades for pulling together a year without me. Plus, the pins-and-needles they exist in while we operate in volatile areas. So, yeah, I sat stoically in my seat, reminding myself to stay humble through a song. If every action carries a price tag, I needed to settle on all this deficit I was creating. First, I needed to do my job and return home safely.

Mournful Things / Preson Phillips

As we entered theatre, I was singled out as the only guitarist our chaplain knew. In Tennessee, I say again, Tennessee—home to the Memphis blues scene, the Nashville songwriting community, and the country music empire—I was the guy.

Leading Contemporary Christian worship was problematic for several reasons. I've played guitar, sang, and written music for years, but mainly to the uncritical reception of my living room. When I find the courage to play in public, I aim to entertain. Worship is NOT entertainment. Good worship artists provide the platform and slip from the musical equation to make space for connection with the Almighty God. I didn't need the added stress of wrestling with ego every Sunday morning.

Second, I didn't deploy to make friends. By leading worship, I engaged in the ministry of listening to other people's problems. Praying with them. Shouldering their burdens. Truth be told, I was furious with God for separating me from my family. With reluctant obedience, I planned my routine: a quiet morning workout followed by breakfast alone, bury myself in twelve-hour shifts, grab a late dinner, evening guitar practice before crashing to stand-up comedy or *The Office*. Rinse and repeat every day for a year. Was it too much to ask to bask in my misery alone?

Also, I listen to, practice, and write music from a rock/metal perspective. Taking this assignment forced me to ration praise, gospel, and CCM into my musical habits. Normally, what I get during an average church service is enough to scratch that itch. Now, I'd have to listen to the genre, select songs, learn the parts, commit to two practices a week, then lead worship on Sundays.

With reluctant obedience, yet again, I scoured for ways to bridge the gap between my taste and the church's needs. In an underground CD my brother Matthew gave me, I stumbled upon Preson Phillips. With eerie semblance to GB, he was the most authentic worship artist I've ever heard. If I had to do this worship thing, I was going to do it like Preson.

Futile Devices / Sufjan Stevens

I'm no stranger to pent-up anger. In fact, I may be a giant baby, pouting when I don't get my way. I knew what I signed up for when I joined the Army, but I also wanted to be there for my son. Boycotting social interaction was my childish attempt to stick it to the system. You want contractual compliance? Fine. Just don't expect me to have fun. Contracts breed results; they don't dictate the attitude upon delivery.

I wanted to be angry and closed off. At first, I committed to that concept, but social interaction pulls with gravitational force toward meaningful existence. Can a cog be effective without understanding its relationship to the machine? In other words, I needed people, and they needed me, to be more engaged.

Regardless, I committed to distance. Oh, there was a part of me that knew it was futile; I'd eventually crack. People aren't islands. With my bottom lip quivering, I vowed to remain one for as long as possible.

How to Love / Lil' Wayne

If you want an accurate snapshot of American culture, try listening to Top 40 radio. Even if I wanted to, I couldn't avoid pop music amongst the comfort items provided to Soldiers. Working out at the gym? If I took my earbuds out, I was guaranteed to hear Usher's "Climax." Cruising the countryside between construction sites? Yep, Flo Rida's "Whistle." Wanna watch *Good Morning America* for a small reminder from home? How about some LMFAO's "Party Rock?"

Taylor Swift. Rihanna. Lil' Wayne. Eminem. Pop music had violently vomited in my life.

A person remains oblivious to cultural norms until they aren't subjected to them anymore. Think about how constantly connected the average American is through text, email, and social media. For my first month in country, I felt phantom vibrations from my right front pocket. My phone wasn't even on me, yet it enticed me with false notifications. At first, I panicked in frantic searches for my electronic ball-and-chain. "Where's my phone? What if someone needs to reach me?" Once I freed myself of its metaphorical links, life became much simpler.

Further, why do Americans drive everywhere? Even a quick trip a few blocks away? It takes, what, five minutes to walk, but we'll still drive it. We'll cruise down to a local gym, hop onto a piece of stationary equipment, then jog toward a destination we can never reach.

As I walked from my worksite to the dining facility late one evening, the veteran homelessness problem hit home. We spend a year away tucking emotions in like messy dress shirts. Second, every item we tetrised into two duffel bags and a footlocker carried us through deployment. When you fully realize the waste, you begin to detest the excess. You begin to see how free you can be without ties to technology. By performing the most American act of service, I began feeling more disconnected from the culture I'd known for most of my life.

I See Everything / La Dispute

Sometimes, we take life for granted. My temporary departure from everyday comfort took me on a glide path from betrayed to bitter to broken. In an instant of quiet conviction, the impetus to sudden change, Jordan Dreyer slapped me with the lyrics to "I See Everything." When I weighed it all out, my situation wasn't so bad. Wading through the worsening journal entries of a teacher losing a child to cancer puts things in perfect perspective.

Yet Jordan becomes the subtle hero. A mere junior in high school, he was aware enough to understand his true condition. If he believed he lacked faith, what did that mean for me?

Jesus Himself said people cannot be effective hiding their light in secret places; it must be displayed for true illumination (Luke 11:33). Instead, I chose selfishness. After leading worship two to three times a week, I disappeared into the shadows of my room. Amidst my lifelong musical dreams, I abused the privilege.

As an officer, I was positioned to provide help to others. I had a responsibility, in every way, to be a resource, a keen eye of protection to this desolate world. Sure, the Army has chaplains covering thousands of stories, but we have to be present for each other. My call to action was clear: abort the pity parade. It was time to suit up and jump into the flames.

I'm Already There / Lonestar

During our deployment, USO hosted a tour to minimize the blow of being away from our families for the holidays. Some of the more memorable acts included: Five Finger Death Punch, Puddle of Mudd, Filter, Daryl Worley, Toby Keith, The Lieutenant Dan Band, Chamillionaire, the Minnesota Vikings and Tennessee Titans cheer squads, and several stand-up comedians. Most musicians have a homage to home-type song, because, surprise, their chosen profession forces long stints on the road. Every band dedicated this piece to us. For a moment, we mettled in unified misery.

Can you understand how wrong it feels to be entertained in a "combat zone?" First, Soldiers are wired to focus on the mission. To me, if any action didn't reinforce engineer support to the Middle East, we shouldn't do it. Second, these same artists weren't playing free shows for our families back home.

No other act carried the guilty gut-punch like Lonestar did. I've covered how they became salve to the wound of Garth's retirement. Sure, this performance was sans Richie McDonald, but this was a dream realized. I tried enjoying the experience by singing along with the crowd.

"Kessel, I thought you were a metalhead," my commander pointed out behind a dopey smile. "How do you know the words?"

My teenage dreams of stardom flashed before me. Inspired songwriting sessions interrupted by the shame of plagiarism. An exciting sprint past an *I'm Already There* album-wrapped tour bus trailed by the embarrassment of begging for signatures on a CD-R. Pursuing romantic relationships behind the impenetrable walls of the friend zone. Every emotion revisited in a span of five seconds.

"Let's just say, I went through a Lonestar phase in high school," I admitted.

Playful jabs aside, I knew the worst was yet to come. Tucked somewhere in the setlist, their homage to home tormented me all evening. I didn't just know the words; every outbound skype call replicated the lyrics. This was gonna destroy me, and oddly enough, I needed it to. I needed to fight off tears. I needed to feel perspective-bending guilt. Amidst the experience, I needed a reminder that I wasn't becoming calloused beyond the point of recognition.

A Media Friendly Turn for the Worst / Norma Jean

Birthdays were a massive ordeal in my family. Where each holiday generated its own set of group traditions, one day per year held special attention. I knew deployment would steal a million little precious moments. Given my silver plate of dates for mid-tour leave, I would've been insane to miss my son's first birthday.

Due to the nature of Army business, we aren't given travel details while on deployment. Loose lips sink ships, so specific information isn't released. We get shuttled to the point of departure and wait for hours, sometimes days, to leave. I was cool with it. I had some personal goals to knock out. For my war trophy, I decided to write and record an album in theatre. While waiting, I scratched lyrical ideas, dinked around with graphic design, and meticulously matched both in artistic pursuit. With nowhere else to go, I found my sole responsibility.

After my flight faced a second weather delay, I wandered, like a zombie, to my temporary bunk for a nap. Maybe some mindless task, like modifying iPod song tags, would lull me to sleep. Norma Jean's "A Media Friendly Turn for the Worst" looped on repeat while I worked.

In the exhaustion, my joy faded. After the temporary fun, the momentary surge of purpose, I'd return to this base to finish my deployment. A trip just long enough to normalize my presence for my son. He was too little to understand the why behind my absence, but old enough to understand I was gone. This was going to hurt. A LOT. I had to prepare for the pain of leaving again.

Out of love, I made a pact with myself. Pain was inevitable, but it couldn't dictate my actions at home. I needed to be present. Sure, meaningful engagement would destroy me upon my return from leave, but I couldn't disconnect to avoid the pain. As I interacted with Soldiers around base, the empath in me sensed them struggling, too. Our emotional pendulum froze somewhere between the pure euphoria of family vacations and missional misery.

Seated in Hell's waiting room, we were gifted ample time to exercise resilience. It was, after all, the only location to transition between dramatic acting roles.

Something in the Way / Nirvana

Since space was limited, I didn't bring many comfort items with me on deployment. A computer, the iPod, an external hard drive, a journaling notebook, some civilian clothes, my Bible, and a hardcover book of Kurt Cobain's artwork, personal photography, lyrics, and journals. Safe to say, I gained an unhealthy admiration for Kurdt that persists today.

A childhood shaped by legendary divorce. Awkwardness caused by social alienation. Poverty. Piscean artistic prowess. Music and pop culture obsessions. The use of humor to diffuse dark situations. With so many striking similarities, I felt an instant connection to his work.

During my mid-tour leave CD binge, I picked up *MTV Unplugged*, *Nevermind*, and *In Utero*. When balanced against the inner workings of Kurdt's soul, *In Utero* becomes the better album. If you ask me, I don't trust Nirvana fans who prefer *Nevermind*. If you ask other Nirvana fans, they'd probably hurl pitchforks at me for neglecting to mention *Bleach* or *Incesticide*.

Let's just say, the Nirvana establishment guards its gates well. Case and point: I've argued with strangers sporting our blessed smiley face. "Great shirt!" I complimented. "What's your favorite album?"

The bewildered teen admitted, "I'm not sure. I just like the shirt."

"Listen here!" I barked. "Nirvana isn't some novelty clothing company. They're one of the best rock bands of all time. If you wanna support the band, buy an album. Would you wear a campaign shirt for a presidential candidate you don't plan on voting for? I sure hope not! Kids these days!" I stormed off, rendering him defenseless.

Anyway, your body takes several days to adjust to time differences after overseas travel. I woke up with my family, but struggled to fall asleep when they did. I used the spare time to learn the unplugged version of "Something in the Way" on guitar.

"It's ok to eat fish because they don't have any feelings." At first, I laughed at the lyrical misinterpretation. There's no way he said what I heard, but yeah, those exact words were scribbled in one of his journals. It was the marriage between Kurdt's sense of humor and his constant insignificance.

How quick are we to dismiss what we don't understand? People with disabilities. Veterans. Mental health concerns. Homelessness. Addictions.

Racial and gender differences. As I listened to the song, I've never felt so overwhelmingly transient in my life. I felt out of place at home. I felt out of place in country. Oddly enough, I identified with that fish. Given the chance, I wondered how many people would justify gnawing at my flesh.

The Family Ruin / Oh, Sleeper

In my leadership positions, I've always hoped to use authority to advance humanity. I'm not perfect, but I never want to abuse influence for negative results. When I heard Oh, Sleeper's "The Family Ruin" (and Blue October's "Razorblade" much later in life), it became clear some leaders are willing to violate vital roles for selfish gain.

Sure, I've witnessed good leaders make poor choices. In my experience, these mistakes were followed with apologies and some semblance of repentance. I've also seen evil people make self-serving decisions. A wolf masquerading in sheep's clothing, though? I'd never watched a seemingly good person topple under the weight of secret evil.

In the Christian faith, reputation's everything. Our belief system doesn't make us perfect, but unbelieving people should see behaviors worth emulating. If we don't practice what we preach, why should they? News flash: we CANNOT perfectly practice what we preach. The standard is too high, but that's where grace enters the equation.

Abusing the privilege with endless trips to the bottomless bowl of grace won't work, either. Even if our actions never compel a person to believe, they should never discourage belief through blatant disregard for our own tenets.

Safe & Sound / Taylor Swift (Ft. The Civil Wars)

As I engaged in community, I found most of my non-work peers were musicians. We spanned the spectrum: Christian music purists, classically trained musicians, CCM/pop people, country fans, and metalheads. Our musical Venn diagram intersected somewhere near Taylor Swift.

Maybe it goes without saying, but I'm not a fan. However, hard rock covers of pop songs are one of my greatest guilty pleasures. Basically, if Taylor Swift threw down to some double bass pedal, overdriven guitars, and a spritz of screaming background vocals, I'd buy her albums. Case and point: I Prevail's cover of "Blank Space." Chef's kiss, my dudes.

The rest of her catalog aside, ol' Taylor nailed the equation with "Safe & Sound." If there's any anthem capable of capturing the emotion of deployment, it's this song. Fear, allegiance, desperation, loneliness, and above all, the potential hope of home looming around the corner. Not to mention, Pandora's box popping open to The Civil Wars discography. Somewhere amidst the prayer circles, rehearsals, and familial-type fellowship, our worship team was dedicated to finding our way, and guiding others, home through music.

Paralyzed / Love & Death

Rewind to 2004, I was a HUGE KoRn fan. A year after I quit them cold turkey for Christianity, I'll never forget finding out Head left the band due to his own conversion. "Tony!" a girl from Campus Crusade called out in the hallway between classes. Her tiny voice shook with excitement, barely damming the good news waterfall behind a dimpled smile. "Have you heard of Brian 'Head' Welch? Yeah? Well, I read an article about him leaving Korn to follow Jesus! Tony, God's answering your prayer for good rock music!"

As he entered into sobriety, Head released the demos that became *Save Me from Myself.* I bought the album and book. They were fine, but his material still had that new Christian scent. Something told me his second record would be a better indicator. Let him mature; Stella's gotta get her groove back.

Fast forward to 2012, "Paralyzed" was released under his new band name, Love & Death. Within the first few notes, I knew I was hearing record deal material. Not a riff, not a chord, just some haunting, reverb-ladened notes. To shake up my repetitive daily routine, I built a new deployment motivation playlist, adding "Chemicals" and "Whip It" as they were released. That first entry, though, was "Paralyzed."

Be Somebody / Thousand Foot Krutch

No matter our intentions, most people focus on creating a lasting legacy. We'd like to think we can leave a mark on this temporary situation called life. For a quick glimpse into a Soldier's head, our entire lifestyle hinges upon sacrifice. Velcroed below the American flag on our uniform, a deployment patch broadcasts you once went somewhere with someone and did something. To a Soldier, it's the ultimate measure of professional significance. Add to that, at my funeral, a flag-draped coffin and twenty-one guns will serve as my final send-off into the sunset. If life is indeed a vapor, maybe I'll be blessed enough to leave my mark in it as deeply as possible.

So, why would I add "Be Somebody" to my motivational deployment playlist? According to Army culture, I was "being" somebody when I used years of training on a deployment. Perhaps, there was a whole section of "somebody" I wasn't being. A father. A husband. A son. A brother. A friend. For an entire year, I wasn't postured to perform any of those roles well. The dilemma was apparent: would everyone else forget about me while I pursued professional significance?

Double Life / We as Human

Have any of you tried to buy a digital album from a foreign country? No, this isn't the start of a cheesy ad read for the hottest new VPN, but it may as well be. I spent three whole days trying to acquire We as Human's self-titled EP. The album wasn't available on iTunes since my IP address wasn't in America. Amazon allowed the purchase until check out, but fraud prevention locked my card and wouldn't process the payment. The workaround was having family in America purchase an Amazon gift card, upload the balance, then make the purchase. The process took three days. I'm sure none of this would've happened if I had a VPN subscription.

After all that tomfoolery, I listened through the EP while following along in a lyric search engine. Justin Cordle was concerned, at least on two tracks, about people professing certain beliefs while living selfish lives in secret. I needed a courageous someone to call out some suspected hypocrisy. It's simple. If you don't believe it, then leave it. Yet as the track count increased, I could feel rage brewing within me. Along with all other deployment anger, I drug my new treasure to the gym for a more productive second pass.

The most skillful playwright couldn't have scripted what happened next. As I rested between sets of leg curls, a fellow Christian, the indubitable Mr. Double Life himself, wandered into the gym. "You make an entrance like a queen…" We as Human narrated through my headphones.

In the distance, Mr. Hypocritical doled out high fives like Oprah Winfrey. "You get a high-five! You get a high-five! Everyone in this gym tonight gets HIGH-FIVES!"

Move along, I thought, as "Double Life" continued playing. *I really don't wanna deal with you right now.*

No such luck. Despite my angry thousand-yard stare, he still approached me with a dopey smile plastered on his face. With a greasy palm raised, his lips read, "How's it going?"

Through a jaded sneer, I reluctantly raised my hand to Justin's continued coaxing over my headphones. "I was there and I know what you did. You can hide underneath that grin…" Slap! High-five delivered. "I see right through you…"

As he strutted to the next person, I sat in disbelief. I've had songs speak to me before, but never with such succinct precision. Some atheists I've met disregard faith-based systems because of people like him. Why should they believe when Doofus over there isn't even trying?

Walk away. Live your double life. I guess Jesus died to cover your obviously blatant sins, too.

Just the Way You Are / Pierce the Veil

While collecting critical evidence of Christian hypocrisy, I also witnessed some of the greatest triumphs of the human spirit. It became too easy to assume the whole barrel would rot from the putrid juice of a few bad apples. Don't get me wrong; none of them were perfect as they were. Simply stated, the way we are always leaves room for improvement. Along with the rest of the chaplain corps, my worship team and I committed to encouraging others to complete their mission.

It's also easy to collapse under preconceived notions. "So-and-so's been heavier most of their life; why would they lose weight now?" "So-and-so always misbehaves when they leave home; how's this deployment different?" Judgment cultivates self-fulfilling prophecy. If a person's believed to be a certain way, they think it for themselves. If they truly believe the lie, they cave to the mere pressure to be better.

When I reflect on how some Soldiers invested in digging against the grain, I have to beam for them. Maybe in the war of self-improvement, all it takes is some sort of attempt.

Someone to Hate / Demon Hunter

Near the middle of my deployment, Demon Hunter released *True Defiance*. I proceeded with my standard deluxe edition order for the weirdest package, by far, I received at my foreign base. Keep in mind, I mix-and-matched five different civilian outfits with one hooded sweatshirt for an entire year. Miss a Demon Hunter release, though? Not a chance. I had to show my boys love from the third world.

Although I've known certain Christians to fixate on Satan's shenanigans, I never have. In my commitment to naivety, I'm sure I missed some evil intentions along the way. However, being in the third world clarified the concept of spiritual warfare. The unforgiving desert's desolation, mixed with total isolation from usual support systems, loudly competes against miraculous whispers from angels.

With help from my new CD purchase, I felt invincible. Sometimes, doing the Lord's work requires a brooding spirit. Just know, when the dust settles, my flock will rise from the inevitable fight, unscathed. Beware wolf in sheep's clothing. Cross me. Test me. Hovering over the bruised carcass, I will spitefully spit on the idol for which you stand.

Bury Me / 12 Stones

Music has always been the contemplative force I use to process life events. Moreover, it's the barometer I use to measure the status of my romantic relationships. Most hits from 90s country radio, The Used's self-titled album, Hoobastank's "The Reason," Blindside's "Silence," Adelitas Way's "All Falls Down," The Ascendicate's "One Day Without You," and 3 Doors Down's "Landing in London." My iPod's packed with proof.

In yet another installment of relational regret, I submit 12 Stones' "Bury Me." Lying on my bunk one Sunday afternoon, I committed to a *Beneath the Scars* listening party. I preferred the heavier stuff over the slow tracks, but when I studied "Bury Me" with intention, I was greeted with a gut punch.

There's no way my wife's childhood dreams of marital paradise included constant stints in a prison of loneliness. Sitting there, alone myself, I couldn't run from my fears. Marriage is a daily choice. Although she knew what she signed up for, she didn't have to keep choosing us. At what critical junction would she realize a better life without me? When would she make the decision to stop hurting at my expense?

Enemy / 12 Stones

St. Francis of Assisi once said, "Preach the Gospel at all times, and when necessary, use words." Christians love this quote. We get to do life our way, then avoid the trouble of stirring up controversy.

As I felt the noose of spiritual warfare tighten, I believed infectious influence would cause my enemies to change. Sound familiar? Yep, I preached the Gospel without words. Sometimes words are necessary. Music helped me face the issue, but how effective is spitting on others' false idols? How long would I sit back doing nothing, hating people's hypocritical behaviors while expecting some sort of change?

Wait—I did do one thing. I hoarded anger. Externally, I presented myself as a beacon of love, joy, hope, and integrity. Then, for a year, I stored every negative emotion. Never dealing with anything in time. Pack it up. Take it home. Deal with it later. You know, the exact action expected from a person with integrity.

Proud of You / 10 Years

While on deployment, I befriended a Soldier with a military career spanning over seven years. On her first tour as a combat medic in 2004, she served in a palliative care unit in Iraq. The mere war stories were traumatizing, but the details were worse.

"Sometimes, I still see their faces when I close my eyes," she told our group over supper one evening.

Most of us were fortunate enough to escape the true brutality of war. How does a person remain sane amongst that level of atrocity? What magic elixir scrubs deeply engrained imagery from random recall?

After a stint in the Washington National Guard, she rejoined the active Army to put food on her children's tiny plates. Sitting in a foreign dining facility, away from them, attempting to provide for them. As we shared life stories and prayer requests, she told us of a custody battle with her soon-to-be ex-husband. Her decision to serve in the military faced scrutiny from the Guardian Ad Litem to the custody case. Still, she smiled. Still, she had faith to fight for a better tomorrow.

Throughout my career, I've stumbled across several stories reminiscent of this one. Oh, the tales your average combat hat-toting veterans have. Some pull at your heartstrings; some make you beam with pride. They need to share, and we, as a society, owe it to them to listen. Like the Soldier here, their resilience will make you see humanity at its finest.

Heart / The Pretty Reckless

Have you ever been sucked into a vortex of weird internet searches? One evening alone, I wasted three hours watching mindless paternity test montages on YouTube. An eighth of a day evaporated from my life. Proud to announce, I admitted my sins to a buddy to declare instant freedom from Maury Povich's obsessive grip.

A few weeks later, I dove down the rabbit hole of Taylor Momsen's career roles after *The Grinch*. I heard she was a musician, but was she any good? Investing an evening's research into her history, I searched IMDb and Wikipedia, scoured The Pretty Reckless' iTunes discography, and streamed live footage on YouTube. All stemming from watching a Christmas movie in June. She wasn't the first; she won't be the last. In fact, I hardly remember what it feels like to forget something.

Breathing / Prime Circle

I've never been a big fan of routine. To me, little variances throughout the day keep a person sharp. However, my journal entries from the time refer to a steady state of *Groundhog Day*. Remember the 90s Bill Murray movie where he relives the same day on repeat? That's life on deployment.

I woke up at the same time every day, worked out at the same time, and ate every meal at the same dining facility table. Every breakfast: biscuits and gravy jumbled with scrambled eggs. Every lunch: two chili cheese dogs with sweet tater tots. I played the same songs on guitar every evening. See? *Groundhog Day*.

The world I once knew lacked familiarity. This contemplative state makes a person reflect upon younger versions of themselves in shame. Did I really need to emphasize retaining certain friendships? Did I neglect better efforts in the meantime? Why did I miss home so much when I left before? Training was much less time and certainly closer.

If I had access to a time machine, I'd go back. Not to change anything, but to better inform the younger version of myself.

London's Bridges / Taken

I spent most of my free time on deployment writing a five-song EP. The project was kick-started by the desperation I felt while leaving work late one night. Walking to my bunk, I passed a female Soldier heading the opposite direction. *"I've got a handle on this again," she says*, I thought as she faked a smile, saluted me, and fought off tears. She looked like she was dealing with some pretty serious stuff. Not being able to shake the feeling, I had to memorialize it. My time in the box needed a defining project.

I painfully skimmed chord progressions, lyrical interpretations, and themes. When it was almost complete, I designed the album artwork. To avoid wrestling the base's practice space from other guitar players, I recorded at 2 a.m. I'd pack a microphone borrowed from the chapel, my guitar, Line 6 UX2, trusty writing notebook, and computer loaded with Audacity.

My hope was to capture the simplicity of the third world in an intimate way. You know, record the songs pure to their original arrangement. If the whole performance wasn't recorded in one clean take, legendary rock producer Bruce Dickinson took over. Stop tape; take it from the top.

When my guitar's single coil pickup destroyed the first few drafts, I had to borrow a buddy's Fender acoustic guitar to keep tracking. Back to napping after work and waking up at 2 a.m. Four sessions later, the raw guitar tracks were complete.

Then, off to vocals, which took forever. If I made one simple mistake, I stopped tape and took it from the top. Where the guitar's a physical instrument, multiple complete performances takes an unnecessary toll on aching vocal cords.

The raw stems still sit on a hard drive in my studio. There's magic in how these songs were captured, but low-quality recordings are difficult to mix. All mixing tutorials would recommend I re-record the performances with better microphone positions. I can't do that now; I'm no longer in country.

Maybe when life isn't so chaotic, I'll mix them. Maybe even reproduce them in full band.

All artistic fear stunts musical productivity. Will people understand the subtle lyrical nuances? How do I stake claim in an industry with so much swelling noise? How can I, a simple dude, ever give people even a shard of what music has given me?

Here / Kari Jobe

After a year out of regular life, I shipped my guitar back home. Without my chief time occupier, I had nothing but time to rationalize my absence. Search the soul through massive music consumption.

I found an increased sense that I didn't belong anywhere. If friends and family made it through a year without me, why did they need me when I returned? Shouldn't bastions of American freedom find solace in planting feet back in the dirt they served to defend? The only people I still felt connected to were the Soldiers around me. Yet I had to leave all these incomplete stories as the Army directed. Mission complete; time to report home.

I'm sure these issues were invented in my head. I never bothered asking friends if I was a forgotten element in their world. Not wanting to appear insecure or needy, some assumptions were made along the way. I also didn't invest time connecting with people who mattered to me.

I've said this before, but my immediate attention's almost always limited to things within my peripheral vision. So, there I was weighing in on where I didn't weigh in. Like the duffel bags I stuffed to return home, I became another fragile item needing delivery.

Forever Fields (Sowing Season) / 10 Years

Sometimes, Soldiers occupy a time or space inconducive to processing momentary emotions. We execute tasks with obedience, stuffing unresolved concerns into what I call an "emotional rucksack." Are you scared? Face the fear and win. Are you angry? Let it go and get the job done. Do you miss your family? Call them during your down time. Otherwise, see you at next formation.

The Army doesn't stifle emotion; we train for resilience and maintain personal awareness. However, the mission can't always account for how we feel.

Day one on American soil, the faint feelings from a year away smacked me square in the face. Jetlagged from a twenty-hour flight. Time lagged from the seven-hour difference. Did I make the right decisions? Should I be proud of our performance? Regretful seeds of reflection germinated, cracking hardened kernels in new growth. Without other options, I set feet to fields to begin harvesting my life's unresolved emotions.

Writing on the Walls / 10 Years

As I reacclimated to post-deployment life, I began mildly testing my abandonment theory. Had most of the world, or at least the one I knew, moved on without me? I'd place a phone call to friends or family. "Can you text me? I can't talk right now."

Message threads tapered off: "Sorry, I fell asleep putting the kid to bed."

My presence no longer seemed necessary. However, the incomplete stories from deployment drove forward. Like investing in a television series, it became easier to stick with the plotlines I knew. Maybe that's what we all were doing.

For months, I had to complete paperwork to leave base. My leadership had to know when I was leaving, where I was going, and when I planned to be back. Now that I was at home, who was I supposed to tell? What if I got lost, maimed, or imprisoned? How would people narrow their search for my helpless carcass? No matter how outlandish, I had this genuine internal struggle while preparing for a drive to clear my head. My poor, unsuspecting neighbor had no clue why I briefed him on my afternoon plans.

I've felt like an alien before, an out-of-touch traveler from faraway lands, but I couldn't even actively participate in my own story. Popular near-death commentaries highlight details from out-of-body experiences. I had one for several weeks. I watched this strange character binge-watching *Scrubs*, the show I started on deployment, from the couch. With a genuine urge to nudge myself into action, I froze under the pressure welling up inside me.

As harsh as it sounds, my existence didn't seem essential to anyone anymore. I didn't need to ask. The writing was on the wall.

The Gift / Seether

Traumatic experience is binding. Somewhere in the pile of mismanaged emotion, I realized my friendship with the female worship leader was far greater than that. Sure, leaving her alone in country hurt, but the concept of permanent separation was debilitating. She was one of few who knew what I knew. She was amongst the few who felt the weight of unfinished business. We weren't just friends. Somewhere along the way, we fell in love.

Having dealt with suicidal ideation before, I recognized the early warning signs. When the vehicle of life high-centers on a mound of emotion, get help. Spinning tires will do no good; you're already stuck.

I engaged in a psychological world tour, sharing internal struggles with anyone who would listen: relatives, friends, and even a therapist. They all said the same thing: what I went through sucked, but having feelings for another woman was wrong. Give it over to God and move on. Reintegrate with my wife and son. Get a job. Solutions always come easy, but let's be honest, a few conversations couldn't fix what I hoarded for a year.

After a whole day sharing my experiences with anyone who would listen, I collapsed on our couch. From the corner of my eye, my dusty guitar caught my attention. Music's always been there for me. I accompanied Shaun Morgan in momentary therapy through "The Gift's" lyrics. Around the refrain, the levee broke on my emotional dam. With it, decades of bitter tears flooded the lush fields of mismanaged feelings.

Maybe I needed to fall apart for a minute. Grab a good cry to release the tension.

When my fit subsided, I picked up my guitar again. The refrain, that seamless transition from verse to chorus, clamped down on me like an iron gate. My strained singing closely resembled the howls of an old hound pinched within its grip. Sobbing for another fifteen minutes, I played through the chords in the chorus. Every regret came flooding back. For a moment, I even understood my mom's condition. People can't hurt you—better yet, you can't hurt people—with a safe standoff distance.

What I thought would be therapeutic kept swirling into deeper, darker places. Sometimes, numbness is the coping mechanism your body needs to survive. Setting my guitar on its stand, I wiped the stray snot from my face to allow apathy to overtake me again.

Only a Memory / Icon for Hire

Have you ever driven in a severe thunderstorm? Rain falling so hard you can barely see through the windshield? Emergency lights pulsing, wipers on full-blast, flipping between headlight settings to cut through the chaos. For a moment, you consider pulling over to let the storm pass. That was my life after deployment. With two hands gripping the wheel, I prayed, somehow, I'd arrive at my final destination.

A whole month passed. I wandered through life as a third-party participant. Applied for, interviewed, and received a job at a technical college as a military admissions representative. Separated from my wife and son to a neighboring town. Living life through the instructions on the back of a shampoo bottle. Wake up. Get ready. Go to work. Come home. Grab a TV dinner cooked in my apartment shared with college kids. Lull myself to sleep to some Netflix stand-up comedy special. Rinse and repeat, day after day.

I planned a transfer to the New Mexico National Guard but still had to out-process from Tennessee. When I left North Dakota, I had the world at my fingertips. This time, my whole world was falling apart. Maybe the thirty-six-hour round trip to Tennessee would give me the clarity to make the right decision. I knew falling in love with another woman was wrong. Even if it was accidental, free from any worldly infidelity, what was I supposed to do with the knowledge I had never loved my wife that way? That I was capable of a love far greater?

Four hours into my trip, a bright glow from my cell phone cut through the darkness. It was a text from my wife: "This song reminds me of our situation from my perspective."

Clicking the YouTube link, arpeggiated notes from a distant piano rang out. "Icon for Hire, 'Only a Memory,'" I whispered. "This is my fault. She wouldn't know them if it wasn't for me."

Listening through the song, I knew she nailed it. You see, despite my evident actions, we explored the option of divorce. Had we drifted too far apart as individuals to ever be successful together again? While pondering one of the most significant decisions of my life, my childhood inadequacies remained. How could I put my son through that? Shouldn't we stay together for the kid like I dreamt my parents would do? A butler pampering a maid in an uncertain race toward death? That's not an idealistic approach to lifelong love.

Still, I knew she was right. She'd probably find the grace to forgive me. I, however, never would. Not after repeating the very history I always hated. This time, no one else was to blame except me.

Pieces / Icon for Hire

A few minutes later, she sent a second text. "This one's from your perspective." Clicking the link, another song from Icon for Hire's *Scripted*, entitled "Pieces," began playing.

You see, my messy life has always made me insecure. My wife, on the contrary, won the near-perfect life lottery. She hadn't experienced death; even her grandparents were still alive. She didn't know divorce; her parents were still married. She didn't know siblings; she was adopted by a family without any other children. She hadn't felt the weight of a wandering lost soul; she grew up in the church. My biggest fear was confirmed by receiving this song: I was the messiest decision she ever made.

Both songs nailed the bullseye of our situation. Sorry, Adam Gontier. You were wrong when you penned the lyrics to "Pain." I'd rather feel nothing than drill at exposed, sensitive nerves.

Sure, my wife's pleas deserved appropriate consideration, but we simply weren't a good match anymore. By her own Freudian confession, we never were. The mess I tend to mettle in was destined to destroy our relationship. Amidst the variety of life choices, I can't blame her for cutting ties from my constant need for custodial services.

Which One to Bury, Us or the Hatchet / Relient K

Some pastors I've spoken with prefer unity sand ceremonies during weddings. They often joke, "If the couple can divide the individual grains of sand, I'll offer them a divorce."

Divorce creates a massive break in communal unity. While dividing personal property, wagers were cast on our joint friendships. Angry phone calls, texts, messages on social media. If people felt the need to choose sides, I felt like they should take hers. After all, it was my wandering heart that created our conundrum. Further, I, the joyful unifier, never asked anyone to choose loyalties.

When a person doesn't defend their friendships, they'll lose 'em. One by one, the departures began, but not without the hurtful jeers from the sidelines. People who always knew I was a dirtbag. People who saw me as persistently self-serving. Well, dang. Why didn't they tell me I sucked when they first noticed it? Try as I may, yesterday's missed chances for self-help can't undo today's regrets.

Staplegunned / The Spill Canvas

I wish I could say my rapidly dissolving home front was specific to me. It wasn't.

The transition to normalcy was difficult for most of my closest friends from deployment. With similar issues, it became easy to touch base. Plus, explaining the entire backstory to someone new was exhausting. One quick message, a simple status check, breathed new life into the shaky baby steps another day in America required. "How do you feel today?" replaced "Why do you feel that way?" Not having to retrace your steps to journey forward casted the illusion of progress.

Despite our evident romantic interest, I continued trauma bonding with my female friend from the worship team. See, she returned home to an aggressive custody battle. The Guardian Ad Litem maintained illegal beliefs that uniformed servicemembers can't provide stability to developing children. Plus, we all have PTSD.

So, like me, she found herself thousands of miles from her support system. Day after rough day, our consolation came from knowing another person, far away from us, shared in the confusing pain we felt.

For all intents and purposes, I became a music consumer again. I didn't have the energy or motivation to create anything new. Reaching for answers, we swapped Bible verses, words of encouragement, and songs. Sure, at my lead, we shared certain rock songs. The rest of the music would make the strangest mixtape of all time. She sent indie, hip-hop, soul-type music. I sent obscure hard rock, calmer heavy metal, and country.

While it's great content, trauma doesn't afford the head space to blaze artistic trails. We begged, borrowed, and stole inspiration from others who already expended energy to say how precisely broken we were at the time.

Warrior / Evans Blue

After a sleepless night trying to drown out racing thoughts to Colin Quinn's *Long Story Short*, the sun sliced through my bedroom blinds. A full work day lay out before me. How was I supposed to be productive with less than thirty minutes of sleep? Sheer exhaustion, coupled with the perpetual weight of failure, sent me into a tailspin. Without explanation, I sent two separate songs to my friend: 10 Years' "One More Day" and Evans Blues' "Warrior." She knew I wasn't doing well.

Our time difference afforded us a brief phone conversation before we shuffled into daily existence. There I was, a Soldier fresh off a non-combat deployment, falling apart. She, a Soldier with actual combat experience, gave patient ears to my tearful lamentations.

Day after day, I spun through the rolodex of veterans with experiences far worse than mine. I was a pathetic, weak vessel. Suck it up, buttercup. When my self-deprecating chest pokes didn't calm the storm, I needed a maternal voice to motivate me. For my parting shot at redemption, I wailed along for some off-key karaoke.

"I am a warrior, not the victim of your pain."

Maybe if I repeated the words enough, I'd believe them. Unravel a bit before strapping on the pretend mask of stoicism. Depositing $5 of gasoline in a nearly empty tank, I knew I'd need to scrounge through couch cushions to refuel again. In the meantime, I had to clean up the mess, pack it away, and sort through the filth later. The public needed my appearance.

The Worst in Me / Like Moths to Flames

When numbness fades, all the other emotions start to surface. Sadness mounted first, but anger lived in its wake. Listen to the lies I told myself: "I don't need anyone's acceptance. People suck. They'll only let you down. I'm better off alone."

I've spent my whole life in indiscriminate pursuit of approval. I don't care who you are—friends, family, strangers in grocery store check-out lanes—I only long to be loved. However, childish temper tantrums don't appreciate the truth. They provide justification to pack a hobo sack with a lone G.I. Joe before running away from home.

For the first time since my Christian conversion, I halted formal church attendance. If people couldn't be trusted, I needed safe distance from vulnerable places. Sure, I had proof of a God Who loves and a Savior Who redeems broken people. Historical evidence of obsidian hearts melting into mounds of helpless goop. I was even proof at one point, but, like I said, cold hearts are never warm when you need them to be. When the numbness faded, I was tossed between ocean waves of indescribable sadness and anger.

My Confession / For Today

I can identify the exact moment I decided to cling to belief in God. The exact moment I traded sadness for a callousness not to be penetrated. Following my robotic routine of daily preparation, I cinched up my tie while listening to For Today's *Immortal*. As I wandered around the room looking for my tie clip, "My Confession" started playing. Why couldn't I just put it back in the tiny box it came in? Such a novel concept: put things in their rightful place. Dresser, nope; desk, nope; bathroom counter, nope. How else was I supposed to appear professional without it?

After several minutes of fruitless wandering, Mattie Montgomery knocked me from my trance: "I've not just seen evidence of Him, I've seen HIM!"

With tears streaming down my face, I collapsed to my knees. I prayed for a village worth trusting in. To rest in my knowledge of Christ's love until I could feel it again. No matter how sad I was, no more tears. Cleaning my face one last time, I closed my prayer. If I left now, I'd have enough time to buy a new tie clip on my way to work.

Poison & Wine / The Civil Wars

As I grew closer to my friend from deployment, the concept of forever grew. Like Joy and John Paul from The Civil Wars, we maintained healthy skepticism.

Love is, at best, a questionable substance to ingest. Its first taste is always sweet to the pallet, but lingering bitterness can inevitably ruin the experience. The friendship, the connection, was all there. I knew her better than anyone else. She knew me. That's the thing with love, though; its flavor changes over time.

Sitting at the imaginary bar, we were being forced into a decision. I changed most of my life for this moment. Cool condensation trailed down the bowl of the glass, resembling the sweat of anticipation. Yet, the inevitable downpour of bitter tears. For better or worse, the misty contents of this cup lead to an uncertain march toward death.

Prior to tipping the glass in a careless toast, appropriate evaluation must take place. The game of love fooled us before. What are your lingering fingers desires for my fragile heart? Where feelings may betray, logically, love makes little sense.

Meltdown / Love & Death

This period of life killed my curiosity for new music. For six straight months, I alternated between two CDs. Thousand Foot Krutch's *The End Is Where We Begin* empowered me some days and kicked me in the teeth on others.

How was I supposed to "be somebody" living in an apartment complex designed for college students? The innocent, incessant questions as to why I wasn't in a house like other adults. The piercing, judgmental glances shot my direction as I spent time with my son. Sprawled out in the messy bed I'd made, this life was nowhere near the glorious rise to victory I had envisioned.

Choking back a total loss of control, I popped in Love and Death's *Between Here and Lost*. Dark themes pinpointed my place: somewhere between deployment and utterly lost.

On the surface, I cast the appearance of a comeback, but my skull's contents told a different story. As the track count increased, Head and Mattie Montgomery persuaded me I didn't need answers; just W8 for the victory. By the CD's conclusion, I catered to invisible bruises enough to hand my insecurities over again. At least until the next drive I took. It didn't matter where I was physically going. Emotionally, I was headed for a meltdown.

Lost Weekend / Write This Down

In 2008, I found Write This Down during their earliest tours around the Midwest. I peddled their EPs to anyone who'd listen. By signing with Tooth & Nail, they gained some deserved mainstream recognition. After moving away from North Dakota, I lost track of them for a while.

A few years later, I was trading music recommendations with my brother when Write This Down came up in conversation. "I'm not sure they're a Christian band anymore," he messaged. "I've heard they're screwing up on the road."

Welp, we pray for redemption, remain forgiving, and speak loving truth if we ever meet them. Sure, platforms bear responsibility, but artists are still beings capable of failure. That was my stance in 2010.

Fast forward to the end of my deployment when I heard blotter of Write This Down's next release. *Lost Weekend?* A title too on the nose to my interaction with my brother. The rockstar lifestyle running rampant with admissions of infidelity and prancing around the party scene?

While I applauded the honesty, it was too raw for Christian audiences. Most of us could relate to the content but would never confess these sins in public prayer requests. Content this transparent would either break paradigms or kill careers. Since submitting my judgmental prediction, I've seen signs of both.

I know the weight of a lost weekend, that uncertain period when actions don't align with observed truth. As a card-carrying Christian, my plight was exactly backward. You can find redemption due to divorce, but Christianity can't plow through one. The apostle Paul says straight up in Romans 7:15, "I don't want to do what is wrong, but I do it anyway *(NLT)*."

Desperate decisions dictate every turn in the endless purgatory of lost. How long would my unresolved, compounding problems drive me away from my point of origin?

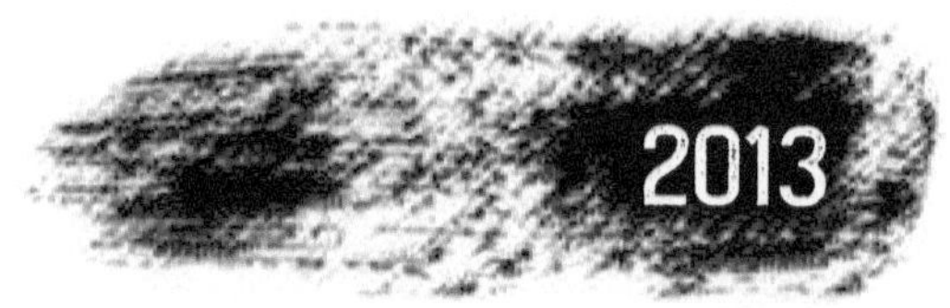

You'll Never Know / Mindy McCready

Most people didn't know about my country music roots. I tricked them into believing I was a lifelong metalhead. In frequent song exchanges with my girlfriend, I dropped the occasional Mindy McCready deep track to impress her with my artistic range. See? I was a legit fan until life pulled me in a different direction.

One monotonous morning in my office cubicle, I cold-called old leads from my desk phone. My girlfriend interrupted with a text message, "Did you hear yet? I'm so sorry." It included a news article detailing Mindy's tragic suicide. A month earlier, her boyfriend made the same choice, from the same spot on their front porch. In apparent grief, she killed the family dog before turning the gun on herself.

The lyrics to "Oh, Romeo" ran through my mind. "Why, Mindy?" I whispered. "You said you wouldn't die this way." Yet there I was, thumbing through the harsh reality of another unnecessary victim.

Sure, her surface-level beauty first drew my young, shallow heart in. However, her real beauty laid in the lessons she taught me about women. Stereotypes I attempted to ignore from the friend zone as a teenager. My precious Mindy discussed these double standards. Hit tracks, like "10,000 Angels" and "What If I Don't," gave perspective to the persistent pests my gender tends to be.

Oh, the media played charades with her sex tape. Dudes, like me, simply aren't scrutinized like women often are. "How could this happen?" some nameless newscaster asked. Those hypocrites televised her demise, then pretended to mourn her loss.

In memoriam, I streamed Mindy's entire catalog. Album after album, I honored yet another fallen star. Bo Burnham said it best: tortured artists invest an entire lifetime dishing out happiness they'll never obtain themselves. The very platform she used to empower others killed her. Another sheep lured to the slaughter drained from my remaining hope for the world.

Eclipsed / Evans Blue

As a child, I begged to know what my parents lacked to make marriage work. Now, I was living it. I can't account for how, or why, my divorce happened, either. I'll tell you all what I've told my son. I was sick, mentally incapable of making sound decisions. I zigzagged through a blur of doors, ducking through others, to maintain momentum. For better or worse, the fog of life consumed me.

After countless discussions, my girlfriend planned to leave active military service. Connecting our lives was one of the few decisions that made sense. We were broken, but fit together just right. For example, she hoped to pursue her lifelong dream of becoming a nurse. I, an expert in academic advising and veteran's education benefits, worked for a college with a nursing program. The little details of our complex puzzle came together.

As we talked more about the future, our conversations usually landed on marriage. Recent divorces didn't discourage us from re-entering the institution. Why delay the orbital intersection of the sun and moon? Why try denying the fusion of celestial light already set into motion? Ripped shreds from two torn family portraits assembled together to form one cohesive unit.

After she cleared her military responsibilities, I flew to New York to prepare for the move to New Mexico. A quick flight out. A 2200-mile trek back with two little boys and a dog I'd never met before. Between packing, loading, and road time, we had plenty of time to normalize the changes. Three days later, we walked through the door to our new home.

In one week, massive changes shook the unstable foundation my life rested upon. I went from weeknights alone to a family of five. From barely breathing to board games and bedtime stories. Sure, we still lived in a college apartment, but my soon-to-be wife was a student. I now had an acceptable answer to the question. We were no longer marking time, but moving toward the direction of our dreams.

Happy Together / Filter

Though it may not be fair to him, my son became ointment to my secret infection. Oh, the roller coaster I rode to find some semblance of comfort. The sheer ecstasy of seeing his small face on Friday evening. The peace of Saturday afternoons playing at the park. Lazy Sunday snoozes while watching *Curious George* with him in my arms. I had a lot of lost time to make up, and boy, did we cram life into those weekends.

Then, came Monday morning. Every week, the pain of letting him go never got easier. As I drove to drop him off, we listened to my tunes to stomp out intrusive thoughts. The little dude never stayed awake on car rides. Why should I have to listen to "The Wheels on the Bus" after he fell asleep? That wouldn't be fair to me; he was listening to my music. Plus, my fellow divorced parents can attest, accidentally listening to kids' music after they leave doesn't bode well with the spirit. You have to prime the pump for the impending gloom looming around the corner.

One particular Monday morning while driving to where his mom and I exchanged him, my iPod threw me Filter's rendition of "Happy Together." My heart froze within my chest. Like any other auditory accident, the experiential air bags deployed, tossing random memories around my car's interior.

There I was, collecting myself to music as I carted my kid around, just like Dad did with me. Glancing over my right shoulder, my son stared out the window at the sage brush dancing in the wind. I may be making this up, but he seemed sad. My past was his current reality. My past, his past. History was repeating. Repeating.

I paused the song to provide my two-year old with an explanation. What did Dad say when I needed comfort?

Nothing. He was holding back tears himself.

I panicked. OK, here goes nothing.

"Hey, bud, sometimes life's tricky," I reassured him. "I'm sorry you have to leave. I wish you could be with me all the time. You understand?" His innocent brown eyes met mine in the rearview mirror. "Love ya, bud," I said, extending my hand for a high-five. "Never forget that." Maybe I was talking for my own benefit. Wouldn't be the first time; has happened a million times since. Maybe I just love the sound of my voice.

After the exchange, I crawled back into my car. I invested the rest of my work commute obsessing the next inevitable step. The divorce, check. Unforgettable time alone with Dad, check. The remarriage, check. Two stepbrothers, HOLY CRAP, CHECK! Vying for Dad's attention, OH NO, check. What's next? Foster home? Not until the first day of the third grade. The next step was the doozy that hurt most.

I solved nothing. If anything, I gained an irrational fear of losing my son to the foster care system. Am I really strong enough to break the cycle? I've already repeated so much of it. Even worse, I gained a false sense of security on the second day of third grade. It's not like reaching a certain milestone makes him untouchable. Walking into work a few minutes later, it seemed like my whole life hinged upon that one linchpin in my personal history.

Zoe Jane / Staind

My fiancée and I raced into life together. She started nursing school three days after arriving in New Mexico. Six weeks later, we were married at a small ceremony through the municipal court. We expected our first child within our first year together. Simple math can prove my point; a pair of thirty-year-olds aren't gonna get any younger. By swiftly establishing our careers and family, we could make up for lost time. Hopefully, if we moved fast enough, we could outrun our traumatic pasts into the contentment we deserved.

Since we didn't get the opportunity with our older children, we saved the gender reveal until our child was born. It was meant to make the process exciting and new, our little way to explore life together.

I've always wanted a daughter. The tender elements of a female's personality resonate much clearer to mine. With three boys, the stakes elevated.

By focusing on little girl names, maybe we'd will our wishes into existence. Early on, I had a few finicky stipulations: her first name had to begin with an "A" to match ours and have two syllables. No more; no less. Also, I handpicked Jane as our hopeful little girl's middle name for two reasons. First, and foremost, I wanted to seamlessly swap our daughter's name into Staind's "Zoe Jane" as I sang her to sleep. Every other aspect of the song mirrored my hopes for her. My wife agreed with these crazy demands as we sifted through thousands of "A" names. Now, we just needed to have a little girl. Otherwise, what a waste of intellectual energy.

The Diary of Jane / Breaking Benjamin

The final inspiration for my daughter's middle name stems from Breaking Benjamin's "The Diary of Jane." I know, some people may question my choice to eternally link my daughter to this song. My wife didn't believe it to be appropriate, either. The Janes we're referencing are two different types of girls. Please put down your pitchforks and allow me to explain.

"The Diary of Jane" reminds me how destructive men can be in a woman's life. Adolescent psychology suggests that young women search for partners who treat them how their fathers did. If I wanted to raise a healthy, confident woman, I had to be present. I had to epitomize love and admiration. Fathers to boys can attest, there's distinct pressure in shaping them into young men. To me, it seems like a less stressful plight to protect a little girl. She doesn't need me to teach her the intricacies of being a woman; that's Mom's job. My success as a father is measured by steering her from dudes merely trying to get into her... diary.

Let me humor a quick sidebar discussion here. I AM NOT hinting that Benjamin Burnley's a chauvinist. Ben, a huge Nirvana fan, knows Kurt Cobain always preached men shouldn't hurt girls when they dance. Case and point: I've seen concert footage where Ben called out a handsy predator in his audience. He refused to proceed until security escorted the guilty party out of the venue. I AM arguing "The Diary of Jane" is a cautionary tale men can draw from to encourage healthy relationships. Soapbox concluded.

On delivery day, we grew to regret our decision to delay finding out our baby's gender. What if we had another little boy? All that energy choosing a female name, yet we barely considered one for a male. We stacked our eggs in one optimistic basket.

After an intense case of Braxton Hicks earlier in the day, getting trapped in rush hour traffic, and a few hours of labor, our first daughter was born. I can assure you, amongst her introductory moments on this planet, I sang both "Zoe Jane" and the acoustic version of "The Diary of Jane" to her. If you ask my wife, she still refuses to admit Breaking Benjamin had anything to do with her daughter's nomenclature. She can say what she wants, though. Through clever negotiation, I got what I wanted.

Blood Host / Scar the Martyr

The further I dove into dad life, the further I drifted from other things I loved. The knee-slapping hilarity of knock-knock jokes substituted for stand-up comedy. Answering kids' inquiries about the universe replaced my car karaoke sessions. That musical noise in the house? Don't need it anymore. Joyous shrieks from hide-and-seek and giggles from living room forts filled the void.

Being a button-downed professional, your friendly neighborhood father of four, kept me far too busy to invest in most releases. For the first time in months, two bands caught my attention. Taking a lunch break to begin my quest, I stopped at Best Buy for both albums I wanted. The hook from Scar the Martyr's "Blood Host" rolled through my head. Contents under pressure? Yep, like a shaken soda stored in a hot car. My life at the time defined by three words.

I couldn't find the second CD on the shelf. A college kid with long, curly brown hair consulted his system. Not in stock. Directing me to order it online, I politely declined. It'd been so long since I had this type of motivation. Let me check a few other places.

Hostage / Dangerkids

My next stop was Hastings (RIP). I wasn't able to find my sought-after CD there, either. Weighing out my next move, I was gonna have to go to the one place I didn't want to go.

Now, I'm no stranger to Hot Topic. My music collection, band shirts, and even pants, at one point, hold the proof. I WAS opposed to going to Hot Topic in a suit. And what, risk looking like a loser collecting lost nostalgia at the local mall? Or worse, a lame dad buying birthday presents for their misunderstood teenager? I really wanted the CD. Off to Hot Topic.

As I walked into the nearly vacant store, the dude behind the counter offered assistance. "Can I help you?"

"Um, I'm looking for Dangerkids' *Collapse*," I replied, motioning to a stack of Justin Bieber albums. "What is THAT? I shop here for obscure rock and metal. Our music has better offerings than Bieber."

Clearly overwhelmed, his sleepy eyes widened as he guided me to a CD rack on the wall. "It's over here. Yeah, we keep stuff in stock that'll sell. If you want rock/metal stuff, we still sell that online."

We finished our awkward conversation: the cashier, a dude wearing skinny jeans, chucks, and a band tee, and I, the awkward professional lamenting the current state of the music industry. Departing the store, I repositioned my Army tie and clip. That was a fun distraction, but reality called me back to work.

I Will Fail You / Demon Hunter

From the outside, my life may've looked glamorous. I had a full-time job helping veterans get into college. My military career was back on track. I moved my family from our tiny apartment into a two-story house. We began routine church attendance again. Demon Hunter even gifted me *Extremist* for my thirtieth birthday. Six days later, it served as the soundtrack for my first marathon.

Normal activities for your average thirty-year-old professional, right? People could review my rise as a textbook case of pickin' yourself up by the ol' bootstraps.

The simple fact remained; I still carried a plethora of unresolved emotions. You know that drawer in every American kitchen? To cast the appearance of cleanliness, you collect spare trinkets into one contained space. Maybe one day, you'll find purpose for all that junk, give it a rightful place, or discard it. I wanted people to believe I had everything figured out but suffered in intense silence. For the past half decade, my life slid on a downward spiral. What disastrous character flaw would finally fail the weak glue I was using to hold my life together?

You see, our beautiful little girl was diagnosed with partial deafness that could ripple into a potential lifetime of developmental delays. How would we know which resources to pursue to improve her situation? With her medical background, my wife understood intervention was necessary, but I wasn't immediately willing to accept help.

Fear began to chew on my spirit. Nonetheless, it was my responsibility to grin and bear it all. I only entertained these dark thoughts in my car, chain-smoking cigarettes on the ride home from work. Then, back into life's junk drawer. For me, the simple act of acknowledging the truth felt like accepting failure.

Nobody Praying for Me / Seether

If a tree falls in the forest and no one's around to hear it, does it make a sound?

What a ridiculous question. One I pondered with great frequency as I descended into a worsening psychological state. Why don't people see through the tree's rough exterior and know it's diseased? Why does it have to make noise to get help? Why wait for it to tumble before acknowledging the problem? Out of sight, out of mind, I guess.

After my ignored cries for help post-deployment, I feared failed attempts to reach out to others would only worsen my condition. A licensed therapist told me I was fine, for crying out loud. To avoid further disappointment, I kept writhing in silence.

Mind you, Christians love praying for people. A Bible study my family attended provided me with community and the opportunity to share my heart. A support system to guide me through my fragile state. In addition to fearing rejection, I was also cautious to become the emotional mess others avoided. My solution: rot from the inside out. I was risking a more tragic fall than I'd ever experienced. My worst fear was that this next one would be the end of me.

Friend / Track of Time

I began challenging my entire ecosystem, taking the brunt of my frustrations out on my wife. For several months, every discussion led to an argument. Every argument ended with empty threats of divorce. Like with most things, I invested as much as it took to convince outside parties I was invested. As long as the façade stood firm, I was fine. The mask I chose to wear eventually shattered into a million pieces.

One Saturday morning, my priorities for our weekend chores resulted in a disagreement. "You never asked what I wanna get done today," my wife stated. "Why do you always have to control everything?"

"You don't have to stay if you feel that way." I fired back, intending to end the argument.

Only, it didn't. Our heated exchange escalated to me blacking out in a fit of rage. For a solid minute, I can't account for a single word I screamed. When I returned to reality, my wife made me leave until I calmed down. No one was physically hurt, but I'll never forget our oldest son's pleas to cease the fight, the betrayal in his eyes as tears streamed down his rosy cheeks.

With nowhere else to go, I took a short drive before returning home to weed our flower beds. A loser of love working out negative energy for positive production. In the sweltering late summer sun, my focus shifted. What kind of maniac breaks a child's heart? If the environment allowed, I was determined to drive myself into heat stroke. Despite my deep belief that no one cared, my wife forced hydration before anything terrible happened.

We spent most of the afternoon avoiding each other. When we made time to talk, I gravitated to my catchphrase. "Maybe I'm meant to be alone. I'm kinda done. With marriage. With life. I dunno."

"What's that supposed to mean?" she asked. The dull glow of our front porch light showcased our impending public argument.

"I dunno. I need time to think about things." Storming off again, we resolved nothing.

As I drove around town, I received several calls trying to lure me from the ledge. My wife. Close friends she contacted for help. I blew them all off. From my perspective, I needed to ruminate in the mess I'd made. After an hour away, I grabbed some vodka and blue raspberry soda from the store. Maybe if I medicated enough to sleep, clarity would come with the morning.

When I arrived home, I grabbed my iPod and a glass, creeping to my home studio. Like my musical aspirations, the vacant room laid waste to my hopes and dreams for the future. No one would even know I was home.

A few mixed drinks later, it became apparent my life wasn't getting better. I tried; nothing worked. Running quick calculations for someone of my physical stature, how fast should I drink a fifth of vodka to kill myself? One hour. With a stopwatch set, I rationed death into manageable swallows. Finishing the final pull from the bottle, I lay down. The dark room spun in concentric circles around me. "Goodbye, cruel world," I whispered. My outstretched arms begged for one more chance to strum the acoustic guitar just beyond my reach.

Midway through the night, I woke up in a pool of vomit. My body decided to reject the alcohol. Sitting in my studio, I felt like a failure. How could I, a trained killer, not possess the skill to terminate my painful life?

I spent most of the next day alone. With kids still scared from my outburst, my wife played the good parent with fun distractions around town. The previous night's hangover pounded within my skull, rendering my productivity ineffective. I slipped into the garage with my iPod to catch a nap on the cold concrete. Through the shuffle function, Track of Time's "Friend" played. I reflected upon decades of departures while actively writing my latest installment. How long would sickness consume me? Why did I keep chasing people away? I broke down as the song repeated through my headphones.

I can't claim to understand fate, but as I unraveled yet again, my family returned home. My wife must've heard my sobs echoing off the metal garage door. A beam of light announced her entrance. "Tony?" she called out. "What's going on?"

"Listen," I begged, handing her an earbud. "I can't lose you. I just want you to be my friend again."

When the song finished, she gave my earbud back. "We can talk about this after the kids go to bed."

For the rest of the afternoon, I played with the kids in our inflatable backyard pool. Their justifiably apprehensive attitudes made me feel like a monster. After all, it was I who shattered fundamental trust in one careless motion. It turns out, destroying a reputation's much easier than rebuilding one. Then, dinner, baths, and bedtime. Rocking my daughter to sleep, I felt a tiny surge of purpose.

Later that evening, my wife and I talked for quite a while. "You wanna be my friend?" she asked. "I'd like to trust you, but the wounds are still too fresh. You need help, Tony."

For the first time in a while, I didn't threaten the situation with separation; however, our demise was hanging in the balance. Meaning, two divorces in less than three years. Negotiating visits for two different kids. I knew the stakes; I just never considered the weight of dropping them so casually in conversation. After our talk, I agreed to sleep on the couch until I earned her trust again.

An hour into restless tossing in our hot living room, I grabbed my iPod and went to the garage. Maybe the cool concrete would help me drift off to sleep. When I pushed play, "Friend" continued looping from my afternoon meltdown. There I was, alone again. Yet no better than before. Within two minutes, I spun out of control.

In my desolation, I sought an avenue for my suffering. Flipping the light on, my original intent was self-harm. A burn, or cut, served as a physical reminder of my psychological torment. If I ever healed, the scar would represent the bridge to my victory. *You promised you wouldn't burn yourself anymore,* I thought. *Screw it. I'll sort through that later.*

Searching the garage for a lighter, I noticed an electrical cord dangling from an outlet on the ceiling. Self-harm would only provide temporary relief. If I stopped existing, my failures would end with me for good.

From a standing position, I wrapped my makeshift noose around my neck and allowed my body to hang. I continued crying as music blared in my ears. My frantic thoughts raced. *I'm sorry you couldn't save me this time.* A few moments later, my fingers and toes began to tingle, like the sensation of limbs falling asleep. The suffering would subside. For me, for others after I was gone. They'd eventually realize I weighed them down.

Tingling faded to total numbness in my arms and legs. The pressure intensified on my neck as I struggled to breathe. For the first time, I considered the actual impact of my actions. What would Jesus say when I reported to Heaven with a bruised neck? What would my Soldiers think about me quitting the mission of life? I may've been a burden to my family, but at least, I was present. I couldn't do this.

When I tried to release the restraint of my noose, I couldn't lift my right arm past my waist. Using my shoulder as a catapult, I flung floppy arms at the cord. Three attempts later, I managed to move the dead weight. My numb fingers were losing grip on reality. Sending the usual cerebral order, I pulled from my shoulder until I collapsed to the floor.

Sobbing in the dim light, my heart pulsed, attempting to restore lost life to my limbs. As sick as it sounds, my sadness shifted to subtle acknowledgment. I couldn't outrun my ending.

When I gained enough strength to move back to the living room, my call was clear. Somehow, someway, I needed to find a path through the pain.

Take the Bullets Away / We as Human (Ft. Lacey Sturm)

Even after attempting to kill myself, I still didn't reach out for professional help. What if the mere mention of suicide tripped some alarm, sending an armed SWAT team to drag me to the looney bin? As the primary breadwinner, I couldn't afford losing our income if they chose to institutionalize me. I'd have to find ways to heal in stride.

Several Mondays later, my boss shared a sales tactic during a weekly conference call. Let me tell you about "The Power of One." Collect one more lead. Schedule one more appointment. Work one more hour per day. Ask one more question during sales pitches. Get one more enrollment. Then, what? Leverage the power of one, one more time.

Long story short, this man demanded every drop of my potentially exerted energy. Even though I prided myself as a good Soldier, decent dad, and husband, I had to risk failure in every other area to be a better military admissions rep. That, ladies and gentlemen, is the power of one. Success was limited to an unobtainable, ever-evolving imaginary portal most normal people never wander through.

In a moment meant to motivate, blood rushed to my head, intermittent audio blaring through my phone's earpiece. Hyperventilation so intense, I had to mute my phone to mask audible gasping. Dizziness so disorienting, I fought the urge to run out of survival instinct. The nervous breakdown I'd been trying to avoid, my first dance with the panic attack, was underway.

When the call wrapped, I hung up without saying goodbye. Snatching my DD-214 from the desk drawer, I staggered to my car in a literal mad dash. Curse the mental health stigma. If I wasn't seen by a therapist soon, the worry surging through my spirit might end me for real.

We as Human's self-titled album became a life staple after my suicide attempts. Every song seethed with a sense of hopeful anguish. As I drove to the Vet Center, I sought consolation from the relatable content in "Take the Bullets Away." I WAS worthless. I WAS filthy, but did I take too long to disarm myself? I had no idea. All I knew, any effort had to be better than loitering near rock bottom.

Before going in to be seen, I wiped the tears and snot from my face. Once the fresh crying look drained from my eyes in the visor mirror, I gathered the courage to wander into the clinic, unannounced. Here goes nothing. One more time.

I Am a Stone / Demon Hunter

I only told my wife and one other person about my weekly counseling appointments: a sweet, older co-worker I affectionately called Mom. She coached me through adult therapy. After conducting a few assessments and establishing a treatment plan, there would be one intense, soul-splitting session. Like resetting a broken bone, the pain would help me heal.

About a month in, my counselor recommended a guided meditation. "Isn't that a Buddhist practice?" I asked. "The word 'meditation' makes me uncomfortable."

"As Christians, Jesus calls us to pray," she said. "Think of it like that. Plus, you need healthy coping mechanisms. Another tool in your toolbox. Let's try this once to see if it works. Deal?"

"I guess you're right," I admitted. "You're the expert. My methods are clearly not working."

Following a mindfulness warm-up, the narrator navigated me toward the location I felt most at peace. Through random recall, I stood at the bank of

Patterson Lake in North Dakota. Then, she directed me to focus on people I hadn't seen in quite some time. I'm not sure why, but my Grandma Marie and cousin Nate came to mind. The ailments they experienced in life were gone, previously frail bodies upright with vibrance. Skipping rocks at the base of the lake, we enjoyed the afternoon.

A few moments later, we sat in the sand watching gentle waves crash to the shore. From behind me, I felt a hand squeeze my right shoulder. A sensation so vivid, I had to open my eyes to check for a physical hand. No one was there.

Closing my eyes again, I turned around, face-to-face with Jesus Himself. Using my shoulder as support, He sat down next to me. Without a word, the fulfillment of intimate conversation developed in silence. All the questions I had for Him escaped me. Just being with Him was enough.

When the exercise ended, I shared the experience with my counselor. Why might my grandma and Nate make an appearance? We theorized that Jesus was my subconscious safeguarding my belief system.

"How do you feel?" my therapist asked.

"Calm," I replied. "The chaos is gone for now."

"Try this exercise any time you feel pressure this week. If you feel trapped in situations you can't leave, try rhythmic breathing in place."

Returning to work on the city's busiest street, Demon Hunter's "I Am a Stone" incited warmth within my heart. I felt loved. I can't explain it, but I reacted the only way I knew how. I engaged in an argument with God. "So, you love me. What am I supposed to do with that?" I shouted.

God asked, "If I love you, can't you love yourself?"

"Nope. I, along with most people, suck."

"Look at that skyscraper. I made it. I made the people who made that building. I formed their thoughts to use the materials."

"So?"

"Look at that car next to you. I made that car. I made the female driving it. The streets. The stoplights. Everything around you. I had a hand in all of them."

"No, duh. I know that. This isn't news. Why do You love me?"

"I made the universe. It spins the way I want. I set it all into motion—"

"I know," I interrupted. "Run the universe. You're doing fine."

"Thanks for giving me permission to run the universe. I know what I'm doing. I know what I want and I love you."

Keep in mind, my portion of this conversation was out loud. A very real lady sat in a very real car next to mine as I sobbed and screamed on one of the city's main drags. Guaranteed, I looked like a lunatic that afternoon. If I ever get the pleasure of meeting her, I owe her an explanation, and perhaps, an apology.

Just like that, God knocked me to my knees. For years, I falsified arrogance, limiting my dealings with feelings of inadequacy to my frequent cigarette breaks throughout the day. The remaining time I danced around the answers to all of life's complexities. In my journey of learning to live again, the first step toward redemption resided in finding ways to forgive myself.

Monster / Unlocking the Truth

As a political scientist, I loved *The Colbert Report*. When Stephen announced his departure from Comedy Central, the show gained relevance. The era, symbolic to this phase of my life, was ending. Just like he couldn't expect to carry his falsified persona into his next gig, I couldn't, either. How does a person walk away from the familiar façade, the characters we created over the past decade, to fully move forward?

For his last few years, I watched every episode until his brand of satire left the air. When I lagged behind, I'd host a private DVR cleaning party, binge-watching several at a time. In fact, two episodes stayed locked in that magical machine until it gave out. His final taping's almost self-explanatory. I called upon nostalgia to exploit the void he left in my life. The other episode probably requires some explanation.

With little interest in new music, I hadn't heard a band that inspired me in quite some time. Unlocking the Truth? That sounds like a band. A good one. After these kids performed their hit "Monster," I sat in awe. From my lazy position on the couch, I googled them for more information. Through frequent performances in Times Square, they signed a record deal and opened on Marilyn Manson's "Hell Not Hallelujah" tour. Their aspirations to succeed in music exceeded mine by a long shot.

I watched that episode every time my motivation waned. What was I doing with my life? When was the last time I even touched a musical instrument? Sure, I built a home studio. Sure, I wrote a few new lyrics while my solitary music production rotted in a vault of endless excuses. These young dudes provided some semblance of artistic inspiration. Not enough to record something new, but for the first time in a while, I found belief in the dream again.

Cold Like That / Garth Brooks

I missed my daughter's first birthday, and most of that Christmas season, due to Army training. Instead of rockin' jingle bells, I clocked in for exhausting twelve-hour overnight shifts at Fort Cavasos. A beast my family's all too familiar with. To ease the burden, I promised the kids to slip our annual almond bark dipping into the schedule when I returned home.

My first weekend back, I shopped for supplies: Oreos, pretzels, marshmallows, peppermint shards, and garnish. The extra effort's always worth the joy those snacks create. Experimenting with ingredients to find the perfect balance. Passing plates of aesthetically pleasing treats during Christmas movie marathons. Selecting the best cookies from the batch for Santa, complete with a few baby carrots for his reindeer. Maybe when they're adults, they'll understand the greatest gift I could ever give them was intrigue for the season.

I made my list, checked it twice, but on my last pass-through Walmart, Garth Brooks' *Man Against Machine* peeked out from an oversized store display. Could it be it's been fourteen years since that autumn night his retirement was announced? That ol' wind had once again found its way home.

Studying the track list, I reminisced the unlikely journey since those innocent teenage days. Becoming a metalhead, going to college, an Army career. All the memories of listening to his music in my room came flooding back. Sure, my family had all heard GB on my iPod, but there's no way they understood the extent of my former obsession. With trembling hands, I dropped the CD into my cart.

Fast forward to Christmas morning, one of the kids hands me a CD-shaped gift. Throwing a sly wink my wife's way, I explained how Santa always brought me Garth's newest release. Let's be real for a minute—I was never surprised to get his albums. It still didn't diminish the joy when I bought it for myself.

A few minutes later, I listened to my new treasure. Time I used to invest scouring liner notes was replaced by assembling children's toys. The words I used to study, still unread to this day. I guess certain aspects of life will always remain the same. Others morph with the demands thrust upon us.

Sever (Unplugged) / We as Human

With continued counseling, life began to normalize. The financial tension of school expenses relieved as my wife graduated and started working swing shifts as a licensed practical nurse. All great signs, especially since we learned of our second pregnancy together. Without the stresses of college and my meltdowns, we were in the right place. Decorate a nursery. Attend baby appointments. Less stringent name selection. With clear heads, we could enjoy the process of having child number five.

Until the first ultrasound.

Underdevelopment to the left side of his heart would force the right side to work harder to compensate. A condition doctors feared was an atrioventricular septal defect in utero, and possibly hypoplastic left heart syndrome, would cause persistent lifelong health issues. A high-risk pregnancy with referrals to several skilled specialists: OB/GYNs, geneticists, cardiologists, pulmonologists, and nephrologists. They all monitored him for appropriate diagnosis outside the womb.

Genetic testing further diagnosed our son with an unbalanced chromosomal translocation. Dad made mention of my mom's "twisted chromosome," but I had no idea what that meant until a doctor explained the results. My cleft lip and palate, and being a little different most of my life, may have been caused by a balanced translocation.

In essence, genetic material had broken off my second and sixth chromosomes and interchanged during development. Our child inherited my abnormal second and my wife's normal sixth chromosome. A lesser-known congenital anomaly with little research to further complications he may encounter as he grew.

Inside the womb, he was safe. Mom's body performed all the functions he couldn't. In the meantime, we had to wait five more months for an accurate picture of his deficiencies and the corrective actions necessary to fix them. We collected as much information as possible to prepare for the journey ahead. Not to mention, the possibility of losing him.

Most parents can relate to these come-to-Jesus moments with their kids. You know the type—they rip away from your protective grip, headed toward traffic. You snatch them away and make sure they're ok. Calm your racing imagination. Provide loving instruction about maintaining safety. They don't do it again and worries subside. That was our previous extent in dealing with the mortality of a child.

As parents, we remain oblivious to death because it's rare for a parent to bury their child. Until you can't. That traumatic accident. A health issue. Then, our attention is piqued. In a weird paradigm, the frailty of life becomes more apparent. While preparing to welcome our little one into the world, we remained on guard for his untimely departure.

Ashes of Eden / Breaking Benjamin

Receiving a grave diagnosis for a child raises some spiritual questions. Was God attempting to capture my attention? Was He punishing me for past sins? Did I not possess the faith to pray this phase away? Could I do anything to take my son's place? Swirling self-doubt, persistent personal blaming, and cycles of suffering took center stage during my therapy sessions.

Social media gave my wife the ability to find an effective support system of people with shared experiences. As we moved into uncertainty, she collected feedback from other parents with "heart babies." The trial and error, the victories, the delays, the medicines, the physicians, the tests, the surgeries, and—most of all—the journey. The process was plagued with terrifying lows. It forced us to plan for things like potential funeral arrangements, heart transplants, and explanations to our other children about how this stuff works without an understanding ourselves.

It's also marked with incredible highs. She logged on to celebrate the victories most parents take for granted with regular kids. When everything feels like life or death, their first steps carry more meaning. Recommending ruthless advocates who will fight for your child. Weaning a medication, brace, or machine from aggressive routine. Every moment with special needs children possesses unparalleled intensity and a severe emotional price tag. A cost, thankfully, unknown to those outside our community.

I used Breaking Benjamin's *Dark Before Dawn* to medicate my tensions. As Ben entered into fatherhood for the first time, every track on the album became an immediate anthem for our corresponding identity crises. How else was I supposed to process this complex information? You guessed it: through song.

Mom / Garth Brooks

During her last month of pregnancy, my wife relocated to the Denver area in the event of an emergency. If our son didn't arrive early, doctors planned to induce a week earlier to begin tackling his medical needs.

To add fuel to the fire, a few days before I left, another family's situation worsened in the Children's Hospital of Colorado heart baby community. The night prior to my departure, their little girl, Macii, passed away. As I read the status updates from my wife, I had one last meltdown. Curled behind the couch, not to be caught by the kids, I prayed for escape from this diagnosis. Begged for comfort for Macii's parents. Sobbed for understanding. What did innocent children do to endure this level of suffering?

The next day, I opted to work to save vacation time, then traveled at night to allow the kids to sleep through the drive. I never accounted for being left alone with my thoughts. With every passing mile, tension built within me.

Imagine holding a human heart in the palm of your hand. Slowly, and I mean slowly, you apply subtle pressure with every ticking second. Pulling into Denver thirteen hours later, my heart was locked in a tight vice. All while acting entirely unphased for the benefit of my family.

Back at Children's Hospital of Colorado, our little girl was admitted with her third bout of pneumonia in two months. Swallow studies confirmed she was silently aspirating liquids thinner than yogurt. To circumvent the problem, her medical care team planned to install a gastrointestinal feeding tube.

With recovery time during our son's delivery, we had a plan to manage the chaos of those first critical moments. On the big day, my parents arrived from North Dakota. My wife's doctor planned to gradually induce her overnight to reduce unnecessary pressure on our son's heart. According to him, we needed to be ready for thirty hours of labor. No matter how crazy things got, we had five adults to cover four kids: two in the Ronald McDonald House, one in the pediatric department, and one incoming. Running the gauntlet of good nights, we seeded affirmations into our final instructions.

From the parking lot, I showed my wife Garth's performance of "Mom" on *Good Morning America*. In a few short hours, we'd have three patients spread across three rooms on three separate hospital floors. With quality time in short supply, we sipped from the last experience we could get.

Think about the song for a minute. Garth sings about God's conversation with an unborn baby. Why leave a warm womb for this cold world? From our child's perspective, this womb held extra protection. His potentially frail heart and lung function were being taken care of. It packed an extra punch when applied to our situation.

Walking what felt like the longest hall in human history, we swapped war stories. Not current sentiment, but details from our extensive military careers. Twenty years in total. With intention, our gaze fixed toward an uncertain portal.

The point of no return.

"Mission number 15128-01 requests permission to SP; time 2000." Adrenaline blinds the terror to go places we ought not enter. We planned. We prepared. We trained. Yet none of that survives the brutality of a first bullet in flight.

The point of no return.

Battle was about to begin. Our ultimate test, the culmination of our collective experience, lay before us. That gate where duty defies all logic and human emotion. At the end of this hallway, we dared not look back. Somewhere along the way, we crossed the threshold to a world that would never be the same.

All Apologies / Nirvana

Our son was born after thirty hours of labor. For his first deed on the planet, he sprayed multiple members of the nursing staff with pee. Intuition told us we had a fighter on our hands. A brave warrior prepared to tackle the atrioventricular septal defect doctors had diagnosed him with.

That first week, we engaged in several intense conversations, often several times per day. Heart transplants, corrective surgeries, donor registries, insurance coverage, end-of-life care. In total, more than twenty departments from his specialty care team guided our steps through this scary maze. We expected a month-long hospitalization, minimum, before they'd consider a local discharge to the Ronald McDonald House. Fingers crossed, my family would stay in Denver for an additional month to establish home health care.

I, the provider, had to mind the fortress six hundred miles away. Sure, there'd be visits, but information gaps controlled the situation. Kissing our son's forehead one final time, my prayers morphed from "Please God, don't take our son," to "Please don't allow him to die while I'm gone." Every goodbye was expressed with sincere finality.

When I returned home, the silence was deafening. There was no one to help. Nothing to do, but callously earn cash. Man's punishment for our sin was to toil the earth, so toil the earth I did.

Rather than face my feelings, I distracted myself with Kurt Cobain's tragic story depicted in HBO's *Montage of Heck*. Every single day, sometimes even twice, I can confidently declare a watch count in the hundreds. I'm not sure what I was looking for, but I coupled this practice with my copy of *In Utero* spinning in the car stereo. Every work commute was soundtracked by the exclamation point of Kurt's career. Judge if you must, but these two customs prevented me from fleeing to Denver whenever I had the slightest doubt about where I belonged.

Since that summer, I've discovered a better answer for my actions. Kurt Cobain was subjected to a frame-by-frame, back-alley psychological assessment. He sang about the legendary divorce setting his frantic life into motion. His perceived rejection. His supposed homelessness. His paradoxical rise to fame. When given a chance to rewrite history as a husband/father, he failed. Every experience was captured through a song, painting, poetry, or journal entry.

Comparing our stories, his life was all too familiar. How many contradictory hopes and fears was I perpetuating? What was I doing with my accomplishments? How often had I invented a scenario in my head for dramatic license? Most importantly, how could I convert my unmanageable filth into relatable art?

Angels Fall / Breaking Benjamin

Where Nirvana was my in-town persona, Breaking Benjamin became my Denver identity. A twenty-six-hour round trip dedicated to one album. While in the hospital visiting my son, *Dark Before Dawn* served as my signal to him that I was present. No other person in his world was listening to rock; it could only be me.

"Angels Fall" will always be his dedicated anthem. Sure, I dream of being a hero to my kids, but I never suspected the opposite was possible. Then, I met this little dude. He has more barriers than most people ever have to face, yet somehow, he doesn't act limited in any way. Not by heart or lung function. Not by decreased energy levels. Not by poor eyesight, a failure to hear completely, or even delays caused by jail sentences in hospital beds. He doesn't care.

Maybe one day, I'll pursue my own dreams with the same level of tenacity he does.

I've Got You Under My Skin / Seether

On my trip to Denver for Independence Day, our daughter was scheduled for craniosynostosis repair. In short, a surgical team cut and peeled back her scalp to break and reform her skull. This procedure would relieve her of potential intracranial pressure, sinus issues, vision problems, headaches, and personality changes. By this point, I felt, short of death, the contents of our darkest dreams were somewhere in the rearview mirror.

During the pre-surgery x-ray, a radiology tech and I had to pin her to a padded table to get necessary imagery. A buzzing spider-like robot hovered overhead, threatening to land on her tiny face. I could almost read her thoughts through the panic in her eyes. "Why are you allowing this, Daddy? Why are you helping them?"

She attempted to wrestle away from us while shrieking the only word she could pull from her limited vocabulary, "Stop!"

Once the last photo was stored safely in their system, she crawled into my arms, her tight grip seeking solace from the trauma we subjected her to.

We'd been adequately briefed on the surgical procedure and what to expect during post-op. Even all this guidance couldn't prepare us for the swelling, the discomfort, and the drainage system her surgeon installed to collect cranial fluid. The inevitable hurt inflicted in the moment would help her later. Now, imagine signing waivers to permit the pain. The whole process opposed my instincts to protect her from unnecessary hardship.

Even after pain meds and sedatives, our daughter still stirred every few hours. Trapped in a world of darkness, she couldn't open her eyes. Couldn't explore the baseball-like stitches in her scalp due to arm restraints. Couldn't change positions due to IVs, monitoring cables, and drainage system. My wife and I spent several sleepless nights cuddling with her in a hospital crib, imprisoning ourselves behind the very bars we authorized.

Within twenty-four hours, surgical swelling reduced enough for our daughter to watch the fireworks outside her hospital window through tiny slits. Her cranial drain was removed, guiding her first steps from shadows cast by the knife. The fiery attitude we'd grown accustomed to returned, but with less fear. We transitioned from mourning her discomfort to worrying she'd hurt herself. The protective helmet, given to her post-op, was a futile guard to the force she became.

While we signed the aforementioned waivers, doctors reassured us of a toddler's resilience. Imagery that haunts us thankfully erases from their developing memories. Experiential caution that paralyzes adult action is a speed bump to them. There's significance in looking up to those small children we look down on. At our daughter's lead, nothing in this world should ever keep us down. Take a momentary tumble, sure. Seize on your knees, not a chance.

Failure / Breaking Benjamin

My family returned from Denver just in time for school. Our son had done well enough locally for doctors to feel comfortable sending him home. Our daughter recovered. While they were sent with stacks of medicines, machines, and specialist referrals, they were home. With victorious fists to the sky, we celebrated survival. A vindictive slap to Darwin's lazy decree that the weak be thinned from the herd. Not in our circle. Swarm the violent survivors. Poise for vicious attack to anyone who dares to disrupt their progress.

Not to appear ungrateful, but excitement soon settles. Without support from hospital staff, all concerns sit squarely on the parents' shoulders. A lot of lost sleep double-checking monitors. Where are his heart rate and oxygen levels? Is he breathing?

Consulting the backs of medicine bottles. Did we deliver the correct dosage with correct timing?

Doubting the accepted course of action. Would they better benefit from moving closer to doctors who understood their conditions? Could we get proper care if we didn't?

Questioning your parental capabilities. Did the other kids feel loved? Were we neglecting certain needs since they were perceived as normal?

Reconsidering career paths. When would the speed of high-pressure sales outpace my ability to keep up? Would my need to progress in the Army be impacted by these delays?

Tucked behind all the questions, the uncertainty, we had little answers. Victory became less apparent. All that remained was the possibility of dire failure, one fell swoop from a total loss. While I'm somewhat ashamed to admit it, my acting skills became very sharpened. To those around me, I appeared happy, confident, and unshakeable. Internally, I had never felt so desperate.

The Heart of a Graveyard / Demon Hunter

In a demented game of Russian Roulette, my paranoia spun like loaded rounds waiting to be chambered. The fatal bullet, matters concerning our son's health, fired into fruition quickly. After two months at home, he was transported back to Denver with what doctors dubbed a superinfection: a viral strain dangerously blended with bacterial and fungal infections. Add already decreased lung function, and he crossed into a health crisis. Do not pass Go. Do not collect $200. Total erasure of every strategic move on the board.

After several days of recovery, I received a frantic phone call from my wife. The shrill alarm of hospital machinery screaming in the background. "Heart rate, pulse, blood pressure, oxygenation, it's all dropping," she informed me. "They have the crash cart next to me to call the code."

"A code?" I asked. "How? He was doing great in the video you sent me yesterday. Like, miracle-level improvement. Playing, laughing, cooing—"

"Heart babies turn quick, Tony. We could lose him tonight. Stay on the phone with me. I can't do this alone."

From inside the room, staff scurried around. Muffled voices shouting instructions. Various alarms shrieking in unbearable call and response. Hospital instrument packaging being torn open on the bedside table. The chaotic synergy of lifesaving measures in progress. I held my breath and prayed.

Then, nothing. All efforts dulled to a deafening silence. Defeat. "April? What's going on?"

"They intubated him, so he's breathing again. He's stable."

From six hundred miles away, I came within inches of listening to my son die over the phone. Nothing to do but listen for the flatline. Extend a sad goodbye to a fairly short hello.

I can't forget having to carry on with life. While my son was in a medically induced coma, pointing all existential energy toward fighting sickness, I went to work. Keeping up with the other kids: homework, baths, fractional family meals, school events, even Halloween. I found my own hum to forge forward.

I was sitting in training for work when I got the call from a Denver number. My heart dropped. My wife was there, why would they call me? "Hello?" I answered.

"Mr. Kessel, this is cardiac surgery at Children's Hospital of Colorado. I have your wife sitting with me, discussing the possibility of open-heart surgery for your son. There's a spot available the day before Thanksgiving if you'd like to take it."

"Heart surgery? He was admitted for a superinfection. Is he even stable enough after his episode the other day?"

"He is, yes. We're confident he's on the back end of that illness. You see, we did an echocardiogram today. His heart isn't getting better with growth. In fact, it's getting worse. I believe occurrences, like we faced the other afternoon, will only increase if left untreated."

"So, the day before Thanksgiving?"

"Yessir. With the holidays coming up, our surgical schedule's full. I had a vacancy open up tomorrow. Your wife tells me you're praying people. I can't tell you what to do, but if you ask me, the time's now. Call it fate or faith, but the stars have aligned."

Running some quick calculations, I had sixteen hours to conduct thirteen hours of travel with three children. Pack, collect the kids from their respective locations, get gas, feed them, then hit the road. If I didn't delay at all, I'd make it with enough time to see him off to a twelve-hour surgery.

"Welp," I replied. "I guess, it's a no-brainer. Let's go."

Sixteen hours later, I saw my son for the first time in two months. With my hand on his heart, like a stack of Bibles, I swore this wouldn't be the last time I saw him alive. We maintained persistent prayer as his hospital bed disappeared into the sterile surgical environment.

Updates came every couple hours. His heart was connected to a bypass machine to perform critical functions. The mitral and tricuspid valves were repaired with septal defects closed ahead of schedule. While attempting to take him off bypass, the surgeon nicked a valvular structure, causing a tear. Back onto the machine. Initial repairs failed, further tearing the artery. After a second attempt, the stitches held tight enough to sustain the blood pressure pounding against it. During post-op discussions, his surgeon clarified the severity of this setback: damage done to the aortic arch is often fatal. Twice within the same week, our son survived despite insurmountable odds.

Four hours later, we settled into his room to begin recovery. To aid the process, his doctors decided to keep him in a medical coma for the first few days. I spent my whole vacation beside his bed.

When Breaking Benjamin got stale, a playlist of my favorite songs soundtracked our silent showing of the Macy's Thanksgiving Day Parade. As the Snoopy float danced down 34th Street, a strange paternal instinct nudged me to check on our son. Every monitor showed favorable stats, but I couldn't shake the feeling.

Something was wrong.

I approached the hospital bed with tears streaming down his face. Because he was intubated, his vocal cords couldn't close to project a need for human contact. There he was: stitches, tape, tubes, cables, IVs, and a gnarly incision resting upon his broken ribcage. Dare I say—I'd never witnessed such heart-wrenching torment in my entire life. When he wanted to cry out for help, he physically couldn't. He was willing to fight but didn't want to wade through the filth alone.

Standing at his bedside that Thanksgiving morning, I descended into my final rock bottom. With Demon Hunter's "Heart of a Graveyard" blaring in the background, I was consumed with overwhelming guilt. A year prior, when I almost ended it all, I didn't dare share with anyone. This infant possessed more moral fortitude than me.

Sure, after several months of continued counseling, I was improving, but his example was the perfect psychological experience to shake me awake. I was a coward for wanting to die. In my child's fight for life, I finally found the purpose for mine.

Deserter / For Today

If there's any indication a person's healing after a mental health crisis, it's a return to what used to captivate them. After an extended absence, For Today's *Wake* began gracing my CD player. The whole album explored the relationship between two brothers—one stays in the faith and one departs. The famed path of the prodigal. The desolation driving glorious return. It was time to mend the burnt-down bridges my lost wandering had caused: with old friends, with family, with those around me.

I didn't just dive into music as a consumer. After spending several months in hospital waiting rooms collecting sounds, photos, and song ideas, I began putting experience to paper. For the first time in my life, I wasn't concerned with whether anyone wanted to buy the product I peddled. After multiple years of torment, I stopped caring about what people might think of me. I finally had a message to carry to the masses.

Am I Awake? / POD

The next CD I dove into was another concept album: P.O.D.'s *The Awakening*. Track after track, listeners follow the main character through Armageddon. Dangerous entanglements through messy affairs, drug use, parental hatred, and the sin lifestyle. For some people, it takes the world ending to return to grace.

As I studied several concept albums, I strung my separate ramblings together to form the base material for my next project. With today's technology, I don't have to dazzle a record label for studio access. Home recording has even taken a massive leap since I recorded my demo in 2012. Through software advances, plugins, music production tutorials, and affordable recording solutions, I don't have to settle for black metal audio quality to pursue my artistic vision. By golly, my musical dream may still be alive!

Truth be told, the eleven tracks are still not recorded, or even entirely written. However, their fragments remain in varying developmental stages within my little black notebook and digital audio workstation. Maybe someday, I'll finish my first full-length concept album.

Mourning Star / Gemini Syndrome

After a miraculous recovery, our son was discharged from the hospital nine days before Christmas. The journey home was plagued with blizzard conditions and several road closures. His portable feeding machine, oxygen, and medical stat sensors plugged into every power outlet inside our minivan. Against all odds, yet again, we made it home in time for a storybook Christmas, just like the ones mentioned in most holiday movies and music.

While my outlook on life had improved, another fear materialized. After nine months of constant doctor's appointments, hospitalizations, and early childhood intervention sessions, my job displayed strong disapproval toward my family's needs. With one counseling statement, I went from a perfect employee record to final warning before termination. I can't say this came as a surprise. Our kids' persistent need for paternal involvement hacked into their precious bottom line. Something had to give. From my perspective, it wasn't going to be my family.

If anything proved as accurate, life's a perpetual battle. We live to die another day. Struggling to support children with special needs is a worthy cause. Somewhere along the way, I acquired the will to fight. Not to sit idly by while the world blurred past me. Sometimes, all you need to raise the stakes is a visible enemy. Although my clock with the company was ticking, I finally identified who I was, what I was fighting for, and who I was fighting against.

This Is the Time / Nothing More

My counselor diagnosed me with anxiety. I'd hate to generalize; however, anxiety's a disease of control. Any situation could trigger a tape of every perceived failure repeating inside our heads. What should be improved? What can be sustained? Sure, I get some of that, but my hang-ups often center around breaches of ethical standards. When people are unsympathetically unwilling to be better, I dwell. What heroic action could I take to generate a different outcome?

The answer's simple. A person can only control what they say or do. Nothing more. Nothing less. It's almost too brilliant for human understanding, especially a person desperately seeking to understand it.

Sometimes, it's hard to console yourself when you're pinned behind a log truck. In your head, you imagine the tie-down snaps or slips. Within a solitary second, a fifteen-foot pole drills through your windshield, right through your fickle skull. How would you react? Would your response even matter?

Now, imagine these events on perpetual loop, bogging you down throughout the day. I liken it to thumbing through a choose your own adventure book. Charting every potential path guarantees you reach the happily ever after.

While my situation was better than it'd been in a while, I simply could not shut off the noise. Despite my hatred for the institution, I self-medicated through alcohol use. Three to four beers every night took the edge off enough to stop me from visualizing every worst-case scenario.

Oh, I knew the risks. Alcoholism runs in my family. It limited my ability to do other things in the evening, like operate a motor vehicle. Immobilizing myself in an actual emergency. None of that mattered. The whispers of my failures, the threat of future let-downs, dissipated enough to get a decent night's sleep. My insecurities would return in the morning, and I'd have to crawl through them again, returning home to my few drinks. I was prepared for the aftermath as long as I didn't have to deal with the noise.

Wrong Side of Heaven / Five Finger Death Punch

The business of building façades is hard to get out of. Let's face it: no one wants to watch you circle the drain forever. As a Christian, I had a particular status to maintain. Too blessed to be stressed. Let go, let God, right? Freshen the paint on that Christian Poker Face.

It's similar for Soldiers. Bootstraps? Grab 'em. Dust off. Move forth and do great things. Transcend standards to pass the next in-ranks inspection.

Oddly enough, one circle faced their situations with honesty. Sure, the conversations were tormenting, but rewarding. The war stories. The survivor's guilt. The fatigue. The rock-bottom conversations of addiction and suicide. The attempts to get better. One group knew the cost of flimsy façades all too well: my Veteran brothers and sisters, former members of the armed forces.

I loved not having to give a backstory. We didn't have to spell out acronyms. Or explain why certain things, like basic training, were necessary. Or answer unsettling questions from civilians: "Have you ever killed someone?" Or apply filters to often unacceptable discussions. Let's face it, I even married a fellow veteran due to this dynamic.

One evening, a buddy and I threw back a few beers, trading tall tales from our respective careers. Like clockwork, we ducked outside for a cigarette every thirty minutes. The conversation turned from playful banter to somber reflection. We concluded we'd both been drowning for quite some time. Vets are great at helping others, but horrible at self-care. With the keen eye of another brother, we'd deploy the life raft when the oppressive waves of past regrets became overwhelming.

There's a reason airlines advise to put your own oxygen mask on before assisting someone else. A flailing soul in the ocean cannot save another. It takes a level head, from firm ground, to perform lifesaving measures. I know from experience. That particular veteran succumbed to the riptide of his personal demons. Despite all the oversight from other vets. All the buddy checks. All the conversations. He eventually drowned.

With this new war waging from the home front, a different form of survivor's guilt exists. Yet, regret is the hidden poison to mental health. The façades we built to hide our guilt will inevitably fall, forcing us to face reality. My veteran buddies taught me that. From solid ground, all we can do is find ways to carry the flag forward with honesty.

Fragile Minds / Silent Theory

In dealing with anxiety, people often advise me not to worry about things I can't control. While they mean well, several strange predictions from my worst-case scenario collection have come true. Our children's medical needs caused my wife to depart the workforce to become a zero-salary, full-time caregiver. Our son's heart condition spiraled into a near-loss of life and emergency surgery.

Threats of termination forced me to take a new job with less pay. Financial crisis tripped revolving doors of dodging creditors, downgrading living accommodations, vehicle repossessions, and power/water turnoff notices. Call it a self-fulfilling prophecy or an avalanche sliding down slippery slopes, but worrying has served me well.

With every miniscule step forward, life slapped us back a few spaces. Redemption isn't always a linear journey. It's a long-term commitment. Like candlestick charts at the New York Stock Exchange, you have to be willing to accept short losses to increase your value over time.

One evening, while counting the cost of my drastic devaluation, I found a new way to self-implode. I'd recently received news that a good buddy died from liver failure due to alcohol abuse. My rusty bucket of bolts sat in the driveway with an undiagnosed overheating problem. After walking to work and earning barely enough money to support my family, I plopped down at my laptop to meet a fast-approaching deadline for an Army assignment.

Per usual, I was accompanied by my trusty, late-night companions: a few lime-flavored beers and Silent Theory's *Delusions*. Bouncing between "Fragile Minds" and "Watch Me Burn," the album's content became a little too honest. Judging from the videos, these gentlemen tapped into a live stream from my life, then wrote about it. With surgical precision, I could feel their scalpels poke at the most tender parts of my soul.

From the king's seat at our dining room table, I had a nervous breakdown. Despite my several dirty dances with panic attacks and emotional meltdowns,

I've never experienced what I felt that night. A surge shot through my spine, sending tingly goosebumps down my arms and legs. My vision blurred, then blacked out. Tremors, similar to electrocution, sent me into an uncontrollable rocking motion. Questioning my ability to manage its intricate parts, my nervous system staged a violent revolution against me.

With a quick convulsion, my right hand struck the glass beer bottle. It thudded to the table, foamy suds flowing in a narrow waterfall to the floor. Tears streamed down my face while a ghostlike howl escaped from my mouth.

"Tony?" my wife called, running through the kitchen. I couldn't see her, but I heard her footsteps pounding on the linoleum. "Oh my gosh, he's having a seizure!"

"I'm... not... I'm... here," I said.

"Let me grab a pillow. You need to lie down."

"No... Just. stay." The final tremor pulsed to a slow conclusion. My vision recalibrated like a microscope shifting focus. Handing me a towel to clean my face, my wife tried to convince me to go to the hospital. I refused. After cleaning my mess and a brief consolation period, I went back to work.

Taking a pull from a fresh beer, I popped my earbuds back in. Halfway through "Watch Me Burn," I spun out of control again. Complete muscle failure. Convulsions. Bitter tears. Heightened mental clarity, granting front row seats to worry's aftermath. The wreckage caused by anxiety, exhaustion, stress, doubt, fear, and my secret identity. I had no idea until I erupted. Like a volcano sits dormant for decades, the natural pressure cannot be contained forever.

I was allowing poison to settle in my veins. I couldn't move on until I forgave those who had wronged me. Until I realized I wasn't a savior to my kids, my family, or anyone else. Until I realized I couldn't avoid hurt in this world. My disease caused me to lose the one thing I could control: me.

Car Radio / Twenty One Pilots

I often wonder where I'll fit in when I decide to release my own music. Throughout my lifetime, lines between genres have blurred. Rap has guitars now. The last time I listened to mainstream country, the singer didn't mention a farm once. Digital recording made metal more technical than ever. Artist features cross genres. It seems the days of musical purity are over.

One morning, my best friend recommended Twenty One Pilots to me. I'd heard the name, but politely declined. With persistence, he narrowed his request, "At least, listen to 'Car Radio.'"

Let me let you in on a little secret. If someone gives me a music recommendation, I have to take it. The gold I might've missed without this rule, so I searched YouTube. "Twenty One Pilots 'Car Radio,' enter." Why's that dude wearing a ski mask? It doesn't matter. I. Must. Listen. Click.

What ensued over the next four minutes was the most confusing musical experience I've ever had. I liked the rap parts, but the electronic stuff? Give the piece a chance. A synthesizer drop developed into metal-like screaming over a dubstep anthem. Were these dudes doing what I thought? They dared exit the neat confines of particular genres?

Through extensive research, I found out Tyler Joseph plays three traditional instruments: bass, piano, and ukulele. The only other guy in the band, Josh Dun, played a real drum kit.

What CD's "Car Radio" on? *Vessel?* Let's give it a go. I'd never been so confused, and impressed, upon completion of an album listening session.

To be honest, I was a little angry. I wanted to be the artist to defy genre in mainstream media. The most ground-breaking album of all time has been banging around the ol' noggin for quite some time. After a little finesse to my production process, a few new instruments, plug-ins, and room treatment, I'd self-produce the genre-defying masterpiece that would resonate with the masses. These cats robbed my opportunity.

I must've listened to the song a hundred times in the weeks to follow. I've spent my entire lifetime hiding behind car radios, cassettes, CDs, iPods, and streaming services. When the persistent noise in my head becomes unbearable, I dissect musical movements, lyrics, and the psychology behind certain singers. If someone ever stole my car stereo, I'd have an interesting road trip. Probably another nervous breakdown.

Despite several decades of music consumption, *Vessel* taught me how to listen to music like a producer. Finding the function each component holds in the context of the song. Monitoring chordal movements. Enhancing certain emotions with unique arrangements. I've forgiven Twenty One Pilots for stealing my piece of the glory. If the general populace can embrace them, maybe they're finally ready for what I have to say.

Screen / Twenty One Pilots

In the lyrics to "Screen," Tyler argues that correct relationship with God, and artists with their audience, requires authenticity. It's funny, but when I was twenty-three years old, I started writing a song with a similar theme. No matter how hard we try to conceal flaws from others, the Almighty's omniscience renders our attempts useless. I couldn't completely learn the lesson because I didn't finish the lyrics.

Digging through my old notebooks, I found the fragments: a riff, some tabs, and a melody. My incomplete piece from long ago filled a massive void to my concept album's track list. Dusting it off, I resumed work on my unfinished business.

Ironically enough, total transparency was my next step towards true mental health. If I can't lie to God, why fake it for friends? Secrets kept me sick. I needed people to know I wrestled with suicide attempts that nearly ended my life. I needed people to know I sought counseling to sift through my issues. I needed people to know I drowned doubt through nicotine and alcohol use. I had exactly nothing together in my life, nothing at all. If I wanted to get better, it was time to face the truth. I was gonna have to install a screen on my chest.

More Than a Memory / Garth Brooks

On April 8, 2017, my wife and I watched Garth Brooks at the PanAM Center in Las Cruces, NM. She gifted me with tickets for my birthday. Even though he performed in my hometown, I was in Roswell drilling with my National Guard unit. For the first time in my career, I skipped final formation to travel to the concert. Tacking ten hours to the end of my work day, I disregarded safe, rational action to wander down memory lane with my hero.

While my fellow audience members, who claimed to be massive Garth fans, only sang along with "Friends In Low Places," I took a three-hour tour. Like perusing nostalgic moments captured to home video, every changing song represented yet another scene from my childhood. The painful first days in foster home. Exploring the embarrassing lengths of my former obsession. The lessons learned from my makeshift house arrest. The helm of these anthems transformed a shapeless child into the makings of a man.

Near the end of the set, Garth dismissed his back-up band for an intimate solo performance. It almost rectified the betrayal I felt in having to reinvent myself after his retirement. We laughed together, cried together, healed together. It was less a concert and more of a therapy session.

On the three-hour trip back to Roswell that evening, I retraced the rest of my steps. What a crazy ride from confused teenager to semi-stable adult. College. Thirteen years in the Army. Fourteen job changes. Two marriages. Five kids. Three different states. Foreign lands. Garth Brooks, 90s country, pop, alternative, nu metal, Christian rock, Christian metal, metal. Every sincere smile bloomed through the watering of life's tears. Success forged through failure. My story matters. I should write it down.

Just like that, the book you're now holding in your hands was birthed into existence.

Sorry, Not Sorry / Gemini Syndrome

After my career change, I placed family on the backburner. Learning aspects of a new job requires greater investment. The way I saw it, if I made myself indispensable, I could rely on reciprocity when the crap inevitably slaps the fan. I volunteered for trips out of town. Worked weekend events. Came in early. Stayed late. Model employees prove their worth.

Sounds like a recipe for disaster, eh? How else would I identify the error of my flawed reasoning? Glad you asked. Through song, of course!

My overhead fluorescent light spilled into the dark hallway as I pounded away at spreadsheets. The other office workaholic had left hours ago. In five more minutes, the program's monthly expenditure report would be complete, ahead of my self-imposed schedule. Gemini Syndrome blared from my dinky laptop speakers. I was lucky enough to soundtrack my transition to this new position with *Lux*. What lessons did *Momento Mori* have in store for me?

"Sorry, Not Sorry."

What was I working for? Funny, colorful currency? As a salaried employee, more time didn't mean more money, just less time with those I love. I can't take it with me, but I never really had it anyway. Plus, it's all digital at this point. With direct deposits and online banking, we don't even get the satisfaction of stacking small cash towers before momentarily staving the insatiable appetite of bill collectors. Why balance the company budget while neglecting mine?

Thanks, Gemini Syndrome. "Let this stupid spreadsheet be tomorrow's problem," I mumbled as I headed home.

Sweet Dreams / Jewel

During my wife's last deployment, her mom bought a Jewel lullaby CD from a store display in Washington. Our two oldest kids heard another Walmart customer demo the album and mistook it for my wife's voice. She's a phenomenal singer. However, her crystalline alto tone is hard to compare to Jewel's unique raspy vibrato. Still, I can see why a small child might confuse them. This hand-me-down disc was responsible for a decade's worth of peaceful bedtimes. I'll agree with whatever they say just to expedite the process.

While rocking my son to sleep one evening, I visualized the imagery Jewel paints in "Sweet Dreams." The soft golden glow shining from a night light. The fade off to sleep. Eerie serenity emanating from every corner of a silent house.

Allowing my imagination to run wild with the scenario, intrusive thoughts tried to rob my peace. Same set-up, only this time, his shallow breathing slowed. With a sharp gasp, a final breath sent his soul ascending into Heaven. My attempts at infant CPR, unsuccessful. His potential for greater things, wasted. What I wouldn't give to trade places. Let him stay, God; take me instead.

Holding him tightly in the dark, I replayed the song several times. The blue illumination from their CD player display screen highlighted his tiny facial features. The innocent simplicity of an unblemished, young life. Unstoppable, yet more frail than a preserved flower petal under the right circumstances. A tale all too common with heart babies. I couldn't bring myself to put him in his crib.

I've given "Sweet Dreams" another listen outside the context of our situation. It's an incredibly innocent song. Raising your kids right. Wishing the best possible future for them. Cherishing precious moments while you can. Still, the musical emotion made it easy, at least for me, to follow the lyrics to some morbid places. I guess all's fair in art. As long as I land in the correct destination, doesn't interpretation grant me the freedom to journey wherever I'd like?

Black Honey / Seether

Throughout my time in the American workforce, I've learned underqualified employees will do anything to protect things they hold sacred. I'm not talking about principles, family, faith, or friendships. I'm talking about shallow stuff: money, power, image. Pick the poison. With shameless flailing for self-preservation, these people have no problem causing collateral damage to save face.

Like ointment, I applied Seether's cover of "Black Honey" to my workplace battle wounds. Of the 1.1 million views the video has on YouTube, I've watched it well over three hundred times. No joke.

During one of these lamentations, reality hit me square between the eyes. Bees only attack when they're provoked. If I didn't appreciate the pain, I needed to stop putting my hand in the hive. It's that simple. In the war of work, I'd keep getting stung. The mindless colony has no other choice than swarm what disturbs their delusion of progress.

What a novel concept! After years of contemplating the condition of humanity, it'd be much easier to conform to lesser ethics. As Garth taught me when I was ten years old, I may never change that. The real psychological victory is blocking this world's attempts to transform me.

Whispers / Taken

The ukulele's the most annoyingly happy instrument in human history. Whenever I hear it, I can't help but think of beach bums tossing frisbees in the sand, lethargic and care-free. It's been a dream of mine to own one, just to write the saddest piece I could muster. The stark contrast was too beautiful to ignore.

Now, none of my musical dreams transpire when I want them to. When the Army sent me to Puerto Rico for official business, I had to seize my opportunity to buy a uke in their natural environment. You'd think, with all the beaches, they'd be everywhere. Nope. Instead of playful strumming, I paraded around San Juan to tourists fist-pumping to "Despacito."

After a trip to the closest music store I could find, I returned to my hotel room with a brand new, electric/acoustic, spalted maple concert ukulele. I spent the entire evening looking up chord shapes and a few Twenty One Pilots songs. I wanted to learn as much as possible as soon as possible.

The next morning, I went to the airport to return home. I didn't buy a case for my new treasure, so I was stuck carrying a uke around airports throughout America whilst wearing a heavy metal t-shirt. Tyler Joseph's right. There's no dignified way to transport a ukulele. Also, you get a lot of judgmental glances from normal people assuming you're some hacky-sack playing hipster. Not my problem. Steer clear of my bucket list and I won't scrutinize yours.

When I got home, I got right to work. After tinkering with my new instrument for several weeks, I wrote a riff carrying a dark undertone. This happy little instrument was capable of producing some sorrowful movements.

Playing through the rough version of the song that became "Whispers," childish loathing blended with the firm confidence of a full-grown man. I've attempted explaining this dual-intentioned noise to my wife for years. Seeded somewhere behind this persistent can-do attitude, rooted in arrogance, lies this crippling fear of failure. My head spun in contradiction, enough to make me stop playing. Who wants to hear this stuff? My dreams of musical grandeur were ridiculous. Why was I even writing an album?

I started recording.

After I finished, I ran right to the living room. Interrupting a late evening marathon of *The Walking Dead*, my wife had to hear this. I'll tell you what I told her that evening. If you wanna wander through the weird neighborhood in my mind, you have to listen to "Whispers." A frame-by-frame commentary of the psychological carousel swirling inside my head. Even in its rough form, it's the residue of my experiences. The first momentum to my next recording project.

The End / Demon Hunter

While writing the entries for this book, I suffered from a nagging feeling I wouldn't live to see thirty-four years old. It wasn't just the imminence of death, either. I imagined untimely, violent departures from this planet. Slipping away waiting for the jaws of life to cut me from a mangled vehicle at the scene of an accident. A bullet plummeting through my brain as an innocent sacrifice to a gas station robbery gone wrong. Exploding with a roadside bomb in a potential wartime loss.

I've explored the concept of death before. Despite my several bouts with suicidal ideation, these intense visualizations only accompanied a deep desire to die. They've never haunted me when I've possessed a will to live. No matter what I did to shoo the feelings away, the morbid fantasies came drifting back. I thought for certain my final curtain call was nigh.

Since I couldn't determine the source of my paranoia, I chose to embrace it quietly. None of us get out of life alive. Sometimes, it's best to invest in people who matter to you. Take a mental inventory. Rectify your list of unresolved conflicts. Brush cobwebs from your wildest dreams and attack with tenacity. If my suspicions were wrong, I could still benefit from clearing some skeletons from the ol' metaphorical closet. If they were accurate, I'd leave with my affairs in order.

In the same fashion these mysterious feelings appeared, they passed after the better part of six months; I did not. Maybe it was some kind of mid-life crisis. Maybe the result of reviewing my history in depth like a tragic reel on repeat while writing this book. If there's anything I learned, it's to stop tip-toeing through existence. Make every moment count. Make every conversation count. Catch the fleeting vapor, known as life, while I still have the chance. Today's mistakes don't have to be tomorrow's regrets. They just might be the emergence of something beautiful.

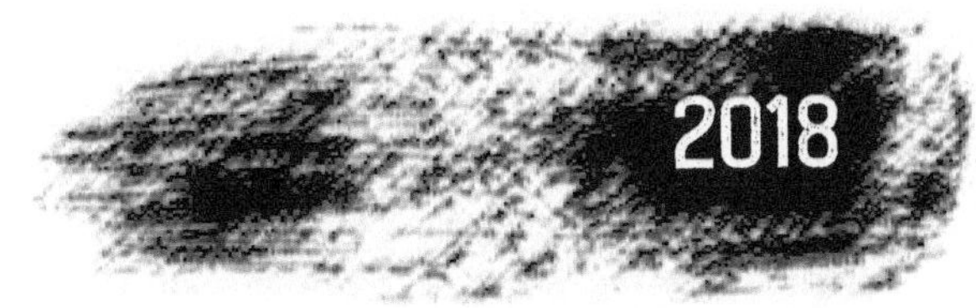

Omitted for Clarity / Karnivool

In reviewing most of these entries, my music obsession appears outside what most people would call normal. After a month of careful deliberation, I decided to take a break to gain a healthy respect for the institution again. To determine whether I genuinely have an addiction. As part of the process of writing my book, I planned to dedicate 1% of that year to total musical silence.

I've heard some addicts binge in one last hurrah before checking into rehab. I was no different. The night prior to my experiment, I shotgunned some Twenty One Pilots, Demon Hunter, Elliott Smith's last known performance, then worked on "Whispers" until midnight. Anticipating the deficit, I loaded my system with enough drug to carry me through the next few days.

Daylight crept through my bedroom window that first sad morning. Peeking through the blinds, menacing clouds blanketed the light from the sun. I thought, *How am I supposed to live without music for THREE WHOLE DAYS?!*

Sorrow welled within my soul as I instantly regretted my decision. As a coping mechanism, I attempted to comfort myself with the melody from Breaking Benjamin's "Torn in Two." *No music means no music, not even from the secrecy of your skull.*

Grabbing my phone, I limped into a pitiful existence. Out of sheer instinct, my pointer finger hovered over the Apple Music icon. "Do you really need something playing every waking minute of the day?" accusing my reflection over the bathroom sink.

A scrawny dude in boxers stared back at me.

My thoughts raced as I retraced my daily routine. *In my car? Some random CD. At work? Audio production tutorials on YouTube. Working around the house at night? More Apple Music. Putting the kids to bed? Blue October's "Calling You" to sooth my son to sleep. That's a lot of violent quiet. Tyler Joseph would suggest someone stole your car radio.*

"Be quiet, you," I ordered, pointing at the man in the mirror. "You have a serious problem."

Three days passed in an agonizing blur. It wasn't fast by any means, but I learned my memory loses clarity without music. Here are my other findings from the experiment:

Have you ever heard Snow's "Informer?" It was huge in the 90s. I can't remember the last time I heard it. That is, until total musical silence. Then, I couldn't get it out of my head. Apparently, the noise I surround myself with has been a silent attempt to stifle this song from my consciousness.

Also, I treat the world like a giant drum kit. Feet pounding the earth in double-bass rhythms. Thumbs tapping every surface available. I wasn't aware until my family made a game out of it. You see, I briefed them before my experiment started. "Don't listen to music around me for the next three days," I said. "If you catch me trying to do anything, keep me honest."

On an afternoon snack run, I sat in our minivan with the kids to avoid gas station anthems blaring over the intercom. My mind wandered to the Mississippi mud ice cream sandwich my wife promised to grab for me. The cool chocolate dessert melting on my tongue in the desert heat. My mouth watered as my daydream was interrupted by our oldest son poking my shoulder.

"Tony, you're drumming again. No music."

Finally, I've attempted tobacco cessation in the past with patches, prescriptions, and gum, all without success. The sharp, snide comments. My easy-going personality lingered near an angry boiling point. To keep the peace, I've kept the shameful vice. Quitting music for three days was worse. Depriving my cranial pleasure center made me moody, depressed, and angry. If I couldn't manage myself, I can't imagine how others dealt with me throughout the experience.

I've said it many times, but I have more than an addiction. Try separating the symphony of life from song. Our genetic make-up won't allow it. The world works on frequencies, rhythm, pitch, melody, and meter. There isn't a person on the planet who can abstain from music. Its powerful force exists whether we choose to acknowledge it or not.

When I discovered Karnivool's *Themata* several years ago, I mentioned how perfectly placed "Omitted for Clarity" was. Eleven seconds of beautiful silence forced the listener to reflect before charging into the finale. The precise sentiment I hoped to accomplish as I concluded this project. A pause heightened my awareness enough to take the final steps into this chapter of my life. I won't EVER do it again, but music holds a more sacred place in my heart because of it.

Amazing / Blue October

There you have it. Thirty-four years scrawled in intimidating black and white. My history is for sale. Like a shotgun blast, I'll never be able to reassemble the neat little pellets into their original protective casing.

Aside from vulnerability, which I'll address later, my second greatest fear was overinflating my story to heroic proportions. I need to be clear—that was never my intention. While I've alluded to my hypocrisy, I need to take a moment to formally point it out. I'm a divorced Christian who wrestled with nicotine and alcohol addiction. Further, I'm an officer in the United States Army who delayed reaching out to a substantial support system after my suicide attempts. Can we collectively agree I am NOT amazing? I'm a giant hypocrite with a decent story.

Music's the centripetal force I gravitate to when I fail. Or when others fail me. It's almost insane to learn, at least on 366 occasions, I've processed most of my life through the lyrics blaring in my various audio players. Believe me, I stuck with the memorable moments. There are several songs I didn't choose to use. However, nothing drives a point through my thick skull like a song can. In full disclosure, I often wander to one of these mechanisms before I take my problems to God. I'm working on that, though.

The biggest lie being told amongst human circles is that we live alone in our various conditions. I'm not the only person who processes their life through music. Who was born with a noticeable birth defect? Whose parents got divorced? Who spent time in a foster home? Who struggled with identity? Who grew up with a parent that abandoned them? Who got into trouble with the law? Who had to bust through glass ceilings after they reformed?

Who attended college as a first-generation student? Who failed to find a band? Who wrestled with mental health issues? Who joined the Army during a catastrophic time in our country's history? Who gave their life to Christ? Who tried beating unsurmountable odds to break the cycle? Who struggled with ego in the professional world?

Who moved across the country to do something new? Who became a parent? Who deployed to a third world country in military service? Who got divorced due to commitment concerns? Who became a part-time parent? Who medicated through alcohol and nicotine use? Who attempted suicide? Who got help with mental health concerns? Who's trying their best to find a way forward?

I used to believe the sad lie that I was alone. In being more transparent with my life, I've learned that's not the case. Hurt people hurt people, so we yank our hands away from the burner of human contact. The disease is the medicine, though. If we truly want to heal, we have to do it within communities of like-minded people. Our stories matter. The most amazing thing we can do with these intense moments of adversity is share them.

Farewell / Brooke Barrettsmith

This book's one of the most inherently selfish pieces of work I've ever completed. It's been nothing but me. Me. ME. Look at me! Look what I can do! Can someone please acknowledge how important I am? I don't intend to get into the business of publishing self-help drivel, but to close the project out, the least I can do is provide you all with one direct moment of inspiration.

Art is the powerful medium humans use to process and present our struggles. Notice, I used the term art over music. People spend hours listening to albums, watching films, studying paintings, flipping through photography, or reading poetry. They may not be willing to listen to the story that inspired the piece; however, our species uses entertainment to escape the realities of life.

Genuine artistic expression requires courage in presenting the darkest, most vulnerable aspects of our lives. Do I really want true restoration or just the pain to go away? Am I mature enough to separate professional critique from personal criticism? Is artistic honesty, from a potentially large platform, even worth it? With my history for sale, I've concluded that brilliant ideas will never see the light of day if creators don't catapult over these fears.

I'd like to propose a challenge to you all. Tell your story through art. Whatever that might mean to you. Paint a picture. Mold the clay. Write a song. Make a video. Get creative. There's an entire audience waiting for the message you have harbored in your heart.

I'm not sure how apparent it was throughout my story, but it reeks with excuses. Life got in the way. I had to provide for my family. I was unwell for a while.

While they're all factual statements, nothing stopped me from producing music. I squandered potential every step along the way. Don't hide behind fear, like me, because people like me owe our entire existence to artists who dared to pursue their dreams. I'm begging you. Please, tell your story through art.

Awaken Love / Lacey Sturm

After six years of editing, I'm finally ready to present the fruit of my labor. In full transparency, this wasn't the original ending. I rewrote this section on my fortieth birthday. If I live an average lengthed life, it's halfway over. I can't keep yet another creative endeavor locked inside the vault.

In making my last pass through this piece, I realized my story was a tad too incomplete for comfort. If you've hung with me for this long, you deserve to know the rest of the story.

Nine months ago, my wife and I celebrated our tenth wedding anniversary. Our five children (ages fifteen, fourteen, thirteen, ten, and eight) are happy, healthy, and productive. Back in August 2023, our youngest son started his second day of the third grade. Not only is he doing well, but all of our kids surpassed my irrational fear of being shipped off to foster home.

His open-heart surgery was our last significant brush with his mortality. I've been cautious to overinflate his story, but he truly is a miracle. His heart surgeon told us he's likely to need another corrective surgery to replace his valve as he grows. However, we remain grateful for the time we have with him.

I left the civilian workforce for a full-time position with the New Mexico National Guard. While this job forced me to leave my oldest son from my first marriage in a different town, it allowed our family to escape the financial crisis created by having special needs kids.

I served as Commander for an Engineer Construction Company. From my dream assignment, I was able to lead a skilled group of heavy equipment operators, carpenters, electricians, plumbers, and masonry professionals.

Two years ago, I promoted to Major and continue to serve as a battalion staff officer. My love for Soldier care and quality training objectives continues to carry my military career forward.

As disastrous as COVID-19 was across the globe, my family also felt its effects. When the pandemic started, I was activated to support relief efforts.

Immediately upon my return home, my family was evicted from our rental property by landlords who sought the opportunity to exploit the exploding housing market for a quick cash grab. After living in a fifth-wheel camper for two months, while supervising virtual learning, we were able to move our five children and four dogs into our first home.

Three out of five of my parents passed away during the pandemic. In June 2020, my adoptive dad died, my step-mom in July, and my adoptive mom in November. None of their deaths were COVID-related, but it was a significant amount of loss within a short period of time.

As for my mental health, it's never a linear journey. Some periods are rougher than others. Upon moving to Roswell for my full-time job, my wife and I were plugged into a phenomenal church. This community of people are exactly what I'd expect from those who follow Jesus.

As church services normalized after the pandemic, my wife and I were asked to lead a mental health peer support group, called Hope for Mental Health. In this role, I became a certified mental health coach. Through several courses in suicide intervention, I now use my struggles to empower others to sift through the filth that life finds us in.

I took my last daily drink of alcohol back in July 2021. Through consistent involvement in Celebrate Recovery, the noise I tried to drown with alcohol consumption dissipated.

In Step Four, we reflect on moments of trauma: where have we been hurt? What ways have our destructive behaviors hurt others? I was surprised to find out that after thirty-eight years on the planet, I still harbored resentment for my mom's departure from my life. My path to mental health restoration had only been playing whack-a-mole with symptoms, never nailing down the real disease.

I'll never forget the morning of December 28, 2021. As I continued to wrestle with the concept of forgiving my mom, I was getting ready for work. After shaving for the day, I stared myself eyeball to eyeball in the mirror and shot up a quick prayer. "God, how am I supposed to forgive my mom when I don't even know her middle name? I don't even know what year she was born. How am I supposed to forgive a woman I don't even know? Forgive a woman who destroyed the concept of unconditional love for me?"

When the continued silence I perceived for thirty-eight years persisted, I went about my day.

Later that evening, my wife and I sorted paperwork, trying to figure out what to throw away and what to keep. An ironic metaphor for the twelve-step process. As we sat on our bedroom floor, my brother Chad sent me a message on Facebook Messenger. "I'm not sure if anyone told you, but Mom passed away this morning."

When I was a child, I used to believe when my mom died, I wouldn't feel a thing. Even after losing three parents in 2020, I had never experienced grief this succinctly. Only this time, I had to face the pain.

The next morning, my sister Lynette contacted me to obtain permission to cremate her. If I agreed, I needed to sign and return a consent form to the funeral home. I waited in my inbox and printed the document immediately. In the upper left corner, the document said, "Name: Mary Margaret Steen." Her middle name was Margaret.

Directly below that, it reads, "Date of Birth: March 28, 1955." She was born in 1955.

As I reflected upon the weight of giving professionals permission to burn my mom's body, the Holy Spirit got ahold of me. With a voice as audible as any other living being, I heard, "I answered the only two questions you had for Me. It's time to forgive your mother."

The process wasn't easy. I had to remind myself to replace hurt with love every time I thought about her. I had to dismiss her rationale behind being gone. I had to be ok with never knowing the reason why. I had to painfully learn that forgiving her wasn't for her benefit. It was for mine. My mental health journey won't ever be complete until I cut ties from this anchor. Today, I can say that her missteps no longer have a hold on me. I've forgiven Mom.

You may be wondering what's in store for me. I don't ever intend to write another book. This is it.

The rubber really begins to hit the road for me in my next chapter. It's time to pay homage to the lessons I've learned. The incomplete songs hanging in my notebook have been neglected long enough. I have enough material. I've made enough excuses. My robust home studio needs my undivided attention now. If you want to know where I'll be in the future, you can find me where you consume music.

This might sound strange, but the last reason I didn't want to completely heal was due to my artistic aspirations. Ariel Bloomer, of Icon for Hire fame, wrote about this concept in her book, *Turn Your Pain into Art.* The music I like to make requires anger, sorrow, and discontent. Picking at my past wounds gave me material to write about. My silly fear that healing would render me artistically ineffective was unfounded. It turns out, this messed-up world doesn't need another artsy martyr. It's capable of generating its own content without my perpetual tendency to self-sacrifice.

That being said, I'm finally ok with who I am today. I'm finally ok admitting I haven't always been, nor will I always be. For our lives to have impact, we have to ruminate in them. Sometimes, over a six-year editing period. Thanks for investing your valuable time to listen to mine. I sincerely hope, through my intense journey of self-discovery, my story has added value to yours.

THANKS FOR READING MY BOOK!

I sincerely hope you enjoyed the experience!

As an independent author, your honest feedback goes a long way to help other customers determine if this book is the right fit for them. In addition, I value your opinion and would love to hear what you thought.

Please consider scanning the QR code below to leave a review on Amazon.

YOUR FEEDBACK MATTERS!

This book would not have been possible for me without God the Father, Christ the Son, and the Holy Spirit. Thank you for eternal grace, immense consolation, and restoration of broken souls. Without you, I am nothing.

To my wife April and five children: Thank you for enduring seven years of writing and editing this book. It wasn't just lost time due to physical work I put in after my day job. For us, healing wasn't just a metaphor used as a literary device. It was real. Picking at the scabs of my past was good for us in the long run, but you were there as I relived things I've avoided for decades. Thank you for enduring my crankiness due to late-night work sessions, my mood swings as I revisited the trauma, and the multiple rereads as I sorted things out. Whether you know it or not, I wrote this book for our benefit. I love you all.

Growing up in musical households, I owe a debt of gratitude to my biological dad (Lloyd), step-mom (Molly; RIP), adoptive dad (Dennis; RIP), and adoptive mother (Donna; RIP). Thanks to all of my siblings: Kurt, Chad, Aaron, Eric, Matthew, Kandy, Missy, Lynette, Christa, Justin, Dawn, Deb, Crystal (RIP), Danny, and Norm. My musical diversity can only be contributed to the various noise you all subjected me to during my younger years.

To my closest friends who have endured years' worth of lyric trading: Sean Fatzinger, Jesse Frenzel, Tyler Stickel, Wes Darnell, Alex Davis, Joe Wright, and Kyle Lynch. You guys are the real heroes. Thank you for being the sacrificial lambs to my constant music obsession. You weren't just great friends; your faithful service gave me an acceptable outlet to avoid awkwardness around normal people.

To anyone I've ever wronged along this collision course of life, I'm sorry. My college advisor, Dr. Michael J.C. Taylor, used to say, "Those who don't learn from history are condemned to repeat it." Yep. Sometimes, I learned these lessons, but long after said replication. This book was never intended to be a scathing review of these hurts. It was an honest attempt to claim my portion of the mess.

Lastly, to the thousands of strangers along my musical journey: fellow concert-goers, YouTube commenters, chat room participants, album reviewers, and song meaning discussers. I'll never see you again. In fact, I barely met you. Just know, along this same collision course of life, you had momentary impact. From the pits, with fists to the sky, I thank you. The world may call us nerds, and we very well may be, but keep marching to the beat of that double-bass pedal. I assure you, it's the rhythm of life.

Tony Kessel is a staunch music enthusiast. Over the past forty years, he has listened to over a million songs. Through incessant dreaming, his rock star aspirations have passed him by. His debut book, It's All In The Lyrics: How Music Helped Me Heal and Find My Voice, is an earnest attempt to recapture his lost youth and restore courage to artistic vision.

Tony serves as a full-time member of the New Mexico National Guard. He resides in Roswell, New Mexico with his wife, five children, three dogs, and red-eared slider. His home studio partner is a bearded dragon named Andromeda.